Critical Border Studies

This edited collection formalises Critical Border Studies (CBS) as a distinctive approach within the interdisciplinary border studies literature. Although CBS represents a heterogeneous assemblage of thought, the hallmark of the approach is a basic dissatisfaction with the 'Line in the Sand' metaphor as an unexamined starting point for the study of borders. A headline feature of each contribution gathered here is a concerted effort to decentre the border. By 'decentring', we mean an effort to problematise the border not as a taken-for-granted entity, but precisely as a site of investigation. On this view, the border is not something that straightforwardly presents itself in an unmediated way. It is never simply 'present', nor fully established, nor obviously accessible. Rather, it is manifold and in a constant state of becoming. Empirically, contributors examine the changing nature of the border in a range of cases, including: the Arctic Circle; German-Dutch borderlands; the India-Pakistan region; and the Mediterranean Sea. Theoretically, chapters draw on a range of critical thinkers in support of a new paradigm for border research. The volume will be of particular interest to border studies scholars in anthropology, human geography, international relations, and political science.

Critical Border Studies was originally published as a special issue of *Geopolitics*.

Noel Parker is Associate Professor in Political Theory and the History of Ideas at the University of Copenhagen, Denmark. His books include *Empire and International Order* (2012); *The Geopolitics of Europe's Boundaries: Spaces, Centres and Margins* (2008) and *Margins in European Integration* (2000).

Nick Vaughan-Williams is Reader in International Security, University of Warwick, UK. His books include *Border Politics: The Limits of Sovereign Power* (2009, 2012), (2011 Gold Winner, Association for Borderlands Studies); *Critical Security Studies: An Introduction* (2010); *Critical Theorists and International Relations* (2009) and *Terrorism and the Politics of Response* (2009).

Critical Border Studies
Broadening and Deepening the 'Lines in the Sand' Agenda

Edited by
Noel Parker and Nick Vaughan-Williams

LONDON AND NEW YORK

First published 2014
by Routledge
2 Park Square, Milton Park, Abingdon, Oxon, OX14 4RN

Simultaneously published in the USA and Canada
by Routledge
711 Third Avenue, New York, NY 10017

Routledge is an imprint of the Taylor & Francis Group, an informa business

© 2014 Taylor & Francis

This book is a reproduction of *Geopolitics*, vol. 17, issue 4. The Publisher requests to those authors who may be citing this book to state, also, the bibliographical details of the special issue on which the book was based.

All rights reserved. No part of this book may be reprinted or reproduced or utilised in any form or by any electronic, mechanical, or other means, now known or hereafter invented, including photocopying and recording, or in any information storage or retrieval system, without permission in writing from the publishers.

Trademark notice: Product or corporate names may be trademarks or registered trademarks, and are used only for identification and explanation without intent to infringe.

British Library Cataloguing in Publication Data
A catalogue record for this book is available from the British Library

ISBN 13: 978-0-415-84324-9

Typeset in Garamond
by Taylor & Francis Books

Publisher's Note
The publisher would like to make readers aware that the chapters in this book may be referred to as articles as they are identical to the articles published in the special issue. The publisher accepts responsibility for any inconsistencies that may have arisen in the course of preparing this volume for print.

Contents

Citation Information   vii

1. Introduction: Critical Border Studies: Broadening and Deepening the 'Lines in the Sand' Agenda
   Noel Parker and Nick Vaughan-Williams   1

2. Theory of the / : The Suture and Critical Border Studies
   Mark B. Salter   8

3. Carl Schmitt and the Concept of the Border
   Claudio Minca and Nick Vaughan-Williams   30

4. Picking and Choosing the 'Sovereign' Border: A Theory of Changing State Bordering Practices
   Noel Parker and Rebecca Adler-Nissen   47

5. Sloterdijk in the House! Dwelling in the Borderscape of Germany and The Netherlands
   Ruben Gielis and Henk van Houtum   71

6. Cartopolitics, Geopolitics and Boundaries in the Arctic
   Jeppe Strandsbjerg   92

7. Off-shoring and Out-sourcing the Borders of EUrope: Libya and EU Border Work in the Mediterranean
   Luiza Bialasiewicz   117

8. Mixed Legacies in Contested Borderlands: Skardu and the Kashmir Dispute
   Antia Mato Bouzas   141

9. Towards a Multiperspectival Study of Borders
   Chris Rumford   161

Index   177

Citation Information

The chapters in this book were originally published in *Geopolitics*, volume 17, issue 4 (November 2012). When citing this material, please use the original page numbering for each article, as follows:

Chapter 1
Introduction: Critical Border Studies: Broadening and Deepening the 'Lines in the Sand' Agenda
Noel Parker and Nick Vaughan-Williams
Geopolitics, volume 17, issue 4 (November 2012) pp. 727–733

Chapter 2
Theory of the / : The Suture and Critical Border Studies
Mark B. Salter
Geopolitics, volume 17, issue 4 (November 2012) pp. 734–755

Chapter 3
Carl Schmitt and the Concept of the Border
Claudio Minca and Nick Vaughan-Williams
Geopolitics, volume 17, issue 4 (November 2012) pp. 756–772

Chapter 4
Picking and Choosing the 'Sovereign' Border: A Theory of Changing State Bordering Practices
Noel Parker and Rebecca Adler-Nissen
Geopolitics, volume 17, issue 4 (November 2012) pp. 773–796

Chapter 5
Sloterdijk in the House! Dwelling in the Borderscape of Germany and The Netherlands
Ruben Gielis and Henk van Houtum
Geopolitics, volume 17, issue 4 (November 2012) pp. 797–817

Chapter 6
Cartopolitics, Geopolitics and Boundaries in the Arctic
Jeppe Strandsbjerg
Geopolitics, volume 17, issue 4 (November 2012) pp. 818–842

Chapter 7
Off-shoring and Out-sourcing the Borders of EUrope: Libya and EU Border Work in the Mediterranean
Luiza Bialasiewicz
Geopolitics, volume 17, issue 4 (November 2012) pp. 843–866

Chapter 8
Mixed Legacies in Contested Borderlands: Skardu and the Kashmir Dispute
Antia Mato Bouzas
Geopolitics, volume 17, issue 4 (November 2012) pp. 867–886

Chapter 9
Towards a Multiperspectival Study of Borders
Chris Rumford
Geopolitics, volume 17, issue 4 (November 2012) pp. 887–902

Please direct any queries you may have about the citations to clsuk.permissions@cengage.com

INTRODUCTION

Critical Border Studies: Broadening and Deepening the 'Lines in the Sand' Agenda

NOEL PARKER
Department of Political Science, University of Copenhagen, Denmark

NICK VAUGHAN-WILLIAMS
Department of Politics and International Studies, University of Warwick, Coventry, UK

The ambition of this special section is to formalise Critical Border Studies (CBS) as a distinctive approach within the interdisciplinary border studies literature. We say 'formalise' rather than 'introduce' because we recognise that there is of course already a strong tradition of applying critical-theoretical insights within that literature. What the field continues to lack, however, is a substantive reference point for scholars working with such approaches to refer to and develop further, and so our hope is to provide such a marker and reinvigorate ongoing debates.

Our initial attempt to set out the motivating concerns and establish avenues of enquiry for CBS was published in the pages of *Geopolitics* in the unusual form of a collectively authored 'Agenda'. This document, the outcome of two workshops in Cornwall and Copenhagen funded by The British Academy, gathered together a range of political theorists, historians, human geographers, anthropologists, and international relations scholars. It reflected common complaints among the group about the growing disparity between the diversity and complexity of contemporary bordering practices on the one hand, and the perception that more theoretical and conceptual work needed to be done in order to keep pace with these developments in academic border studies on the other hand.

THE HARVEST FROM ALTERNATIVE BORDER IMAGINARIES

At only seven pages long, however, the 'Agenda' was necessarily brief and speculative rather than a substantive contribution to the literature. The aim of this special section, therefore, is to speak directly to the 'Agenda', but also to broaden and deepen it. By broadening, we refer to the need, as noted in some of the articles presented here, to put the rather more abstract Political-Theoretical suggestions of the 'Agenda' in conversation with already-existing currents of scholarship in other disciplinary contexts – most notably Geography, Sociology and Anthropology. With regards to deepening, we mean the task of progressing the insights of the 'Agenda' by 'applying' them against the backdrop of specific theoretical debates and empirical border sites, and then reflexively feeding those results back into our initial formulations in order to push and further refine the main tenets of a CBS perspective.

Although CBS represents a heterogeneous assemblage of thought, the galvanising force running throughout the 'Agenda', the articles gathered here, and what we consider to be the hallmark of the approach more generally, is a basic dissatisfaction with the 'Line in the Sand' metaphor as an unexamined starting point for the study of borders. In general terms this is the research problem that the 'Line in the Sand?' programme attempted to tackle and all the articles offer a series of innovative – and sometimes provocative – proposals apposite to the task of developing new border imaginaries, theories, and methodologies.

A headline feature of each of the pieces is a concerted effort to decentre the border. By 'decentring' we mean an effort to problematise the border not as taken-for-granted entity, but precisely as a site of investigation. On this view, the border is not something that straightforwardly presents itself in an unmediated way. It is never simply 'present', nor fully established, nor obviously accessible. Rather, it is manifold and in a constant state of becoming. For that reason, we are committed to exploring alternative border imaginaries.

As Mark B. Salter notes in the opening contribution to this special section, 'the line' in this context has long been the 'dominant thinking tool' of border studies, understood in simplest terms as the razor-edge of the nation-state where mutually recognised sovereignties meet and yet do not overlap. While, as Henk van Houtum and Ruben Gielis note in their article, the 'container-box' model of the nation-state was always an idealisation whose empirical accuracy had to be called into question, there is a growing sense among critical scholars of border studies that this 'territorial trap' is now even more inadequate for conceptualising the spatial and temporal coordinates of everyday life. As Parker and Adler-Nissen (this issue) put it, there is an increasing 'disaggregation' between the territory and function of state borders.

A wealth of evidence presented in these pages and elsewhere supports the view that the thinness of the 'Lines in the Sand' metaphor belies the thickness of the border in its contemporary multiform complexity. Although the traditional image of the border as a line in the sand is under considerable theoretical and empirical pressure this does not mean that borders are straightforwardly a 'thing of the past'. Parker and Adler-Nissen refer to the 'puzzling persistence of (state) borders', albeit in guises – some visible, some invisible – that already confound the line metaphor and challenge us to rethink the nature and location of the border. If, then, as Salter suggests, the forward slash between 'inside' and 'outside' can no longer be read in terms of a line in the sand, what resources do we have for developing alternative border imaginaries, and what are the implications of these imaginaries for critical border research?

One of the pressing tasks confronting the CBS scholar, therefore, is to develop tools for identifying and interrogating what and where borders are and how they function in different settings, with what consequences, and for whose benefit. In this context, CBS urges two twinned moves: a shift from the *concept of the border* to the *notion of bordering practice*; and the adoption of the lens of *performance* through which bordering practices are produced and reproduced.

First, as outlined by Parker and Adler-Nissen (this issue), the notion of *bordering practices* refers to 'the activities which have the effect . . . of constituting, sustaining, or modifying borders'. Such practices can be both intentional and unintentional; carried out by state actors and non-state actors including citizens, private security companies, and others engaged in the conduct of what Chris Rumford has called 'borderwork' (Rumford, this issue); and, further, with greater and lesser degrees of "success" depending from whose perspective that issue is evaluated. A focus on practice entails a sociological line of enquiry, which might emphasise attention to 'the everyday' – the processes through which controls over mobility are attempted and enacted – and the effects of those controls in people's lives and in social relations more widely.

Second, the shift in focus in CBS towards bordering practices draws on the language and the imaginary of *performance* for an alternative paradigm for (re)thinking border politics. Borders do not simply 'exist' as lines on maps, but are continually performed into being through rituals such as the showing of passports, the confessionary matrix at the airport, and the removal of clothing. Reconceptualising borders as a set of performances injects movement, dynamism, and fluidity into the study of what are otherwise often taken to be static entities: 'The uniform and straight lines in the sand, that borders were once thought to be, are now better understood as a complex choreography of border lines in multiple lived spaces' (Gielis and van Houtum, this issue). Moreover, practices of bordering and de-bordering are not just performed as theatrical spectacles, but are also shown to be *performative* of particular socio-economic and political realities and subject-positions. Borders are intimately bound up with the identity-making activities of the nation-state and other forms of political community. The modern political subject is 'bordered' in the same way as the state of which s/he is a citizen and this marker is performed through identity cards, national insurance numbers and so on. In this way, as Parker and Adler-Nissen note, there is an important and inescapable access by states bordering practices into individual bodies – a connection that is intensifying in the light of new, increasingly invasive, biometric technologies.

However, as Salter insists, the permeation of bordering practices throughout society does not mean that the border is necessarily everywhere – or more accurately, 'the border is not everywhere for everyone' (Salter, this issue). Thus, for example, in the case of the EU's borderwork, Bialasiewicz shows that despite the technocratic and depoliticised language of "efficiency" and "customer experience", the human cost of allowing "trusted travellers" to glide freely into and across EUrope has its corollary in that 'the Mediterranean has ... become Europe's graveyard' (Bialasiewicz, this issue). Yet, at the same time, both Gielis and van Houtum in the context of the German-Dutch borderlands (this issue) and Bouzas in the case of Kashmir (this issue) show how 'border-dwellers' can also radically problematise the idealised homogenous nation-state form, and offer the basis for rethinking political community beyond the old coordinates of the modern state/state system.

Borders are increasingly 'off-shored' beyond the physical territory of the state and 'out-sourced' to other state and non-state actors (Bialasiewicz, this issue); and on this basis a core hypothesis of CBS is that 'borders between states are increasingly not what or where they are supposed to be according to the [modern] geopolitical imaginary' (Minca and Vaughan-Williams, this issue). Spatially, borders – understood here minimally as a control over the movement of people, services and goods by a sovereign authority – increasingly form a continuum stretching from within states, through to the conventional 'flashpoint' at airports, ports, and territorial outer-edges, and beyond to 'pre-frontier' zones at the point of departure.

Temporally, too, borders are not as fixed as our animating metaphor otherwise implies, but ever more pre-emptive, risk-assessed, and designed to be as mobile as the subjects and objects in transit that they seek to control. The increasing technological sophistication with which controls on movement are carried out, the diversity of geographical locations where these controls take place, and the speed at which decisions about what and/or whom is considered legitimate and/or illegitimate are all factors commonly cited in support of the view that new border imaginaries are required. Contemporary bordering may be able to 'concertina' time.

The identification and interrogation of the aporetic and undecidable nature of contemporary bordering practices is another central feature of CBS scholarship. As one might expect, the link between bordering practices and violence is a core theme running deeply throughout many of the contributions in this special section: the border as a spatialisation of the violent underpinnings of the state (Minca and Vaughan-Williams); the violent performativity of bordering practices designed to exclude, abandon, and/or kill the 'Other' (Salter, Parker and Adler-Nissen, Bialasiewicz, this issue); and the colonial legacies of partition and past violence (Bouzas, this issue): all loom large in this context. Read in this light, borders are memories of past and present violences etched into social landscapes, which are often concealed by sovereign power – or 'sutured' to borrow Salter's powerful metaphor.

On the other hand, bordering practices – and the various forms of contestation and resistance they often give rise to – are not treated simply as normatively 'bad' phenomena. Rumford, for example, highlights the ways in which borders are also sites of 'cultural encounter' rather than simply a mechanism of division and exclusion. Indeed, even in some of the world's most persistently troubled border-zones, such as the India-Pakistan region, the border can be said to act as an 'interlinking and cooperative space' (Bouzas, this issue). On this view, as Salter might say about Bouzas' material, 'borders then knit the world together' even though the colonial 'sutures' remain living after-traces of past violence.

Methodologically, the empirical thrust of CBS research is conversant with anthropological approaches to the phenomenology of the border and indeed several of the pieces included here reflect extensive ethnographic fieldwork – for example Bouzas' interviews with migrants in the border villages near Kargil, Pakistan and Gielis's time spent with Dutch migrants in Kranenburg.

BORDER IMAGINARIES BEYOND THE LINE

The essays collected here offer a rich reservoir of alternative border metaphors and vocabularies beyond the 'line in the sand' motif. Pursing the two moves referred to earlier provides a space to tease out alternatives. Hence, the contributors take as their inspiration a wide range of resources of both a critical-theoretical and empirical nature as called for by the original multi-authored 'Agenda'.

The special section opens with Salter's critical review of Giorgio Agamben as a theorist of the inside, R. B. J. Walker as a theorist of the line between inside and outside, and Carlo Galli as a theorist of the outside. Salter notes the popularity of Agamben, particularly his border concepts of the ban, camp, and generalised state of exception, in much of the theoretical literature produced by CBS. As well as offering a *tour d'horizon* of the use of Agamben in CBS, Salter provides a critical and highly provocative commentary on the limitations of the Agambenian-influenced literature, and argues that ultimately it fails to adequately account for the figure of the international and its continued significance.

In their contribution Minca and Vaughan-Williams explore the otherwise overlooked concept of the border in Carl Schmitt's work. While the decision on the exception – perhaps the paradigmatic 'line in the sand' – has been covered extensively in secondary commentaries of Schmitt's earlier work, engagement with his later usage of the concept of the *nomos* has been comparatively rare. Minca and Vaughan-Williams investigate *nomos* as a spatial-ontological device that refers to the relationship between order and orientation and they consider the possibility of the emergence of a new global *nomos* characterised precisely by the proliferation and differentiation of borders.

Parker and Adler-Nissen take a Derridean tack on the undecidability of borders and, ultimately, all identities – which indicates the presence of *actors* trying to make differences *appear* to be more definite than they are. With that perspective, the prime issue is which agents might make borders *seem* settled, and why it might be beneficial to them to do so. In an epistemological register rooted in Kratochwil out of Luhman, they argue that there would be benefits to any collective particular, especially states, in actively maintaining the border's substantiality. But this has to be done on a number of distinct 'planes of inscription', since these planes are increasingly 'disaggregated'. A prime instance is the 'sovereignty games' of states within the European Union, where sovereignty is instrumentalised to shore up nation-state distinct identities.

Gielis and van Houtum map the concept of 'dwelling' in the extant literature in terms of a continuum of approaches to the border from the 'Heideggarian nest' on one end of the spectrum (associated with concepts of 'being' and bordering) to the Deleuzian 'line of flight' at the other (marked by endless becoming and de-bordering). For Gielis and van Houtum practices associated with 'the border' are always already caught in abeyance between the two extremes and so here we are necessarily dealing with a constantly shifting and ultimately ephemeral 'line in the sand' (Gielis and van Houtum). As a bridge between the Heideggerian and Deleuzian extremes, they draw extensively on the work of Peter Sloterdijk to generate new border thinking capable of grasping the experience of dwelling in contemporary borderzones: 'Dwelling can be seen as a place which is constantly changing from a secure bubble-like place into a multidimensional foam-like place and back again' (Gielis and van Houtum, this issue).

Strandsbjerg draws on the work of Bruno Latour to call for a 'cartopolitical turn' in CBS. This could imply that the relationship between borders and space which is current among CBS scholars has to be amended. He argues that there is a greater need for CBS to problematise how particular conceptions of *space* are stabilised and solidified in order to better appreciate the historical and material context in which bordering practices are (re)produced. This piece is anchored in the latest developments in the Arctic which, as a consequence of Global Warming, give access to rich mineral resources.

Bialasiewicz offers a detailed analysis of EU border-work in the Mediterranean with a specific focus on the 'off-shoring' and 'out-sourcing' of EUrope's borders in the Libyan case. She draws attention to a certain creativity in the way the European Union carries out its 'border-work', such as projecting border-work out to far beyond the recognised borders of the current Union. This highlights, in particular, the role of EUrope's neighbours in new strategies of securitisation (notoriously, Libya under Gaddafi), drawing attention to some of the actors, sites and mechanisms that make the Union's border-work possible. Her analysis draws critical attention to the creation of '"off-shore" black holes where European norms, standards, and regulations simply do not apply' (Bialasiewicz, this issue). She also traces the responses of various humanitarian NGOs to the unfolding situation in the aftermath of the Arab Spring and emphasises the human cost of European border security. The EU's border-work is still developing.

Bouzas' case study of the India-Pakistan border brings an important post-colonial and conflictual backdrop against which the violence of past and present bordering practices are analysed. 'Seeing like a border' involves, as Bouzas explores the backdrop of the Kashmir conflict, engaging more directly with the problematics of 'political space, of inclusion and exclusion', which gives rise to a more explicit analysis of 'the state's strategies of territorialisation in the periphery' (Bouzas, this issue). It also urges border scholars to pay much closer empirical attention to 'the ways in which local populations have been kept on one or other side of the line and their experiences of it' (Bouzas, this issue).

Finally, rounding the special section off is Rumford's call for CBS to adopt a 'multiperspectival view' as an alternative to 'seeing like a state' (in James C. Scott's ringing phrase from 1999) when analysing the border. He argues that this view gives full scope to the possibilities made available by the end of the Cold War. 'Seeing like a *border*', as he dubs this position, would mean that the border could become a field of action on the part of non-state actors – notably, the ordinary citizens who dismantled the Wall or have been involved in numerous less vaunted episodes before and since.

ACKNOWLEDGEMENTS

We would like to thank all of the contributors to the special section for helping us to realise the 'Lines in the Sand' project in this form, all the many participants at our workshops in Cornwall and Copenhagen, The British Academy for providing financial assistance (SG-50847), and the Editors of *Geopolitics* – particularly David Newman – for support and patience throughout the publication process.

Theory of the / : The Suture and Critical Border Studies

MARK B. SALTER

School of Political Studies, University of Ottawa, Ontario, Canada

Borders are crucial sites of political and spatial contestation: and in an attempt to evade the lamentation for an ideal model of a single line or the empty insistence of the dominance of that line, this article argues that the trope of the suture better captures the dual world-creating functions of the border. By examining the critical border theories of Agamben, Walker, and Galli, the suture better focuses analytical attention towards the role of borders in the creation of both sovereign states and the system of sovereign states.

INTRODUCTION

The new theoretical touchstones for critical border studies – debordering and rebordering – emphasise the processes of border-making, or in other words the performativity of the border.[1] All borders are performative: they must be created and given meaning through their delimitation and transgression.[2] The "inside/outside"[3] of the sovereign state is not the same as the "hyphen-nation-state"[4] or the "bounding of the bordering process"[5] because the sovereign "/" creates the separate spaces of domestic law and the international metacommunity. The slash, chasing forward on itself, creates a division and a unity between the inside and outside. The line has been abandoned as the primary metaphor of border studies, and I propose here that the suture – as a process of knitting together the inside and the outside together and the resultant scar – better evokes the performative aspects of borders. The article first sets out the death of the line as the primary metaphor, develops the theory of the suture, and then examines the role of the border in Agamben as a theorist of the inside, Walker as a theorist of the /, and Galli as a theorist of the outside, and the work in border studies that they have inspired. We argue that despite the reliance on Agamben's discussion of the ban and the threshold, his scant work the border lacks any engagement with the international. Walker's powerful work on the mutual constitution of inside/outside through "boundaries, borders, and limits" does not provide any way of distinguishing between sovereign borders and other kinds of boundaries or limits. Galli argues that borders have become the predominant geopolitical ordering principle, and in effect making a similar argument to Balibar,[6] that borders are everywhere. In each of these cases, the process required to both separate and unite the inside from the outside, and the radical influence that this has on the status of law and the right to have rights, is underplayed. As a thinking tool, the suture orients our analytical attention toward the performativity of the sovereign border to create both sovereign states and a system of sovereign states, and reinforces both the legal abandonment of that seam and the differences in the navigation of that performative space made possible through social capital.

Understanding sovereign state borders as a suture can inform our analysis of bordering in a way that admits the changes in contemporary practices but reaffirms the unique world-building characteristics of sovereign borders. Sutures are never always or completely successful, just as stitches in a wound may lead to healing but also leave a trace of their own through the scar. When we move from one territorial sovereign to another through the border, when we move from one population classification to another through examination and confession, when the sovereign authority to include or to exile and the sovereign responsibility to protect become disconnected, in all these moments of rupture, the suture of sovereignty is revealed. Indeed their very failure reinforces the grand narrative of sovereignty: borders are created by the assertion of sovereign states, the naturalness of which is immediately undermined by the fabrication and necessary transgression of the border. The border naturalises the violence that was necessary to create it. The exclusion of the outside is always already included in the delimitation of the inside, as Agamben would frame it.[7] This 'inclusive exclusion' of the outside has been engaged by a number of philosophers and social critics – but what interests me most is how these two are made strange and knit together both at the same time. The incompleteness of the suture, the scar, are haunting reminders of the surplus. The suture is a way of rethinking critically the dilemma that R. B. J. Walker has posed in his latest ouroboros, *After the Globe: Before the World*:

> anyone seeking to reimagine the possibilities of political life under contemporary conditions would be wise to resist ambitions expressed as a move from a politics of the international to a politics of the world, and to pay far greater attention to what goes on at the boundaries, borders and limits of a politics orchestrated within the international that simultaneously imagines the possibility and impossibility of a move *across* the boundaries, border and limits distinguishing itself from some world beyond.[8]

Walker's formulation of the question provides a much more nuanced foundation than competing models of the changing nature of borders, by connecting borders not simply to their function but also to their world-making character. Debrix claims that the suture functions like ideological interpellation: "The moment when ideology is effectively implemented, recognized, and internalized by the individual subject . . . suture can be seen as having the same effects as interpellation. It facilitates the identification of the subject-as-spectator with an imaginary representation, but necessitates the work of a material/visual text in a real contextual framing to take place . . ."[9] In these models, there is an ideology of the border as that suture that interpolates all border-crossers and observers as border-subjects and world-makers, individuals who must be able to validate their identity and status to cross the border and in doing so authorise sovereign states. Borders then knit the world together, but also knit us as subjects into the bordered world.

As Vaughan-Williams and Parker state: "[Borders] are increasingly ephemeral and/or palpable: electronic, non-visible, and located in zones that defy a straightforwardly territorial logic."[10] A preclearance area at an international airport illustrates both the utility of critical border studies in undermining the traditional assumptions of geopolitics and the performativity of the border.[11] Travellers are pre-screened by airline agents and border officials prior to departure on international flights, often against no-fly lists or passenger profiles that reflect anxieties about illegal immigration and false asylum claims, health concerns, and security threats. Traditional models of the territorial state borders are confounded by the presence of border functions that are not at the edges of the state. State authorities, private actors, and individuals each create the meaning for the border in its transgression: making particular claims for decision or status. Critical border studies refer to these processes as both debordering and rebordering: Sparke explains this as the "discontinuity between the repeated, often reactive, rearticulations of the territorialized nation-state on the one hand and the neoliberal transnationalizing of the state on the other,"[12] borrowing from Appadurai's notion of "disjuncture".[13] The Gordian legal status of preclearance areas is often complex and unclear, different from claims to entry or status on the territory of the state. While (admission, identity, or status) claims made on the territory of the state are within the law, claims made from without are abandoned from the law, and thus even when debordered or rebordered, the performance of the state border has a profound effect.[14] The romantic nostalgia for the border as a line indicates its weakness as a theoretical tool.[15]

The End of the Line

The line has been the dominant thinking tool of border studies. Take Williams' recent book, which starts: "The line in the sand . . . possesses many of the characteristics we tend to associate with territorial borders in international politics. This idea is a powerful one, so powerful, in fact, that it is often taken for granted."[16] Even when borders are taken to be multiplying or multiplicitous, the dominant metaphor remains the line and in particular the performative nature of the line to divide: "No political border is more natural or real than another. Rather, all borders are human constructions and as such derive their function and meaning from the people they divide."[17] Newman is one of the most important traditional border theorists, and he argues that "this transition from the study of the line per se to the social and spatial functions of those lines as constructs that define the nature of inclusiveness and exclusiveness, which would appear to characterize the contemporary debate concerning boundaries and borders."[18] Even when Bigo imaginatively uses the topological metaphor of the torus, it relies upon the line: "This cylindrical model benefits from extreme simplicity in the representation of in the alignment between inside, internal . . . and outside, external . . . all is resolved on the borderline of the state, a line as thin as possible, a no-man's land, a paper line, a line of sovereignty."[19] But the idea of the border as a line is under increasing empirical and theoretical pressure.[20]

When borders are represented as lines, the analytical focus becomes the two sides of the line, what is divided or crossed or transgressed, rather than the system in which that line can have meaning. Sassen traces the circuits of authority and rights within a territorial frame to demonstrate that while "the nation-state remains the prevalent organizational source of authority and to variable extents the dominant one . . . critical components of authority deployed in the making of the territorial state are shifting toward become strong capabilities for detaching that authority from its exclusive territory and onto multiple bordering systems."[21] Globalisation and the disaggregation of territory, authority, and rights then becomes about the disjunction between lines. But, the globe in Sassen's model is simply the container for states, rather than a constitutive system of systems: borders then are the functional divisions between different appeals to authority, rather than a way of structuring the condition of possibility for authority at all. Similarly, Balibar's treatment of borders focuses entirely on the inside. Borders, he argues are overdetermined, polysemic, and heterogenous.[22] We cannot disagree that "no political border is ever the mere boundary between two states, but it is always *over*determined and, in that sense, sanctioned, reduplicated, and relativized by other geopolitical divisions"; that borders "do not have the same meaning for everyone"; or that "some borders are no longer situated at the borders at all."[23] Rather we say that this entirely internal focus structurally limits the possible insights available from this schema because the line is not a processual or systemic metaphor. For Balibar, the outside is individualised through citizenship status, race, class or gender, not the outside of an international system itself. Brown's analysis, on the other hand, attempts to juxtapose the processes of supposed debordering due to globalisation with a resurgent practice in the construction of physical walls, the reinforcing of lines. Because "the migration, smuggling, crime, terror, and even political purposes that walls would interdict are rarely state sponsored, nor, for the most part, are they incited by national interests. . . . they appear as signs of a post-Westphalian world"[24] However much we are sympathetic with Brown's use of psychoanalytic theory to understand the impulse to wall, the relentlessly externalised focus structurally limits the possible insights, when the international is entirely untheorised or empirically described as simply a realm of danger.[25] Each of these theorists strain the metaphor of the line past its breaking point: the line simply does not provide analytical purchase on the functions of inclusion and exclusion or the co-constitution of the inside and outside.

Critical border studies have largely abandoned the line as its dominant.[26] In particular, there has been a shift away from legalistic boundary drawing and cross-border economic trends towards the performativity of the border, the ways that borders are given meaning through practices. This encompasses work done on border zones and cross-border regions, and also multiple borders, such as within the European Union or other integrating regions. Others in geography have turned to Bauman and Castells, using hydraulic metaphors of flows and networks, and argued for "networked borders."[27] Analytical focus has shifted from the line – written on a map or on a landscape – towards the policies and populations that are defined and cross those borders. Vaughan-Williams advocates for the analytical frame of a "generalized biopolitical border" in which the sovereign power to include and exclude is, essentially, mobile and dispersed and focused on the body.[28] This article models the "/" between inside/outside: the sovereign border read as a suture remedies the solipsistic tendencies to view borders either exclusively as internal or external.

/ as Suture

Traditionally, borders drew the line between the safe spaces of the political from the dangerous anarchy of the international (regardless of the objective threats faced in either of these realms). However, separate from the empirical challenges to this simplistic notion of borders that we can marshal, there is a more elemental weakness to this trope: "There are no simple lines, no zones of zero width, between insides and outsides, even when exceptions are declared . . . the outside is always somehow inside, the inside somehow outside, whether in diagnoses of life supposed within modernity, or in diagnoses of life between modernity or that which is supposedly outside. Limits simply cannot work politically if they are hermetically sealed."[29] And, Hermes is an apt patron: messenger to the Greek pantheon, the god of boundaries, travellers, and strangers – noted for oration, persuasion, charm and change. The suture better represents this messaging, transition, implication between the inside and the outside.

Individuals see the world as a pleasing or dystopian organisation of population, territory, and responsibility. The grand narrative of sovereignty resolves pressing questions about identity, ethics, and community. However, as an individual crosses between sovereign states – the border, the airport, the colonies, the refugee camp, the processing centre, the interstitial spaces of Guantanamo Bay, Guam, Diego Garcia, etc. – there is a displacement within the grand narrative of clearly demarcated, exhaustive, and ethical sovereign states that manage their relations according to law and force. Everyday life within states renders these fundamental questions about boundaries obscure or hidden, but when an individual crosses that border, the assumptions about belonging, identity, sovereignty, territory, law and force are suddenly apparent.[30] These interstices are the abject of the global: the disgusting surplus of the sovereign regime that lays bare the colonial legacy of contemporary globalisation and the undercurrent of force that troubles the smooth water of authority. The grand narrative falters, and seems not simply arbitrary but radically unstable: why are there states, borders, sovereignty – how do I, the traveller, fit into this world of sovereign states? The use of film theory can be instructive, as Debrix, Dittmer, Shapiro, Weber and others demonstrate.[31] Suturing is the description of the process of stitching the audience into a film – whether through editorial representations of the camera-as-eye or narratively through sympathy with a character. Debrix connects the suture in Lacanian psychoanalysis to Althusserian interpellation, and in particular the trick that the suture explains: the subject is not present on the screen or in the discourse about the world, but "may allow himself/herself to be fooled by the apparatus."[32] Žižek explains:

> The signifying structure has to includes its own absence: the very opposition between the symbolic order and its absence has to be inscribed *within* this order (orig.,), and 'suture' designates the point of this inscription.[33]

Sovereign states need to stich in subjects to the narrative of the state, precisely at the moment when they are most exposed to its decision and in greatest vulnerability of being abandoned by it. Individual border crossers internalise the discourse of the sovereign state, its possibility, its stability and its promise of protection, at the very moment that the sovereign state seems impossible.

Badiou also writes of the "suture" in which "instead of constructing a space of compossibility through which the thinking of time is practiced, philosophy *delegates* its functions to one or other of its conditions, handing over the whole of thought to *one* generic procedure."[34] Thus the suture of philosophy to its political geography has meant that the understanding of borders has come to dominate geopolitics and yet reduced in the actual analysis. All of the particularities of border practices and the minutiae of exceptions are subsumed with the generic model of exclusive sovereign territoriality. But, in addition to listing these anomalies like preclearance areas at airports, we must understand the discursive and political dynamics of rendering these anomalies anomalous. It is easy to see how this concept can be useful for interrogating geopolitics and borders.

Building from critical work on the construction and maintenance of the inside/outside boundaries that are so crucial for group and sovereign identities, the concept of the suture focuses our analytic attention on those moments of tension, anxiety, displacement, rupture or abandonment. And, following the recent trend towards analyses of performativity, there is an emphasis on the practices through which both individuals and states are sutured into the sovereign state and the globe. Žižek again: "Suture is usually conceived of as the mode in which the exterior is inscribed in the interior, thus 'suturing' the field, producing the effect of self-enclosure with no need for an exterior, effacing the traces of its own production: traces of the production process, its gaps, its mechanisms, are obliterated, so that the produce can appear as a naturalized, organic whole."[35] At the airport, one's citizenship or refugee status becomes suddenly apparent and the mask of hegemony slips: the belonging that so many assume to be inherent, or at least reliable, comes to be interrogated and put into radical question.[36] Just as the border-crossing subject stiches him/herself into the narrative of belonging, so too does the sovereign state incorporate the subject as a border-crosser than can be accepted or rejected, defining what populations can move. What was understood as an abstract code for the geopolitical organisation of communities is suddenly represented as a series of contingent and violent claims to inclusion and exclusion. And, at that moment of rupture, the world of citizens, states, and identities must be knitted back together. The suture is the neglected limit of politics and international relations, the actual face of order and order, order and chaos, inside and frontier, inside and outside.

The suture connects the two spheres of possibility in part by making visible the dividing line between the spaces, but also insisting on its own presence and character as an exception. The border is possible without forcing the collapse of the sovereign state because it is described as exceptional. The sutures are portrayed as exceptions to the general paradigm of sovereignty. But, for everyday life and individuals in transit, a sovereign order is made possible through their very visible joining and exceptionality – the transit is not empty of meaning: the border is not a "non-place."[37] The suture is pregnant with meaning – not only by what it creates and separates, but also in the way that it connects and distinguishes. It renders visible the raw power that must be exerted to hold the two together and apart. Agamben speaks specifically to the raw decisional power exercised by the sovereign, particularly in exceptional spaces.

Agamben: Borders, Thresholds and the Ban

Agamben has become one of the most important contemporary social theorists of border for two reasons, though he rarely takes the border on as an explicit subject in his work.[38] Agamben's discussion of Schmittian sovereign power and the camp play two signal roles in current writings on contemporary politics, space, and borders.[39] Borders represent the physical limits from which individuals can claim the right to have rights, and the lines to which sovereigns (mostly) confine the exercise of their absolute power to ban. We can find Agamben's most productive thoughts on the border in terms of the ban, which signifies both "the insignia of sovereignty and expulsion from the community."[40] The ban is both a statement of inclusion and a statement of exile. For Agamben, the ability to define the biopolitical as a matter of governance, and the ability to exclude – in different forms – life from the community, are the signals of politics. While for the most part, Agamben focuses on the legal exclusion of certain groups in the camp, or through the processes of extraordinary rendition or by statute as refugees, we must accept that, though the camp represents an internal spatialisation of the state of exception, the border is the threshold that represents the spatialisation of the external, the international as a permanent state of exception.[41] He says: "The originary juridico-political relation is the ban, not only is a thesis concerning the formal structure of sovereignty but also has a substantial character, since what the ban holds together is precisely bare life and sovereign power"[42] For Agamben, this ability of the sovereign to exclude an individual from political life, to ban them to bare life in which they can be killed but not sacrificed or exiled, is "more original than the Schmittian opposition between friend and enemy, fellow citizen and foreigner."[43] And, for Schmitt, the enemy was precisely someone "who no longer must be compelled to retreat into his borders only."[44] Thus, the ban represents the subjects who can be abandoned, left the exposure of the effect of the law without any recourse within the law.

We see this vulnerability as individuals pass across the suture, through camps, borders, or transit zones, spaces in which subjects hold no rights that are not mediated through the recognition or interpellation of a sovereign. Refugees and citizens are equally vulnerable, in status, if not in resources: there is no prima facie way to require the recognition of the sovereign. At these moments of examination – when subjects are called on by the agents of the sovereign to perform their claim to rights – individuals attempt to suture themselves into the fabric of the community, always already having left that community. Border crossers are always performing some version of their expectations of sovereign authority.[45] There is an in-built anxiety when facing these moments of suture: will the actors and the audience co-perform the sovereign play of identity and difference? All citizens possess the rights of citizenship, but some are more vulnerable to de-citizenship than others.[46] Because this tension cannot be resolved, or rather that tension is productive because it is not resolved, then other objects come to stand in for the suture. The passport functions symbolically as the bridge across the interstitial space, a talisman that protects the bearer undergoing a right of passage, a shield against sovereign abandonment. In law and in fact, the passport is none of these things, nor is citizenship, nor is belonging.[47] We are all equally vulnerable to exile, to sacrifice, to being rendered *homo sacer*. And, while the majority of *Homo Sacer* is concerned with the camp as the internal space of exception, the border is the external space of exception – where sovereign power does not limit itself either at the line or in the space beyond. Agamben's notion of the ban as the primary border function – the process through which the sovereign decides the degree to which it will grant the individual, the appellant, rights – thus matches the empirical observations made by Balibar and others: the essence of sovereign power is the ability to decide whether who counts as human. The border counts as one of those spaces of decision.

The international sphere – though constitutive of the threshold of sovereignty – is almost completely absent from Agamben's political theory.[48] The thresholds that are so important to the sovereign, and the ability of the sovereign to include and exclude, are not defined against emptiness, *terra nullius*, the desert, the sea, or outer-space. Sovereigns are mutually constituted by a metacommunity of other sovereigns: the ability of the sovereign to declare the law is dependent on the absence of law at the meta-sphere. "Metacommunity" is a more useful term than international relations or world politics term to describe the inter-sovereign environment, despite being a slightly clumsy neologism, because it does not inherit the modern notion of the "nation," "globe" or "world" and allows comparisons between different kinds of inter-communal societies, including those in Ancient Greece which are determined more by a distinction between Greek and barbarian than between Athenians and Spartans.[49] The expansion of the contemporary metacommunity – structured around the ideal of juridically equal sovereign states – has only emerged over the past fifty years with the onset of decolonisation and the maturation of international law through the United Nations. Before that, the metacommunity was characterised by formal juridical inequality amongst sovereigns. In the contemporary scene, most scholars would readily admit that some states were more sovereign than others. But, from the point of view of modern international law, sovereigns in their interactions do not have the constitutional or political power to ban or to exclude another sovereign. Sovereignty functions in international law to nominally protect the absolute right to ban, because the rules of the inter-sovereign metacommunity are a fundamentally different type than domestic sovereign relations.[50] To our mind, the example of the passport demonstrates this: while passports are assumed to represent belonging and the legal status of citizenship, they are in fact representative of the inter-sovereign metacommunity. The passport is the request (not requirement) of one sovereign to treat the citizen well – but there can be no obligations on that foreign power, except those limitations or obligations to which the foreign sovereign binds itself. The passport is nothing but a reinscription of the absolute power of the sovereign to decide on the right to have rights, and the mutual construction of that power between sovereigns. The border similarly represents that mutually constituted limit of the sovereign's ability to decide to decide. The transgression of a particular border may trigger war or United Nations sanctions, but it precisely does not cause the system of sovereign states to unravel.

Agamben illuminates his nascent theory of the constitution of the inter-sovereign metacommunity when he discusses the refugee question. As Arendt argues in the aftermath of the First World War, the metacommunity asserted a complete monopoly on the legitimate definition on citizenship and statelessness, first through the practice of the Nansen passports and the League of Nations High Commission for Refugees and later through the United Nations High Commissioner for Refugees and the 1951 Geneva Refugee Convention.[51] In these institutions and practices, sovereigns reaffirmed their absolute right to define citizenship, that is the claim to inclusion, and to define and manage those individuals outside of that system without limiting their rights to exile, to prohibit entry, or to render individuals stateless. Agamben attempts a reversal of this move: "Inasmuch as the refugee, an apparently marginal figure, unhinges the old trinity of state-nation-territory, it deserves instead to be regarded as the central figure of our political history."[52] However, Agamben misses precisely the *inter-sovereign* character of this move. It was not a single sovereign making a decision to ban a particular group that became stateless or refugees. Rather, sovereigns came together within these institutions to decide the mutual and shared bounds on the exercise of their own absolute power. The refugee question cannot be comprehended or explained without the metacommunity of sovereigns. It is precisely these inter-sovereign dynamics of the metacommunity that Agamben neglects, and this neglects stems from his reliance and reading of Aristotle, who – despite his relationship with one of the great imperialists of the Classical age – did not devote a great deal of his writing to inter-state relations.[53]

Agamben starts *Homo Sacer* with Aristotle and the separation between bare or naked life and political life.[54] First, Agamben draws the distinction between bare life (*zoē*) and the political life (*bios*), arguing that the basis of metaphysics and politics is the inclusive exclusion of bare life in political life. The distinction in *Politics* Bk III that is crucial for Agamben is "for the sake of mere life (*zoē*) (in which there is possibly some noble elements so long as the evils of existence do not greatly overbalance the good) mankind meet together and maintain the political community."[55] This he sees as a correction to Foucault's characterisation of biopolitics as the primary turn to modernity. Agamben traces the inclusion of bare life into political life, and consequently the necessary vulnerability of politics to the potential reduction to mere biological existence back to Aristotle. Political life in this reading is more than bare life, even if contemporary politics has elided the difference so that the condition of political life now is equivalent to bare life. Inclusion – in both the space of the state and of bare life in political life – and the potential for the ban or exclusion is the essence of the political. Agamben, in this move, suffers the same mistaken assumption as Sassen, Brown, and Balibar, focusing entirely on the law as a domestic or internal function, and representing the border as being entirely and exclusive defined and decided by the sovereign. The most important inside/outside or inclusion/exclusion function of contemporary sovereign is the border between the state and the international.

Aristotle is the real source of Agamben's neglect of the international, because the ancient Greek philosopher grounded his understanding of the possibility for a *polis* on the division between Greeks and barbarians, humans and slaves, the *polis* and a community: the former has a shared sense of justice, the latter does not. Agamben misses, however, that the strategies for the maintenance of political community are different, whether a state is "happy in isolation" or whether it is part of a metacommunity.[56] And Aristotle is ambivalent on the issue of the metacommunity: in one sense, his commitment to all men as possessors of freedom lays the foundation for cosmopolitanism, expanded upon by the Stoics; in another sense, his division of men into men capable of freedom and barbarians who are "slaves by nature."[57] This fundamental division between slaves and men is crucial to understanding Aristotle's conception of politics, and completely misread in Agamben.

Aristotle relates borders to self-sufficiency and war. "Everyone would agree in praising the territory which is most entirely self-sufficing . . . it should difficult of access to the enemy and easy of egress to the inhabitants . . . [the city] should be a convenient centre for the protection of the whole country . . ."[58] When he describes the requirements of the polis, he ranks "first, there must be food; secondly, arts, for life requires many instruments; thirdly, there must be arms, for the members of a community have need of them, and in their own hands, too, in order to maintain authority both against disobedient subjects and against external assailants; fourthly, there must be a certain amount of revenue, both for internal needs, and for the purposes of war . . . sixthly, and most necessary of all, there must be a power of deciding what is for the public interest, and what is just in men's dealings with one another."[59]

Agamben misses war in general, and the constitutive role of borders in the creation of war (as opposed to domestic security or emergency). But he also misses the importance of war to Aristotle's conception of politics: "The whole of life is further divided into two parts, business and leisure, war and peace, and of actions some aim at what is necessary and useful, and some at what is honorable ... there must be war for the sake of peace."[60] We can see Agamben start to refer to external threats, and the difference between "peace and war (and between foreign and civil war)," but it is never an integral part of his argument.[61] But, Agamben quickly elides foreign wars and the contemporary war on terror that he terms "a global civil war" – allowing the state of exception to "increasingly as the dominant paradigm of government in contemporary politics."[62] Agamben takes Aristotle's state and his discussions of war to be about the sovereign only, and not about the relations between sovereigns.

But, crucially, Aristotle continues: 'Courage and endurance are required for business and philosophy for leisure, temperance and justice for both, and more especially in times of peace and leisure, for war compels men to be just and temperate, whereas the enjoyment of good fortune and the leisure which comes with peace tend to make them insolent."[63] The external conditions of the metacommunity have a determinative effect on the creation of subjectivity. The international – and the role of the border in limiting the *polis* and the war-facilitating anarchy – play a determinative structural constitution of the subject and the possibility of politics.

Agamben argues, "Order must be established for juridical order to make sense. A regular situation must be created, and sovereign is he who definitely decides if this situation is actually effective."[64] Agamben neglects the co-constitution of inside/outside in this moment. The establishment and definition of order is always both inward and outward looking. The sovereign is, in essence, the border making itself and defining that which it includes and excludes – and defines that which is ordered inside and that which is anarchical or disordered outside. Every decision, therefore, is both political and inter-political (engaging the metacommunity) – describing the conditions and the possibility of an inter-political. Agamben continues, "Politics is now literally the decision concerning the unpolitical (that is, concerning bare life)."[65] The border is precisely that suture between politics and the unpolitical, the inside and the outside – knitting them together. Agamben's invocation of Aristotle's division between *zoē* and *bios* radically underestimates the consideration of the metacommunity, the inter-political realm (be that inter-city, inter-state, world or global).

The majority of interesting and compelling work on Agamben in border studies, and critical geopolitics in general, share this neglect of the international. While Agamben's concept of the camp and the ban have been used to analyse Guantanamo Bay, refugees, and borders, there is very little work on the *international* constitution of these spaces of exception.[66] Even the productive way that Vaughan-Williams uses Agamben specifically to introduce the idea of a "generalized biopolitical border" seems to downplay the constitution of sovereignty through its interactions with other sovereigns.[67] The work in critical border studies that uses Agamben as its theoretical base, sometimes inherits his solipsistic focus.

In sum, Agamben is an important theorist of contemporary politics and sovereign power, and while concerned with thresholds and the ban, his work on the border is entirely lacking any understanding of the international. The dual suturing function of the border is absent: to both separate the domestic sovereign from other sovereigns and bind the sovereign to other sovereigns in a metacommunity. We found the source of this blindness to the role of borders in the creation of the state/metacommunity in Agamben's misreading of Aristotle. We turn now to Walker to engage more fully with this double-move of the border to suture the inside and the outside.

Walker: The Boundaries, Borders, and Limits of the /

Walker's *Inside/Outside: International Relations as Political Theory* is one of the most important books in IR of the past twenty years. It argues that the constitution of political theory and international relations as mutually constituted ways of knowing about the world in turn reflect "the limits of the contemporary political imagination" and express "an historically specific understanding of the character and location of political life in general."[68] Politics and the pursuit of the good life are written as possible only within the bounds of the sovereign state; anarchy, violence, and insecurity exist outside of the state. Political theory is only possible within the community; IR is required for relations between polities. Both political thought and IR must be understood as theories about borders: the maintenance of political of community, the strategies of survival within and between political units; the ways in which political, social, or economic groups might transcend national geographies. The actual role of borders is implicit rather than explicit (at least until *After the Globe, Before the World*); although Walker writes that IR is a "discipline concerned with the delineation of borders," this is meant primarily in a philosophical sense.[69] Similarly, one of the multiple meanings of sovereignty is given "as a given, as the outer limit of a society, a limit occurring as a geographical frontier and maintained by procedures of defence and diplomacy . . ."[70] While *Inside/Outside* is primarily a book about political theory, Walker insists that critical theorists must engage with the grounded, everyday practices of those defence and diplomatic relations: "Claims to sovereignty involve very concrete political practices, practices that are all the more consequential to the extent that they are treated as mere abstractions and legal technicalities."[71] The concept of the "work" that these practices do becomes crucial for understanding sovereignty as performative.[72]

Walker's latest book focuses more specifically on the border:

> it is a line that cannot be evaded, transcended or ignored. As a constitutive limit of modern politics in territorial space, it is also a constitutive limit of both modern political practice and the modern political imagination As a demarcation, however, it is also the site of a mutual

production, and much of what is interesting about it concerns the very active and diverse practices of mutual production that are enabled once the demarcation has been made.[73]

He affirms that modern political theory assumes that borders are both "spatial and legal . . . must be congruent, all in the same place, or at least all aligned at the edge of the same abstract space."[74] Like many border theorists, he argues that this assumption is undermined by the material practices and imaginations of globalisation. The book is alive to suturing effect of borders "that may seem to have zero width . . . but which nevertheless host the most intense practices of sovereign authorization that are simultaneously internal and external . . . they must also be understood as very intensive sites at which considerable work must be done so as to affirm and enact the reality of the ideal . . ."[75] Boundaries, borders, and limits play a signal role in Walker's core argument that the modern political imaginary of the world as a system of sovereign states is inescapably tied to the notion that the globe that is constituted through exclusive claims to sovereignty and territory, and that to try and think outside of this set of nested insides and outsides would require a whole-scale revision of political thought.

Walker's argument focuses on the problematic work of borders to both divide states and constitute a globe. "The reimagination of contemporary political life especially depends on a willingness to think about boundaries less as sites at which very little happens except the separation of one political community, or state, or condition, from another, than as very active sites, moments and practices that work to produce very specific political possibilities of necessity and possibility on either side."[76] Let me ask a different kind question: how do the boundaries, borders, and lines connect and unite that which they separate? What is the actual suturing work of the border? Here is my point of critique: because Walker relies on the language of "boundaries, borders, limits" the argument stuck is a dichotomous circularity: a snake eating itself, simultaneously asserting and undermining its own categories of inquiry; world, globe, inside, outside. Borders, and the modern political theory that underpins them and gives them meaning, fix subjectivity, sovereignty, a system of sovereign states, and whatever the imagination of the global is that exceeds that international system. This figuration provides an excellent viewpoint to understand how borders limit the political imagination, but it has already ceded the chief point of its political critique: it cannot imagine possibilities that are outside the border as division. In contrast, focusing on the suture – the practices of at once knitting together, separating, and distinguishing multiple insides from multiple outsides and the resultant site of rupture and repair – allows us to contingently define the dual functions of the border as tentative separation and as incomplete unification. The suture is thus a thinking tool that helps us operationalise Walker's argument. Borders tie together the domestic, the international, and the global, rendering those lines both a visible sign of state legitimacy in the face of the international and invisible as a sign of the artificiality of the state and the international.

Work is being done in this vein. Rumford's project on 'borderwork' illustrates this dynamic tension. Local groups of "ordinary citizens" are able to both inscribe and overcome borders by strategically taking advantage of different national and European policies to protect a commercial product or regional identity.[77] This borderwork is possible because the borders these citizens perform are multiple, functioning to connect that region to larger networks and to divide that region from local competitors. In his work on Protected Geographical Indications, we see non-state groups invoking the bordering protection of the EU for their local economic products, such as Melton Mowbray pork pies or Stilton cheese. What is particularly useful in this example is the capability to connect, rather than only divide. Galli, however, pushes this notion of multiplying borders much further.

Galli: Political Spaces

Galli is a renowned Italian commentator on Schmitt who argues that "with September 11, 2001, the political thought of Schmitt is dead . . . the Global War commences only where Schmittian political theory is exhausted."[78] He makes two interrelated arguments: that the global war on terror deterritorialises the friend/enemy distinction that was stabilised by borders and that faced with the empirical challenges of globalisation we must theorise politics and space "without the geometric-political coordinates provided to us by modernity. Globalization is indeed essentially border-crossing, the breach of boundaries and the deformation of political geometry."[79] Rather than argue for the disappearance of borders, Galli argues that we must theorise politics and space in a different relation because borders have ceased to hold their constructive qualities.

In his genealogy of modern geopolitics, Galli argues that space is deeply imbricated in politics: "Politics concretely organizes the spaces of liberty, citizenship, law enforcement, and institutional efficacy. Politics extends the spaces of dominion, traces lines of exclusion, designs internal and external borders, and determines the centre and the peripheries, the 'highs' and 'lows' . . ."[80] Tracing the way that Machiavelli, Hobbes, More and Montesquieu each develop uniquely modern imaginaries of space as geometric and smooth, and coterminous with sovereign power, Galli arrives independently at Walker's conclusion, without any degree of self-reflexivity, that "the modern State forms itself precisely in order to expel war to the exterior and to delimit a pacified space at its interior."[81] This inside/outside dynamic is mirrored by Galli's summary of Schmitt's *Nomos of the Earth* that the smooth 'peaceful' state of European public law is made possible through the definition of a chaotic warlike external space of colonial competition.[82]

He argues, "Politics must be spatial before it can be anything else, but this does not exactly mean that politics draws its measure from space, or that it actually takes root in it. Rather, it means that politics must engage with space through the *cut*, which is to say the violence of uprooting, distribution and the creation of 'sides.'"[83] Galli emphasises this arbitrary separation of the space of sovereignty from the void of the international in terms of the 'cut': "The fact that the disconnected political space must necessarily be 'cut' by sovereign decision (and never simply closed or ordered) is a sign that Schmitt takes seriously the non-spatiality of the modern . . . the state is also in crisis *externally*, for the statualization of the world does not produce any order in and of itself, given that it is a simple juxtaposition of multiple sovereignties."[84] Borders are precisely the suture to this cut. Consequently, the real challenge of globalisation to politics is precisely that a cut is not possible. He argues, "For better or worse, every corner of the world is today in direct contact with the world as a whole. Globalisation is, at every point, an *immediate short-circuit* between the local and the global; it is the coincidence of both inclusion and exclusion, assimilation and segregation."[85] Technology and the collapse of space acts as a permanent and undefined suture – connecting the local not to a specific place or authority but to everywhere. Where Galli diverts from both Walker and Agamben is by describing the undoing of modern space: "These figures (peace and war, internal and external, State and Society, political power and economic power, civil production and military destruction) all become confused in one and the same 'volcanic magma,' in a dimension that is neither smooth nor striated . . . all of modernity's political geometries were surpassed."[86] So, borders are multiple and everywhere, but have somehow lost their constitutive function to create insides and outsides, because such a distinction is meaningless under the conditions of globalisation and the global war on terror.

Galli ends his analysis of political space by engaging with the notion of "nomad subjectivities," and a connection to Nancy's notion of frontier to contrast to the modern model of "geometrico-political" borders.[87] Arriving at the mobilities turn in geography from a different direction, he argues that contemporary politics are characterised by movement.[88] Despite a reliance on Schmitt elsewhere, Galli's diagnosis of a globalised world as being characterised by border crossing and requiring new models of space and politics because of the "obsolescence of the distinction between internal and external", the law entirely drops out of his analysis.[89] Whether we use Agamben, Walker, or Schmitt, the question of the law, or the right to have rights, is crucial to our understanding of borders and political space. When Galli invokes the frontier as "an expression of subjective identity whose limit is not a limitation" he attempts the border function as a limit, but without any of the closure implied in fixity.[90]

Work on "acts of citizenship" follow this logic.[91] In this reading, citizenship is not simply a legal status that must be granted by the state, but is also a legal position that can be occupied.[92] When states make status decisions, be it at a school, church, hospital, or place of work, then that place assumes a border function for those individuals. Acts of citizenship occur when the position of citizen is appropriated and occupied by individuals, again in any space, against state actors.

For Galli, then, the empirical facts of globalisation and the global war on terror render borders meaningless, because there is no longer an inside and an outside. In making this claim, he completely misses the political work done by borders to render those meaningless borders meaningful – because those borders still persist and have dramatic effects. Galli argues in essence that borders have not been superceded by globalisation, but rather that every space is a space of the border, a suture between the internal and the external. While constant movement and nomad subjectivities provide a theoretical way out of the problem of closure, fixity, and exclusion, Galli fails to account for the real legal consequences of the border. If the modern border dynamics of inclusion/exclusion have become generalised, then we are left with a genuine ethical problem of the place of rights. If everything is suture, is there ever any foundation for law?

Together/In-between/Apart

The border is at once a division and a knitting together of legal spheres, sovereignties, and authorities. We argue strongly that, against Balibar and Galli, the "border is not everywhere" – or rather the border is not everywhere for everyone. We must accept that although there are multiple boundaries, and different populations experience these boundaries in radically different ways, there is something unique about the state border – and that is the possibility of appealing to law. The state border closely mirrors Agamben's exemplar of a state of exception: border crossers are subject to the law but not objects in the law – a law that is indistinguishable from the force of exclusion and the tyrannical petty sovereign decision. There is no appeal that is not also bound by the sovereign. And, we would emphasise that this is exactly as true of the citizen as it is of the refugee – both share the same legal vacuum at the border. No subject can make a claim on the sovereign that the sovereign *must* recognise – we are all bare life, denuded of political potentia, at the moment of crossing, the moment of examination. This is the suture of the human and the citizen. Following Arendt, "human" rights are a grand trick to re-assert the authority of the state to define itself as the sole arbiter of rights. The passport and the refugee adjudication process (whether done by states or by UNHCR) play exactly the same function – they are communications between sovereigns as to who will exercise dominion and assert the *potential, the possibility* to hear a claim – not to grant it. The state border is the sine qua non of sovereignty, the political and the human.

Walker argues that within modernity, we have no way of thinking outside the world/international dichotomy, and Agamben by a different route is even more pessimistic about the possibility for thinking differently. Galli suggests, echoing the work of Deleuze and Guattari, that there is a possibility for

> nomad subjectivities that are opposed to space, that carry an identity that does not coincide with stability or identification with the state [. . . which] seek mobility, possibilities of not adhering, of seceding, of struggle, of plural, temporary, or partial citizenship. For these subjectivities, the geometric-political effectiveness of static and statual borders is lost, and borders could be anywhere – wherever space is a 'space of transition,' wherever it is more conflictual than definable on the basis of logics of security.[93]

However, we must admit that even as citizenship stretches and strains, it remains a way of connecting rights, responsibilities, and provides a foregrounding for democracy – even as it is fundamentally tested and put into question at borders. Thus, what does the notion of suture provide for our understanding of borders that does not reify the pessimistic notions of absolute exposure and does not kick rights into a free play of nomadology?

We want to make two tentative conclusions, and suggest one direction for new thinking. First, the suture is useful for understanding the way that borders are made to appear and disappear. The / between inside and outside is not so much a break, rather it is a knitting of the limits of political communities – always in reference to other communities. One of the puzzles for us, then, is not how war and anarchy are made separate from the political life of the city, but rather how the relationship between the normal and the abnormal – politics as a continuation of war – are mutually imbricated and made both necessary and different. Second, the border suture is a permanent line of exception that has come to be disaggregated across space/time, the border effectively hides and reinforces the exposure to decision that all border crossers are subject to. And, in addition to the distinctions made between those that are seen – that perform the correct rituals of confession and obeisance – there is a continual and eternal deferral of that decision: we are only ever admitted provisionally, which might be the grounds for a political empathy between insiders and outsiders, citizens and refugees. Border studies, and in particular critical border studies, have taken inspiration from Agamben, Walker, and Galli, but overly focused on the border as a division, rather than as a condition of possibility for sovereignty itself. Promising work, such as that by Vaughan-Williams, Rumford, and Nyers, can advance that agenda by connecting borders to the practices of sovereignty.

ACKNOWLEDGEMENTS

I acknowledge the Social Sciences and Humanities Research Council and the Centre for Research in the Arts, Social Sciences, and Humanities, University of Cambridge for their support for this project. Elements of this argument have been presented at Durham, Keele, and Aalborg Universities, and the University of Ottawa (particularly my seminars on geopolitics and states of exception). Earlier drafts were presented at the "(inter)disciplinarities: The "New Relationality" conference at the University of Victoria, and as the Inaugural Lecture of the "Critical Border Studies Series" at York University. My thanks go to the reviewers, my students, and multiple audiences.

NOTES

1. C. Rumford, 'Theorizing Borders', *European Journal of Social Theory* 9/2 (2006) pp. 155–169; D. Newman, 'Borders and Bordering: Towards an Interdisciplinary Dialogue', *European Journal of Social Theory* 9/2 (2006) pp. 171–186; J. Agnew, 'Know-Where: Geographies of Knowledge of World Politics', *International Political Sociology* 1/2 (2007) pp. 138–148;
2. M. B. Salter, 'Places Everyone: Performativity and Border Studies', *Political Geography* 30/2 (2011) pp. 66–67.
3. R. B. J. Walker, *Inside/Outside: International Relations as Political Theory* (Cambridge: CUP 1993).
4. M. Sparke, *In the Space of Theory: Postfoundational Geographies of the Nation-State* (Minneapolis: University of Minnesota Press 2005).
5. D. Newman, 'On Borders and Power: A Theoretical Framework', *Journal of Borderland Studies* 18 (2003) p. 15.
6. É. Balibar, 'What Is a Border?', *Politics and the Other Scene*, trans. by C. Jones, J. Swenson, and C. Turner (London: Verso 2002) pp. 78–84.
7. G. Agamben, *Homo Sacer: Sovereign Power and Bare Life*, trans. by Daniel Heller-Roazen (Stanford: Stanford University Press 1998).
8. R. B. J. Walker, *After the Globe, Before the World* (New York: Routledge 2010) p. 3.
9. F. Debrix, *Re-Envisioning Peacekeeping: The United Nations and the Mobilizaton of Ideology* (Minneapolis: University of Minnesota Press 1999) pp. 122–124.
10. N. Parker, L. Bialasiewicz, S. Bulmer, B. Carver, R. Durie, J. Heathershaw, H. Van Houtum, et al. 'Lines in the Sand: Towards an Agenda for Critical Border Studies', *Geopolitics* 14/3 (2009) p. 583.
11. M. B. Salter, 'Governmentalities of an Airport: Heterotopia and Confession', *International Political Sociology* 1/1 (2007) pp49–67; Agnew (note 1); H. H. Hillier, 'Airports as Borderlands: American Preclearance and Transitional Spaces in Canada', *Journal of Borderlands Studies* 25/3,4 (2010) pp. 19–30.
12. Sparke (note 4) p. 164.
13. A. Appadurai, *Modernity at Large: Cultural Dimensions of Globalization* (Minneapolis: University of Minnesota Press 1996).
14. M. B. Salter, 'When the Exception Becomes the Rule: Borders, Sovereignty, and Citizenship', *Citizenship Studies* 12/4 (2008) pp. 365–380.
15. I am grateful for Chris Rumford's prompt on this point.
16. J. Williams, *The Ethics of Territorial Borders: Drawing Lines in the Shifting Sand* (New York: Palgrave 2006).
17. A. C. Diener and J. Hagen, 'Borders in a Changing Global Context', in A. C. Diener and J. Hagen (eds.), *Borderlines and Borderlands: Political Oddities at the Edge of the Nation-State* (Lanham, MD: Rowan and Littlefield 2010) p. 189.

18. D. Newman, 'Boundaries, Borders, and Barriers: Changing Geographic Perspectives on Territorial Lines', in M. Albert, D. Jacobson, and Y. Lapid (eds.), *Identities, Borders, Orders: Rethinking International Relations Theory* (Minneapolis: University of Minnesota Press 2001) p. 151.

19. D. Bigo, 'The Möbius Ribbon of Internal and External Security(ies)', in M. Albert, D. Jacobson, and Y. Lapid (eds.), *Identities, Borders, Orders: Rethinking International Relations Theory* (Minneapolis: University of Minnesota Press 1999) p. 114.

20. A. Paasi, 'Bounded Spaces in a "Borderless World": Border Studies, Power and the Anatomy or Power', *Journal of Power* 2/2 (2009) pp. 213–234.

21. S. Sassen, *Territory, Authority, Rights: From Medieval to Global Assemblages* (Princeton: PUP 2006) p. 419.

22. Balibar (note 6).

23. Sassen (note 21) pp. 79, 81, 84.

24. W. Brown, *Walled States, Waning Sovereignty* (New York: Zone Books 2010) p. 21.

25. E. Haddad, 'Danger Happens at the Border', in P. K. Rjaram and C. Grundy-Warr (eds.), *Borderscapes: Hidden Geographies and Politics at Territory's Edge* (Minneapolis: University of Minnesota Press 2007) pp. 119–136.

26. C. Johnson, R. Jones, A. Paasi, L. Amoore, A. Mountz, M. Salter, and C. Rumford, 'Interventions on Rethinking 'the Border' in Border Studies', *Political Geography* 30/2 (2011) pp. 61–69.

27. Rumford, 'Theorizing Borders' (note 1) p. 157.

28. N. Vaughan-Williams, *Border Politics: The Limits of Sovereign Power* (Edinburgh: Edinburgh University Press 2009).

29. Walker, *After the Globe* (note 8) p. 146.

30. O. Löfgren, 'Crossing Borders: The Nationalization of Anxiety', *Ethnological Scandinavica* 2 (1999) pp. 5–27; Salter (note 11).

31. Debrix (note 9); J. Dittmer, *Popular Culture, Geopolitics and Identity* (Plymouth: Rowman and Littlefield 2010); M. J. Shapiro, *Violent Cartographies: Mapping Cultures of War* (Minneapolis: University of Minnesota Press 1997); C. Weber, *Imagining America at War: Morality, Politics and Film* (London: Routledge 2006).

32. Debrix (note 9) p. 106.

33. S. Žižek, *The Fright of Real Tears: Krzysztof Kieślowski between Theory and Post-Theory* (London: British Film Institute 2001) p. 32.

34. A. Badiou, *Manifesto for Philosophy*, trans. by Norman Madarasz (Albany: SUNY Press 1999) p. 61.

35. Žižek (note 33) p. 55.

36. G. Agamben, 'Beyond Human Rights', *Means without End: Notes on Politics*, trans. by V. Binetti and C. Casarino (Minneapolis: University of Minnesota Press 2000) pp. 26. Salter (note 14);

37. M. Augé, *Non-Places: Towards an Anthropology of Supermodernity* (London: Verso 1995).

38. See, amongst others, N. Vaughan-Williams, 'The Generalized Bio-Political Border? Reconceptualising the Limits of Sovereign Power', *Review of International Studies* 35 (2009) pp. 729–749.

39. O. Belcher, L. Martin, A. Secor, S. Simon, and T. Wilson, 'Everywhere and Nowhere: The Exception and the Topological Challenge to Geography', *Antipode* 40/4 (2008) pp. 499–503; D. Bigo, 'Detention of Foreigners, States of Exception and the Social Practices Of Control', in P. K. Rajaram and C. Grundy-Warr (eds.), *Borderscapes: Hidden Geographies and Politics at Territory's Edge* (Minneapolis: University of Minnesota Press 2007); S. P. Eudailya and S. Smith, 'Sovereign Geopolitics: Uncovering the "Sovereignty Paradox"', *Geopolitics* 13/2 (2008) pp. 309–334; R. B. J. Walker, 'Lines of Insecurity: International, Imperial, Exceptional', *Security Dialogue* 37/1 (2006) pp. 65–82. See also Vaughan-Williams and Minca, this volume.

40. Bigo argues that Agamben has fundamentally misunderstood Jean-Luc Nancy's explanation of the ban; Bigo, 'Detention of Foreigners' (note 39). Agamben, *Homo Sacer* (note 7) p. 111.

41. Ibid., pp. 169–170.

42. Ibid., p. 109.

43. Ibid., p. 110.

44. C. Schmitt, *The Concept of the Political* (Chicago: University of Chicago Press 1996) p. 36.

45. N. A. Wonders, 'Global Flows, Semi-Permeable Borders and New Channels of Inequality', in S. Pickering and L. Weber (eds.), *Borders, Mobility and Technologies of Control* (Dordrecht: Springer 2006) pp. 63–86.

46. W. Walters, 'Deportation, Expulsion and the Police of Aliens', *Citizenship Studies* 6/3 (2002) pp. 265–292.

47. M. B. Salter, *Rights of Passage: The Passport in International Relations* (Boulder: Lynne Rienner 2003).

48. Schmitt himself was far more concerned with the international, but this is outside the ambit of this article; C. Schmitt, *The Nomos of the Earth in the International Law of the Jus Publicum Europaeum*, trans. by G. L. Ulmen (New York: Telos 2003).

49. M. B. Salter, *Barbarians and Civilization in International Relations* (London: Pluto 2002); T. Todorov, *The Fear of Barbarians: Beyond the Clash of Civilizations* (Chicago: University of Chicago Press 2010).

50. This is one of the key points of Walker's recent work that we think is underplayed – the ways in which the co-constitution of the inside and outside relies upon an underlying assumed unity – if not of a universal sovereignty then of a common humanity.

51. H. Arendt, *The Origins of Totalitarianism* (New York: Meridian 1958); N. Soguk, *States and Strangers: Refugees and the Displacement of Statecraft* (Minneapolis: University of Minnesota Press 1999).

52. Agamben, 'Beyond Human Rights' (note 36) p. 22.

53. Because Agamben uses Schmitt so extensively in his understandings of power and politics, he should be more attuned to the Schmittian concern with international law, international relations, and geopolitics; C. Minca, 'Giorgio Agamben and the New Biopolitical Nomos of the Earth', *Geografiska Annaler: Series B, Human Geography* 88/ 4 (2006) pp. 387–403; Vaughan-Williams, *Border Politics* (note 28).

54. Agamben, *Homo Sacer* (note 7) p. 28.

55. Aristotle, 'Politics', in R. Mckeon (ed.), *The Basic Works of Aristotle* (New York: Random House) Bk III: Ch. 6, S1278b, p. 1182.

56. Ibid., Bk VII, Ch. 2, S1325a, pp. 1298–1299.

57. Ibid., Bk I, Ch. 4, S1254a, p. 1132.

58. Ibid., Bk VII, Ch. 5, S1327a, p. 1285.

59. Ibid., Bk VII, Ch. 5, S1327a, pp. 1285–1286.

60. Ibid., Bk VII, Ch. 14, S1333a, p. 1298.

61. G. Agamben, *State of Exception*, trans. by K. Attell (Chicago: University of Chicago Press 2005) pp. 22, 42–43.

62. Ibid., p. 2.

63. Aristotle (note 55) Bk VII, Ch. 14, S1334a, p. 1299.

64. Agamben, *Homo Sacer* (note 7) p. 16.

65. Ibid., p. 173.

66. Minca (note 53); F. Johns, 'Guantánamo Bay and the Annihilation of the Exception', *The European Journal of International Law* 16 (2005) pp. 613–635; R. Ek, 'Giorgio Agamben and the Spatialities of the Camp: An Introduction', *Geografiska Annaler: Series B* 88/4 (2006) pp. 363–386; C. Aradau, 'Law Transformed: Guantánamo and the 'Other' Exception', *Third World Quarterly* 28/3 (2007) pp. 489–501.

67. Vaughan-Williams, *Border Politics* (note 28).

68. Walker, *Inside/Outside* (note 3) p. 5.

69. Ibid., p. 15.

70. Walker, *After the Globe* (note 8) p. 169.

71. Ibid., p. 13.

72. C. Weber, 'Performative States', *Millennium: Journal of International Studies* 27/1 (1998) pp. 77–95; L. Bialasiewicz, D. Campbell, S. Elden, S. Graham, A. Jeffrey, and A. Williams, 'Performing Security: The Imaginative Geographies of Current US Strategy', *Political Geography* 26/4 (2007) pp. 405–422.

73. Walker, *After the Globe* (note 8) p. 73.

74. R. B. J. Walker, 'Lines of Insecurity: International, Imperial, Exceptional', *Security Dialogue* 37/1 (2006) p. 70.

75. Walker, *After the Globe* (note 8) p. 52.

76. Ibid., p. 32.

77. C. Rumford, 'Introduction: Citizens and Borderwork in Europe', *Space and Polity* 12/1 (2007) pp. 1–12.

78. C. Galli, *Political Spaces and Global War*, in Adam Sitze (ed.), trans. by Elisabeth Fay (Minneapolis: University of Minnesota Press 2010) p. 182.
79. Ibid., p. 103.
80. Ibid., p. 5.
81. Ibid., p. 38.
82. Ibid., p. 41. See also L. Odysseos and F. Petito (eds.), *The International Political Thought of Carl Schmitt Terror, Liberal War and the Crisis of Global Order* (London: Routledge 2007).
83. Ibid., p. 93.
84. Ibid., p. 91.
85. Ibid., p. 160.
86. Ibid., p. 88.
87. Ibid., pp. 124–125.
88. P. Adey, 'If Mobility is Everything then it is Nothing: Towards a Relations Politics of (Im)mobilities', *Mobilities* 1/1 (2006) pp. 75–94; M. Sheller and J. Urry, 'The New Mobilities Paradigm', *Environment and Planning A* 38 (2006) pp. 207–226.
89. Galli (note 78) p. 108.
90. Ibid., p. 125.
91. E. F. Isin and G. M. Neilsen (eds.), *Acts of Citizenship* (London: Zed Books 2008).
92. C. Moulin and P. Nyers, '"We live in a country of UNHCR" – Refugee Protests and Global Political Society', *International Political Sociology* 1/4 (2007) pp. 356–372.
93. Galli (note 78) p. 124.

Carl Schmitt and the Concept of the Border

CLAUDIO MINCA
Cultural Geography Department, Wageningen University, The Netherlands

NICK VAUGHAN-WILLIAMS
Department of Politics and International Studies, University of Warwick, Coventry, UK

The paper investigates the promise of Carl Schmitt's concept of 'nomos' for developing new spatial imaginaries apposite to the study of 'the border' in contemporary political life, as per the aims of the 'Lines in the Sand' research agenda. Schmitt introduced the idea of a 'nomos of the earth' to refer to the fundamental relation between space and political order. There have been various historical expressions of the nomos, from the Respublica Christiana, *to the* jus publicum Europaeum, *to a post–World War II (dis)order yet to be adequately theorised. We aim to explore the relatively overlooked spatial ontology of Schmitt's work and suggest ways in which it might prompt alternative ways of thinking about borders and bordering practices as representative of broader dynamics in the relation between space and political order.*

INTRODUCTION

Any attempt to grapple with the political salience of the 'line in the sand' metaphor at the core of this special section arguably requires an engagement with the legacy of Carl Schmitt's thought.[1] Schmitt, an influential German jurist and political philosopher of the past century, was a theorist of lines and line-drawing practices *par excellence* and yet this aspect of his work is relatively neglected. In *Nomos of the Earth in the International Law of the Jus Publicum Europaeum* (2003 [orig. 1950]; hereafter '*Nomos*') he refers to the historical persistence of the establishment and maintenance of lines of division via the demarcation of fields, pastures, and forests in the working of the land in ontological terms.[2] Schmitt argues that it is precisely through the making of such 'fences, enclosures, boundaries, walls, houses, and other constraints' that the nature of the relation between 'order and orientation' in social life – what he calls the 'normative order of the earth', or *nomos* – is manifested, in all societies, in all communities, in all times.[3] It is the nature of this fundamental 'division of the earth', and the juridical-political order it determines, that Schmitt seeks to grasp by his deep engagement with the concept of *nomos*.

The literature on Carl Schmitt is by now vast and articulate. In the past decade or so, a flow of articles and books dedicated to several key aspects of his work has appeared, and this tendency has intensified recently.[4] The 'Schmittian' debate is rich and well consolidated, especially with regard to his work on the concept of the political, theory of the sovereign exception, and critique of liberalism. Several biographies have also helped to shed light on the historical and political context of his work, and on the controversial relationship between the popularity of his ideas and his direct involvement in and explicit support for National Socialism.[5] However, only after the publication of the English translation of *Nomos* in 2003 was adequate attention given to Schmitt's theorisations of space and 'the spatial' in relation to 'the political'. This was reflected in numerous interventions questioning the nature of the new global political space in relation to Schmitt's work, both in International Relations, and, only very recently, in political geography.[6] While the discussion on Schmitt's spatialities promises to become robust and possibly better contextualised, not enough has been written so far, at least in our opinion, on his particular understanding of the concept of the border and its implications for studying bordering practices today. It is our aim in this article to begin to address this lacuna.

Our starting point is that the changing nature and location of *borders* between states in contemporary geopolitical configurations is indeed suggestive of the working out of a new global *nomos* hinted at so tantalisingly in Schmitt's later work. For Schmitt, one of the central features of the era of the *jus publicum Europaeum* ('European public law') – the period he identifies between the 'discovery' of the Americas and World War II – was a supposed strict division of European soil into clearly identified and mutually recognised territorial units.[7] Central to this division, for Schmitt, was a specific concept of the border, assumed, ontologically and symbolically, to be located at the outer-edge of the modern sovereign state.[8] As a growing body of work – including the 'Lines in the Sand' project at the origin of this special section – has sought to demonstrate, however, borders between states are increasingly not what or where they are supposed to be according to this geopolitical imaginary.[9] In response to the need to 'extrapolate new border concepts, logics, and imaginaries', as identified in the 'Lines in the Sand' agenda,[10] we will thus critically engage with the idea of the '*nomos*' as originally discussed by Schmitt for opening up novel lines of ontological and socio-spatial enquiry into contemporary bordering practices.

The question of the border, intended as the ontological (and very concrete) 'gesture' of inscribing a division between an inside and an outside, is present in Schmitt's work in different forms, sometimes implicitly, some other times (especially in *Nomos*), in a more explicit fashion. We will therefore treat this issue in reference to two specific aspects of Schmitt's oeuvre: first, his understanding of the 'political community' and of sovereignty in relation to his reading of the constitution of the modern state; second, his speculations on the nature of a new *nomos*, a global spatial order that would presumably follow the collapse of the *jus publicum Europeum*. More elements of his work could be recalled, but these two, in our opinion, are particularly instructive in showing how Schmitt's conceptualisations can assist in grappling with the spatialities of today's global politics and in particular the nature of the contemporary global biometric border regime. While some recent and prominent treatments have implied the historical novelty of ever more varied and technologically sophisticated 'walling' practices since 9/11, the introduction of the Schmittian concept of *nomos* to the lexicon of border studies offers what we consider to be a more sophisticated approach.[11] Our central argument is that Schmitt's treatment of *nomos* provides critical border studies scholars *both* a powerful theoretical diagnosis of the persistence of line-drawing practices in human organisation *and* an historically sensitive disposition towards the way in which this logic plays out in the light of technological advancement.

ORDERING AND BORDERING

Schmitt was greatly preoccupied with the question of order. He was also concerned with the nature of what he considered to be a truly 'political' community. A large part of his early work, but not only, is dedicated to these questions. The entire discussion on the formation of 'the political', together with his most celebrated definition of the relationship between 'friend and enemy', as developed mainly in *The Concept of the Political* [1927] are based on a very specific reading of what a political community is supposed to be.[12] Schmitt was indeed convinced that, with the separation between religion and politics implicit in the post-Westphalian order, the secularised state was deprived of any deep, ontological, legitimacy. However, if sovereignty was to be transferred to the people, as implicit in the constitution of the modern state, then a new concept of 'the political' had to be formulated in order to make this very 'people' act and feel like an actual community, a unified political community. An important part of his work is thus dedicated to the importance of unity for the national community, and in particular for the German people.[13]

This condition of unity, however, must not be understood as a sort of return to some imagined origin,[14] quite the contrary; for Schmitt, with the triumph of secularisation and the disappearance of 'the transcendental' in politics and in the constitution of the state and of sovereign power, there was simply no original moment or event to be reconstituted in order to unify or reunify a political community. Rather, the question of unity had to be seen as a political strategy adopted in order to be able to identify, in concrete terms, who was a friend and who was an enemy – that is, to produce 'the political' in the Schmittian declination of this term.

The border is, in many ways, a pillar in this definition of the political community, a border here deliberately conceived as both a metaphorical space and a physical 'line in the sand'. First of all, the border is understood as a sort of material manifestation of how, in a certain moment and space, the state (and its related political community) can identify itself, can see and manage the 'here' and the 'there'; and can, in other words, 'spatialise the political'.[15] Again, whilst Schmitt does not seem to believe in a sort of cartographic fixity of these categories, at the same time he suggests that, precisely for the need to understand in concrete terms the spaces of the political, the border is a real 'line in the sand' in the production of a political community, a community that can then engage in war with the Other and, indeed, act 'politically'.[16] The border, then, is the symbolic and physical line in the sand that helps to produce the imaginative political geographies of enmity that sit at the foundations of his theory of the political. Actual borders, moreover, are visible, clear, 'concrete', spatially defined: all qualities greatly appreciated by Schmitt. Borders are also the result of the spatial appropriation of land, which, for him, is a fundamental ontological gesture in the constitution of any political community.[17]

The border, for Schmitt, is then both the visible result of a primordial appropriation of the land and a concrete line in space, with immediate and immanent effects, something fundamental to any form of social organisation and of 'the political'. The theoretical foundations of this 'primary spatialisation'[18] deserve some further thought. Schmitt, while never entirely endorsing a fully fledged 'organic' theory of the state (in the Ratzelian tradition), at the same time often returns to the question of how to treat the supposed coincidence of nation, state and territory as the quintessential modern political formation, a key element in any formulation of international politics as well. He clearly expresses his concerns regarding the tensions that inherently transverse the formation of the secularised state and of its spaces. These concerns are presented in his work in different ways. First, since in the modern state there is no coincidence between law and the state itself[19]; for Schmitt, this distance must be compensated for by institutionalised borders, with their reassuring cartographic fixity. Second, the modern state as a political territorial formation is marked by a deliberate, and for Schmitt rather problematic, separation between institutions and society, between economy and politics, etc. As a consequence of these artificial separations, the body of the nation, for Schmitt, is too often presented as a sort of biological body contained by specific borders, as if a potential equilibrium could be obtained, at least in perspective. This has consequences in international politics as well, since it implies a global system of nation-states in a sort of potential stable status quo of political and national formations.

Schmitt's scepticism towards this interpretation, that he sees also as the result of the decline of the global order generated by what he famously calls *jus publicum Europeum*, comes from the fact that he believes the modern state to be a constitutionally *incomplete* project, a formation affected by lack of ontological legitimacy, but also by an idea of the people as sovereign – albeit a sovereign power that inherently exceeds its very possibility of finding a stable and permanent condition. He expresses this view on several occasions, but in particular in his 1935 *Staat, Bewegung, Volk* (Movement, State, People) where he describes a dynamic biopolitical understanding of the Nazi State-in-the-making and its flexible and mutable spatialities. This is also where he delineates the fundamental principles of a new national-socialist constitutional order. The new German community in the making for him had to consist of three key elements: the state, as administrative apparatus; the 'movement', as the political leadership (read: the party) operating in the name of the people; and the people, that is the civil society, literally consisting of a multitude 'living in the shadow and under the protection of decisions reached in the higher regions of the political order'.[20]

For Schmitt, in the secularised state, a state fully founded on immanence, the principle of sovereign power is based on an original act of violence, a revolutionary act, and the border represents in many ways the spatialisation of this very violence. This violence is aimed at realising a form of concrete order produced, again, not so much by a supposed internal harmony of/in the national community, but rather by a 'cut', a caesura in the territorial and biological body of the nation, a partition that originates an actual political space.[21] Schmitt is, in fact, firm in his belief that normality and order are produced by an act of concrete differentiation. The border, the line in the sand, is for him a crucial element of this differentiation: an 'exceptional' space, a zone of anomie excluded from the 'normal' juridical-political space of the state, but nevertheless an integral part of that national territory.

This very idea of 'normality' is indeed key to Schmitt's renowned formulation of the sovereign exception, recently re-interpreted by philosopher Giorgio Agamben, among many others. According to Italian political philosopher Carlo Galli,[22] in this formulation Schmitt presents a detailed analysis of the constitution of the metaphorical and concrete borders of modern politics but also of the ways in which those very borders should be endlessly transgressed. Galli is indeed convinced that one of the major contributions of the German legal theorist to contemporary political thought is precisely his lucid deconstruction of the secularised state and, at the same time, his related understanding of the exception as the only way to furnish the state with a degree of legitimacy. The exception, in fact, not only constantly questions the relationship between the inside and the outside that the institutions of 'borders' should have stabilised, but becomes a true principle of transgression and reformulation of the very meaning and functions of the border itself – transgression and reformulation that Schmitt reads as ways of re-establishing a reactionary order while, for Galli and others may be read in different terms as well.

The border, in this case the border of the state, has of course an effect on the relationship between the 'us' – whether the national community, the State, the German People, Western Civilisation, or, in the case of the enmity lines, the regulated space of the *jus publicum Europaeum* – and 'the Rest'. The border for Schmitt has also another crucial performative dimension. The border is, in fact, the site where the 'decision' – a fundamental element in Schmitt's theory of power – is enacted and where it shows perhaps its most visible face.[23] It is here that extra-legal violence is revealed as the ultimate ground of the 'normal' juridical-political order of the state for the crown jurist of the Third Reich. Schmitt is indeed convinced that due to the constitutional lack of an ontological foundation (that is, the lack of the transcendental) in the secularised state, the border becomes a sort of strategic fiction, a 'line in the sand' based on a fictional belief in the existence of a fundamental right to the land, of a pre-existing order that must be maintained or re-established. This overwhelming and constitutive tension between the (lack of the) 'ontological' and the actual representations of the state as a legitimate formation translates into a tension precisely on the border; only the act of decision, *about* and *on* the border makes it possible to overcome that untenable tension. The border is therefore the result of a fictional but very effective decision, a site that reveals, in its very performativity, a dialectical tension between the sovereign decision and a fictional representation of order. For Schmitt, the border is where this tension comes together, where any attempt to 'freeze' the fictional order of the immanent state, to stabilise it, to hide the lack of a deeper ontological form of legitimacy, is translated into 'concrete' space.[24]

THE *NOMOS* OF THE EARTH AND THE QUESTION OF BORDERS

Whereas Schmitt took the modern sovereign state as the tacit ground for his analysis of the limits of authority, sovereignty, and territory in earlier texts, *Nomos* implies a modified position, although his obsession on the ways in which Geneva and Versailles had treated Germany was present in several of his pre-war writings.[25] In *Nomos* he problematises the straightforward inside/outside topology associated with the spatio-normative order of the *jus publicum Europaeum*. But while Schmitt is in no doubt that the old

Eurocentric *nomos* had come to an end, he does not equate this demise with the abandonment of planetary division: 'The new nomos of our planet is growing irresistibly. . . . To be sure, the old nomos has collapsed, and with it a whole system of accepted measures, concepts, and customs. But what is coming is . . . not boundlessness or a nothingness hostile to nomos'.[26]

The concept of '*nomos*' is a derivation of the Greek word *nemein* meaning 'to take or appropriate".[27] In German *nemein* translates as *nehmen*, which, in turn, is linked to the verbs *teilen* (to divide or distribute) and *weiden* (to pasture).[28] The idea of *nomos*, then, encompasses these three dimensions – the appropriation, division, and cultivation of land – as the 'primal processes of human history, three acts of the primal drama'.[29] For this reason Schmitt refers to *nomos* as a 'fence-word'.[30]

> Every new age and every new epoch in the coexistence of peoples, empires, and countries, of rulers and power formulations of every sort, is founded on new spatial divisions, new enclosures, and new spatial orders of the earth.[31]

Schmitt's history of the normative order of the earth is structured around three distinct epochs each characterised by different border logics. Up until the 'age of discoveries' of the late fifteenth and sixteenth centuries, there was no concept of the 'globe' as we think of it today. *Respublica Christiana* was a spatial order reliant upon divisions between the soils of the medieval West, the soils of the heathens, and the soils of Islamic empires. In this context modern assumptions about the congruence between authority, sovereignty, and territory made little sense. Rather, Medieval Europe was characterised by messy and often overlapping spatialities. Common among *all* peoples, according to Schmitt, was the assumption that *their particular society* was at the 'centre of the earth'. Outside those societies was a space conceived of in terms of a chaotic and barbaric zone: 'practically . . .', Schmitt argues, 'this meant that in the outer world and with good conscience, one could conquer and plunder to a certain boundary'.[32] It is in this sense, therefore, that the border existed as demarcation between inner and outer worlds. The 'discovery' of the American continent in 1492, however, created 'free space' for the appropriation, division, and cultivation of colonial lands by Europeans. In turn, this posed the need for new global spatial ordering, which stimulated the emergence of a second *nomos* on Schmitt's account: the *jus publicum Europaeum*. With the circumnavigation of the globe came new cartographic representations based on a core geographic differentiation between land and sea, and the advent of a modified border logic: that which Schmitt refers to as 'global linear thinking'.[33]

The emergence of the 'globe' as a new form of measurement enabled the conceptualisation of borders on a global scale. Central here was the division of global space into two zones: the *jus publicum Europaeum* on the one hand; and the 'New World' on the other. The European powers behind this partitioning sought to 'bracket' war to the outside of the New World where only the law of the strongest applied.[34] In turn, this had the effect of reducing the scope for and intensity of conflict within Europe, which became rendered merely 'analogous to a duel'.[35] Schmitt's global lines were a set of divisions that carved up territory *within* the European order. Thus, Pope Alexander VI's *inter caetera divinae* in 1494 was a pole-to-pole line that granted lands in America to Spain. Similarly, the *partition del mar Océano*, of the same year, saw the Atlantic split between Spain and Portugal. Later, in 1559, came the Anglo-French 'amity lines'.

The *jus publicum Europaeum* went hand in hand not only with a central division between European and non-European spaces, but also with a juridical-political order based upon centralised, spatially self-contained, sovereign states. At the heart of this new European spatial order was the concept of the border of the state, which, at least in Schmitt's account, provided for political unity, an end to civil wars, and clear demarcations between jurisdictions:

> The core of the *nomos* lay in the division of European soil into state territories with firm borders, which immediately initiated an important distinction, namely that this soil of recognized European states and their land had a special status in international law.[36]

With the end of World War I and the related breakdown of that normative spatio-juridical concept of global order, however, the world entered a period of crisis resulting from the emergence of a vapid border-less universalism. The declining juridical significance of the categorisation of peoples as 'civilised', 'half-civilised (barbaric)', and 'wild peoples (savages)' was a factor in the eventual dissolution of the *jus publicum Europaeum*.[37] These categories had formerly accompanied firm distinctions between European and non-European zones of juridical-political order, but their abandonment meant that the spatial relation between the European motherland and overseas colony became increasingly blurred. As a result of this blurring, Schmitt points to the emergence of a new global universalism, which arose alongside the ascendancy of liberal economic thinking and commercialism, free trade and labour, and, crucially, *the absence of an overarching normative spatial order*: 'In short: over, under, and beside the state-political borders of what appeared to be a purely political international law between states spread a free, i.e. non-state sphere of economy permeating everything: a global economy'.[38]

The dissolution of the *jus publicum Europaeum* emerged in all its evidence during the Paris Peace Conferences of 1918–1919. Symbolic of the new space-less universalism was the ill-fated League of Nations. Schmitt criticises the architects of the League precisely for their failure to offer a viable alternative to the previous *nomos* and to realise the importance of establishing a coherent spatial order: 'Instead of bracketing war, a net of intentionally vague, formal compromises and cautiously worked stylized norms was assembled, and, in turn, was subjected to an ostensibly purely juridical interpretation'.[39] What followed, therefore, was the emergence of profound global *dis*order, which became reproduced by the very universalist norms and institutions that sought to overcome these problems. The prospect of a third *nomos* preoccupied Schmitt towards the end of his 1950 text, but, as we shall explore in the following section, his speculations hinged around the *changing* nature of border logics rather than the *obsolescence* of borders per se.

SHIFTING BORDERS AND THE COMING GLOBAL *NOMOS*

Despite his relative scepticism towards the modern state and its political foundations, Schmitt nonetheless insisted in his attempts to identify a possible *nomos* for the German people and for a newly pacified global political space. This preoccupation is expressed in different moments and in different passages of his scholarly trajectory, but it became particularly important both during his 'Nazi phase', and during the postwar period in his writings dedicated to international politics and questions of space. This apparent twist away from the theorisation of 'the political', due also to his changing life circumstances, takes indeed two major forms: first, his attempt to imagine a biopolitical solution to the historical problems of the German people (despite his reluctance, in general terms, to appeal to biological and racial categories in order to support his juridical and political claims)[40]; second, his later, more geopolitically oriented writings on the concept of greater space, the *Großraum*, and the problem of 'world order' in the post-war period.[41]

First, in order to establish the biopolitical dimensions of Schmitt's pre- and interwar thought it is instructive to turn to Cavalletti's account of his work. In the same way that every spatial concept, for Schmitt, is necessarily political and vice versa, the concept of population from the eighteenth century onwards must be understood as a spatio-political term with a positive 'intensity' capable of drawing a peculiar amity line.[42] According to this new concept of population, which Cavalletti argues was fully embraced by Schmitt, each and every relation between population and the environment was only made possible via a 'primary' spatialisation of the human species.[43] Such a primary spatialisation produces an understanding of the human that is immediately political: 'population' is a calculative concept, which defines an endless series of caesurae in the body politic.[44] From this moment on any relation between population and territory loses its traditional geographical meaning and becomes a kind of geo-biopolitics: 'space becomes vital and life becomes spatial, in an intensive way. . . . The density of life is the concept that denominates life fighting with life . . . density intended as a form of primary (original?) spatialisation that permeates every spatial-political organism'.[45] Space-population and space-density, on Cavalletti's account, are key concepts in a particular vision of the world that came to inform Schmitt's biopolitical understanding of the national community. Indeed, Schmitt adopted these ideas via the writings of Italian fascist demographer Luigi Valli, whose book – *Il diritto dei popoli alla terra* (1926) – was read and cited by Schmitt in his National-Socialist interpretation of the Monroe Doctrine of greater spaces published in 1939.[46]

Second, as noted above, in his writing on the *nomos* and new global spaces produced by different forms of universalism, Schmitt abandons his focus on the state as the locus of the political, with all its implications, and moves towards the analysis of other possible spatial formations that may help in replacing the lost *jus publicum Europeum* in favour of a new subdivision of the planet into many *Großraume*.[47] The important point here is that, with his theorisations of the nature of the German *Großraum* in support of Hitler's *Geopolitik* of expansion, and especially his specification of the *nomos* of the earth that followed, Schmitt seems to identify the answer to some of the problems of the political present in the understanding and the adoption of an adequate and properly formulated spatial theory. The lack of ontological foundations to the contemporary political condition could then be somewhat compensated for by an adequate conceptualisation and implementation of spatial theory, a spatial understanding of the workings of the political: locally, but especially globally.

Since the decline of the *jus publicum Europaeum* had allowed for the emergence of a sort of space-less global politics based on a spatial measure, Schmitt believed that a new spatial order, a new set of criteria of spatial differentiation aimed at creating some degree of mutually recognised and accepted order, were needed. This was the key, for Schmitt, to peace and stability, together with a new form of legitimacy based on a 'concrete situation' and not any more on the predominant space-less and neutral universalism of post-war global institutions. As well as the growth of a world economy, Schmitt identifies several other symptoms of the coming of a new global *nomos* following the end of World War II and the planetary division between East and West. One is the dawn of a new technical-industrial era, which facilitated not only warfare on land and sea, but also *air* as 'the force-field of human power and activity'.[48] Another related symptom is the growing political, legal (as well as economic) influence of the US beyond its territorial delimitations as conventionally understood. While Schmitt concedes that 'every true empire around the world has claimed . . . a sphere of spatial sovereignty beyond its borders', he argues that the extension in the 1930s of the US security zone up to 300 miles from its shores constituted a *Großraum* of new proportions.[49]

Far from the kind of 'borderless world' arguments peddled by some globalisation theorists during the 1990s, however, Schmitt's three prognoses for the emergence of a new *nomos* are each characterised by distinctive border logics. The first is one that predicts the victory of one of the superpowers and the coronation of a new planetary sovereign: 'He would appropriate the whole earth – land, sea, and air – and would divide and manage it in accord with his plans and ideas'.[50] In this scenario planetary division is not abandoned, since the victor is presented as presiding over a global space striated by lines drawn unilaterally. The second future imagined by Schmitt is one whereby the victor administers and/or guarantees the balanced structure of the previous *nomos*, as in the case of *pax Britannica* in the nineteenth century. Here again borders are not elided, but predicted to operate like magnetic fields of energy and influence that stretch beyond the physical territorial limits of the state. Third, Schmitt presents a final option that involves the combination of several independent power blocs constituting future world order: one where the state has been displaced by greater spaces vying for the ability to control planetary division. In each case the fundamental logic and activity of line-drawing is not rendered obsolete à la borderless world advocates. Rather, it is *transformed* according to historical outcomes.

A NEW GLOBAL *NOMOS*?

If, as Schmitt's analysis implies, the changing nature and location of borders between states is symptomatic of broader structural shifts in the, as Schmitt would have it, 'spatial consciousness of the earth', then recent work on the transformation of contemporary bordering practices chimes with his speculations on the emergence of a new *nomos*. While there is certainly evidence to suggest that older forms of bordering – consistent with the inside/outside logic of the *jus publicum Europaeum* – continue to exist, a growing number of writers (as noted below) seek to draw our attention to the proliferation and differentiation of borders. Indeed, it is especially against the backdrop of the ongoing 'war on terror' since 9–11 that this line of argumentation has been developed and illustrated. In this context, it is often said that bordering practices – understood broadly in terms of wherever and whenever a check is made on the mobility of people, services, and goods – have become sociologically 'thicker' entities that belie the 'thinness' of the line in the sand metaphor. Indeed, there are several ways in which this metaphor has been found wanting in the light of recent contributions to interdisciplinary border scholarship (including the other pieces in this special section).

First, in spatial terms, the notion of a territorially fixed barrier is radically at odds with the mobility of contemporary bordering practices, which are increasingly designed to be portable as the people, services, and goods they monitor. There is, in other words, an increasing geographical diversification of the border, with (Western) states commonly juxtaposing each other's controls, off-shoring checks on mobility to overseas territories, and/or, conversely, dispersing those checks throughout 'domestic' space. Complicating traditional border tropes even further is the fact that bordering practices are today not about preventing but facilitating the faster transit of a trusted few at the expense of an array of suspicious Others.[51]

Second, and intimately related to these developments, the static 'line in the sand' metaphor does not adequately reflect the temporal sophistication of technologies designed to filter 'good' from 'bad' according to pre-emptive risk assessments and identity management systems. Indeed, 'the border' can now be understood as a continuum of controls on movement stretching not only between domestic and foreign space, but also from 'now' literally into 'the future'. Another aspect is the sheer speed at which automated checks based on techniques such as iris scanning, fingerprint detection, and backscatter whole body x-ray machines can make decisions about who and/or what is considered legitimate/illegitimate, and therefore included/excluded from mobile communities.[52]

Third, empirical observations about the spatio-temporal transformation of the border have been matched by calls for more sophisticated theoretical vocabularies and imaginaries.[53] In response, and reflecting a broader sociological 'turn' in the International Relations literature, the border has been recast as a set of sovereign rituals through which the fiction of the modern subject, state, and state-system is continually (re)produced, performed into being, and whose contingency is ultimately concealed over and forgotten about.[54] In this context some recent theorisations have drawn on the register of the 'virtual' in order to capture the way in which border security apparatuses attempt to *simulate the effects of* maximum security in the West.[55] Indeed, building upon Schmitt's account, these analyses gesture towards the existence of a new 'virtualised' *nomos*, which is performed through the pre-emptive biometric practices of Western states dispersed globally.

In the light of these developments how does Schmitt's treatment of the border add to our understanding of contemporary bordering practices? On the one hand, it might be objected that the profound changes to the nature and location of borders undermine the congruence between sovereignty, law, and space, which provided Schmitt with the necessary coordinates for his paradigmatic diagnoses of friend/enemy relations as the essence of the political, notions of a 'true' political community based on insider/outsider distinctions, and treatment of the sovereign as he who decides on the exception within a given territorial jurisdiction. On the other hand, however, Schmitt's later formulation of the concept of *nomos* already noted the unravelling of these coordinates as a basis for diagnosing what he considered to be the post-war crisis of world order, and offers critical border studies scholars a distinctive theoretical framework.

Noting the increasing multi-dimensionality of the border, R. B. J. Walker has recently argued that future political analysis will need to 'think much more carefully about how complex practices of drawing lines have come to be treated as such a simple matter'.[56] In particular, Walker enjoins scholars of border studies to consider in greater depth precisely the role that *some* borders do in conditioning the possibility of *other* borders. It is in this regard that Schmitt's theorisation of *nomos* is potentially most instructive as what we might call a 'meta-border' concept. Thinking in terms of *nomos* extrapolates away from the border understood merely in terms of a thin 'line in the sand'. Rather, the lens of *nomos* adds greater thickness – spatial, temporal, and historical – to the analysis of contemporary bordering practices and the spatial consciousness they reflect. The adoption of this lens avoids the trap of reading the changing nature of borders in any given historical era as *sui generis*. This trap not only characterised much of the 1990s globalisation literature noted earlier, but also more recent treatments of the war on terror. Wendy Brown, for example, similarly reads the 'proliferation of walls, and walls within walls' as a novel phenomenon arising from the weakened condition of the nation-state.[57] By contrast, a Schmittian reading would emphasise that the desire for walling is not new and that current bordering practices reflect *both* sedimented logics of division *and* new manifestations of spatial order and orientation made possible by technological advancements.

CONCLUSION: ON BORDERS, THRESHOLDS, AND WEREWOLVES

Let us try to wrap up our argument and see what can be learned from Schmitt's lesson. Perhaps the main question facing scholars of border studies today is whether Schmitt's oeuvre can be of any use in the understanding of the contemporary global spaces of the political in the light of the declared or undeclared articulations of the so-called war on terror. In addition, we may want to ask how his theory of the sovereign exception can be helpful in the interpretation of the geographies of permanent exception that have emerged in the aftermath of the attacks on the Twin Towers. In the contemporary shifting global 'condition', a condition that Schmitt would have possibly read as the result of the definitive triumph of technology over politics, is his early definition of state borders still valid? How does his understanding of the border as spatial device, as a strategy, as a site where the violent effects of a 'decision' are the only actual source of true legitimacy, engage with the contemporary political geographies of exception, with new forms of conceptualisation and management of the border?

Carlo Galli, for example, whilst recognising a prophetic element in Schmitt's understandings of the changing nature of global politics and its spatialities, at the same time remains sceptical about the use of Schmittian concepts and categories in order to decipher the contemporary order, including the question of borders. In our view, this criticism is acceptable only if Schmitt is read merely as a sort of meta-geographer. However, if we follow Agamben's interpretation of the Schmittian sovereign exception, the contemporary border can also be read as a threshold, a reading that resonates to some extent with Schmitt's early speculations.

The border conceived as a threshold is literally a line in the sand, in the sense that it can be described as a site where 'the sovereign' can activate/produce the exception, within a logic that is only apparently functionalistic, but that in practice translates into a potentially endless series of arbitrary decisions, sovereign decisions empowered by the 'fracture' produce by the exception.[58] In the contemporary scenario of production (and biometric management) of 'new' forms of borders, it may be of some use to recall Schmitt's reflections on the enactment of the sovereign decision, aimed at realising an impossible order, *on* the border and *through* the performativity of the border. The sovereign decision on/at the border today might thus be read as a strange attempt at re-spatialising the political, with the difference that the contemporary 'enemy' seems to have no location, no spatiality, only a strange combination of presence and absence; this a-spatial enemy, the opposite of the telluric partisan as famously theorised by Schmitt in the 1960s, is thus imagined and treated more as a projection, a ghost.[59] In the present political configuration and in the biometric transfigurations of the border, we are still witnessing endless sovereign 'gestures' attempting to mark out borders, to spatialise the (ghostly) enemy, but they present themselves, unlike Schmitt's old state borders, as true lines in the sand – strangely mobile, porous, visible and invisible, virtual, but at the same very 'concrete', as Schmitt would have it. They come and they go, and they pervade, albeit with different intensities and effects, all available spaces. Every piece of land drawn into the global war on terror, as we know, has the potential to be literally converted into a temporary, unstable and yet very concrete border, where the sovereign decision and the related space of exception can be mobilised and performed.

The ghostly enemy of the contemporary border regime disturbingly recalls the werewolves, to use Agamben's jargon, that inhabit beyond/outside the Hobbesian border, a figure that Schmitt recalls on several occasions.[60] We might say that on the contemporary border-threshold, a border that reappears whenever a sovereign decision is taken, we are all potential werewolves, or *homines sacri* as Agamben would have it. It is precisely in this sense that these borders can be conceived – following Schmitt's formulations and Agamben's successive interpretations – as thresholds, as unstable sites of materialisation of the permanent exception and of potential profanations. In a strange dance between the violent and concrete effects of a new, temporary but potentially all encompassing 'global order', and the global functionalist fantasies of full control of bodies and spaces – of bodies in space – friends and enemies seem to become literally ghosts who travel through our public spaces and across our multiple borders, ghosts that can materialise in any moment, here or there, in a space-in-between that resembles more and more the fictional tensions of order described many years ago by Carl Schmitt.

NOTES

1. The biblical metaphor of the 'line in the sand' refers to the drawing of a border in the ground beyond which no one dares to cross. It captures various commonplace assumptions about borders and their relationship with territory, sovereignty, authority, and spatiality. The 'Lines in the Sand' network seeks to problematise these assumptions and question their continued salience in the light of contemporary political practice – see N. Parker, Luiza Bialasiewicz, Sarah Bulmer, Ben Carver, Robin Durie, John Heathershaw, Henk Van Houtum, et al. 'Lines in the Sand? Towards an Agenda for Critical Border Studies', *Geopolitics* 14/3 (2009) pp. 582–587.

2. C. Schmitt, *The Nomos of the Earth in the International Law of the Jus Publicum Europaeum*, trans. by G. Ulmen (New York: Telos Press 2003 [orig. 1950]) p. 42. See also C. Minca, 'Carl Schmitt and the Question of Spatial Ontology', in S. Legg (ed.), *Spatiality, Sovereignty, and Carl Schmitt: Geographies of the Nomos* (London and New York: Routledge 2011); and R. Rowan, 'A New Nomos of Post-Nomos?', in S. Legg (ed.), *Spatiality, Sovereignty, and Carl Schmitt: Geographies of the Nomos* (London and New York: Routledge 2011).

3. Schmitt, *Nomos of the Earth* (note 2) p. 42.

4. See, for example, D. Chandler 'The Revival of Carl Schmitt in International Relations: The Last Refuge of Critical Theorists?', *Millennium: Journal of International Studies* 37/1 (2008) pp. 27–48; W. Hooker, *Carl Schmitt's International Thought: Order and Orientation* (Oxford: Oxford University Press 2009); L. Odysseus and F. Petito, *The International Political Thought of Carl Schmitt: Terror, Liberal War, and the Crisis of Global Order* (London and New York: Routledge 2008); G. Slomp, *Carl Schmitt and the Politics of Violence, Hostility, and Terror* (Basingstoke and New York: Palgrave Macmillan 2009).

5. See G. Balakrishnan, *The Enemy. An Intellectual Portrait of Carl Schmitt* (London: Verso 2000).

6. See S. Legg (ed.), *Spatiality, Sovereignty, and Carl Schmitt: Geographies of the Nomos* (London and New York: Routledge 2011).

7. Ibid.

8. See R. B. J. Walker, *Before the Globe/After the World* (London and New York: Routledge 2010); R. B. J. Walker, *Inside/Outside: International Relations as Political Theory* (Cambridge: Cambridge University Press 1993).

9. See, inter alia, L. Bialasiewicz, *Europe and the World: EU Geopolitics and the Transformation of European Space* (Aldershot: Ashgate 2011); N. Parker, 'From Borders to Margins: A Deleuzian Ontology for Identities in the Postinternational Environment', *Alternatives: Global, Local, Political* 34/1 (2009) pp. 17–39; C. Rumford (ed.), 'Global Borders', *Environment and Planning D: Society and Space*, Special Issue (2010); M. Salter, 'The Global Visa Regime and the Political Technologies of the International Self: Borders, Bodies, Biopolitics', *Alternatives: Global, Local, Political* 31/2 (2006) pp. 167–189; N. Vaughan-Williams, 'The UK Border Security Continuum: Virtual Biopolitics and the Simulation of the Sovereign Ban', *Environment and Planning D: Society and Space* 28 (2010) pp. 1071–1083; N. Vaughan-Williams, *Border Politics: The Limits of Sovereign Power* (Edinburgh: Edinburgh University Press 2009); W. Walters, 'Border/Control', *European Journal of Social Theory* 9/2 (2006) pp. 187–193.

10. Parker et al. (note 1) p. 583.

11. See W. Brown, *Walled States, Waning Sovereignty* (New York: Zone Books 2010)

12. See C. Schmitt, *The Concept of the Political*, trans. by G. Schwab (Chicago and London: The University of Chicago Press 1996 [orig. 1927]); C. Schmitt, *Political Theology: Four Chapters on the Concept of Sovereignty*, trans. by G. Schwab, 3rd ed. (Chicago and London: The University of Chicago Press 2005 [orig. 1922]).

13. See Schmitt, *The Concept of the Political* (note 12).

14. See R. Esposito, *Communitas. Origine e destino della comunità* (Torino: Einaudi 1988).

15. C. Galli, *Lo sguardo di Giano* (Bologna: il Mulino 2008) p. 32.

16. Schmitt, *Nomos of the Earth* (note 2) pp. 35–36.

17. Ibid., see the Introduction.
18. See A. Cavalletti, *La città biopolitica* (Milan: Mondadori 2005); also, Minca (note 2).
19. This is also Galli's (note 15) view p. 20.
20. Balakrishnan (note 5) p. 184; see also G. Agamben, *State of Exception* (Chicago and London: University of Chicago Press 2005); C. Schmitt, *Un giurista davanti a se stesso* (Neri Pozza: Vicenza 2005) "Introduction" pp. 19–24.
21. On this aspect of Schmitt's work see G. Agamben, *Homo Sacer: Sovereign Power and Bare Life*, trans. by D. Heller-Roazen (Stanford, CA: Stanford University Press 1998); and Agamben, *State of Exception* (note 20).
22. Galli (note 15) pp. 140–141.
23. See Roxanne Doty, 'States of Exception on the Mexico-U.S. Border: Security, Decisions, and Civilian Border Patrols', *International Political Sociology* 1/2 (2007) pp. 113–137; Salter (note 9); N. Vaughan-Williams, 'Borders, Territory, Law', *International Political Sociology* 4/2 (Dec. 2008) pp. 322–338.
24. See also, Galli (note 15).
25. C. Schmitt, 'Forms of Modern Imperialism in International Law' (orig. 1932), in S. Legg (ed.), *Spatiality, Sovereignty, and Carl Schmitt: Geographies of the Nomos* (London and New York: Routledge 2011); and C. Schmitt, '*Großraum* versus Universalism: The International Legal Struggle over the Monroe Doctrine' (orig. 1939), in Legg (ed.), *Spatiality, Sovereignty, and Carl Schmitt: Geographies of the Nomos* (London and New York: Routledge 2011). Schmitt, *Nomos of the Earth* (note 2) p. 355.
26. Schmitt (note 1) p. 355.
27. Ibid., p. 67.
28. Ibid., pp. 344–345.
29. Ibid., p. 351.
30. Ibid., p. 70.
31. Ibid., p. 79.
32. Ibid., p. 352.
33. Ibid., p. 87.
34. Ibid., p. 94.
35. Ibid., p. 141.
36. Ibid., p. 148.
37. Ibid., p. 234.
38. Ibid., p. 235.
39. Ibid., p. 243.
40. See Minca (note 2); Barnes and Minca, 'Nazi Spatial Theory: The Dark Geographies of Carl Schmitt and Walter Christaller', *Annals of the Association of American Geographers* (forthcoming, 2013); Agamben, *State of Exception* (note 20); and Cavalletti (note 18).
41. Barnes and Minca (note 40).
42. Cavalletti (note 18).
43. Ibid., p. 79.
44. Ibid., p. 79.
45. Ibid., pp. 202, 206.
46. Ibid., p. 210; Schmitt 1992; 1995. See also Minca (note 2).
47. See Barnes and Minca (note 40).
48. Schmitt, *Nomos of the Earth* (note 2) p. 354.
49. Ibid., pp. 281–282.
50. Ibid., p. 354.
51. See L. Amoore, 'Biometric Borders: Governing Mobilities in the War on Terror', *Political Geography* 25 (2006) pp. 336–51; N. Vaughan-Williams, 'Borderwork Beyond Inside/Outside? Frontex, the Citizen-Detective and the War on Terror', *Space and Polity* 12/1 (April 2008) pp. 63–79; N. Vaughan-Williams, 'Off-Shore Biopolitical Border Security: The EU's Global Response to Migration, Piracy, and 'Risky' Subjects', in L. Bialasiewicz (ed.), *Europe and the World: EU Geopolitics and the Transformation of European Space* (Aldershot: Ashgate 2011).
52. See L. Bialasiewicz (note 9); D. Bigo, 'The Möbius Ribbon of Internal and External Security(ies)', in M. Albert, D. Jacobson, and Y. Lapid (eds.), *Identities, Borders, Orders: Rethinking International Relations Theory* (Minnesota and London: University of Minnesota Press 2001) pp. 91–116; W. Walters, 'Mapping Schengenland: Denaturalising the Border', *Environment and Planning (D): Society and Space* 20/5 (2002) pp. 564–580; Vaughan-Williams, 'The UK Border' (note 9).

53. See Parker et al. (note 1); and C. Johnson, R. Jones, A. Paasi, L. Amoore, A. Mountz, M. Salter, C. Rumford, 'Interventions on Rethinking 'the Border' in Border Studies', *Political Geography* 30/2 (2011) pp. 61–69 for reviews of this literature.

54. See J. Edkins, *Trauma and the Memory of Politics* (Cambridge: Cambridge University Press 2003); Salter (note 9); Walker, *Before the Globe* (note 8).

55. F. Debrix, 'Baudrillard', in J. Edkins and N. Vaughan-Williams (eds.), *Critical Theorists and International Relations* (Abingdon and New York: Routledge 2009) pp. 54– 65; M. Dillon, 'Virtual Security: A Life Science of (Dis)Order', *Millennium: Journal of International Studies* 32 (2003) pp. 531–558; Vaughan-Williams, 'The UK Border' (note 9); L. Amoore, 'On the Line: Writing the Geography of the Virtual Border', in C. Johnson et al. 'Interventions'.

56. Walker, *Before the Globe* (note 8) p. 6.

57. Brown (note 11) p. 1.

58. See P. Giaccaria and C. Minca, 'Topographies/Topologies of the Camp, Auschwitz as a Spatial Threshold', *Political Geography* 30/1 (2011) pp. 3–12.

59. See Galli (note 15) on this.

60. Schmitt, *Nomos of the Earth* (note 2) p. 95

Picking and Choosing the 'Sovereign' Border: A Theory of Changing State Bordering Practices

NOEL PARKER and REBECCA ADLER-NISSEN
Department of Political Science, University of Copenhagen, Denmark

We argue that the continued persistence of borders is an effect of their constitutive role for the many dimensions of a social particular. States cannot choose to have a border; but they can and do make choices amongst the materials available on the various planes of inscription for bordering. For contemporary states the planes have become increasingly disaggregated, in the sense that they do not fall into place at one and the same border. Thus, states have to pick and choose different articulations (often inconsistently) on different planes. We illustrate these ideas with instances, present-day and historical, of bordering. A corollary of there being more need to pick and choose is that articulations of sovereignty change. So, sovereignty is increasingly the material of 'sovereignty games', where sovereignty is used as a political instrument. In sum, our theory directs attention to state bordering on different planes of inscription.

INTRODUCTION: THE PUZZLING PERSISTENCE OF THE BORDER

It is a familiar assumption that globalisation transforms states' discrete existence under what we can in shorthand refer to as 'Westphalian' order. As the most straightforward manifestation of the separate existence of states, borders are clearly implicated in this development. An early, radical position on this transformation was to contend that globalisation meant that the days of states' discrete existence, and a fortiori their borders, were numbered. But most serious studies of globalisation soon adopted the view that states were not, in Michael Mann's formulation, 'dying', so much as 'diversifying' under changing circumstances.[1] Indeed, put in terms of borders and bordering, what R. B. J. Walker calls 'the politics of the line' remains very much with us.[2]

Whilst borders may have become more difficult to determine than they have been in the past, they seem certain to survive *in some form or other*. Increasing difficulty might well have its origin in the kinds of things that globalisation and integration theory have put the spotlight on: technological developments in transport and communication; economic, especially financial integration across state borders; trans- and supra-national legal regimes; transnational cultural, intellectual and human flows; and so forth. But maybe that only means that the surprising *continuance* of borders has to be formulated with those factors in mind.

Our purpose in this article is indeed to explore the continued persistence of *state* borders. Rejecting the idea that globalisation, or regional integration, etc., simply undermine state boundaries, we try to find a way through the wide variety of political manifestations taken by what appear as *state* borders. We aim to set up a theory of states' 'bordering practices'; extrapolate the implications; and then check its purchase on reality – primarily with the present-day examples of 'sovereignty games' in mind.

So how do states sustain their borders? The strategy of the paper is to propose a definition of boundaries where borders appear as a sub-category. On this basis, we envisage a field of actions which states can engage in. Then we will identify theoretically a range of possibilities as to *why* states *might* want to engage in 'bordering' – or, we will choose to say later, to 'inscribe' their borders. We then reformulate states' difficulties with bordering as a condition resulting from 'disaggregation' between the various planes of inscription of their borders. Finally we take sovereignty games in Europe as an instance of when states engage in the types of action previously formulated in theory. The upshot of this is to indicate that our theory of bordering practices can cover a range of those contemporary practices which are untheorised in existing ways of looking at states and their borders.

The 'Lines-in-the-Sand' critical agenda calls for alternative epistemologies, ontologies and topologies[3] to those promoted by 'the politics of the line'. For some, this requires that we aim to deconstruct and challenge taken-for-granted assumptions about state borders guaranteeing order and justice.[4] But in addition, the very persistence of a 'politics of the line' requires an explanation. The level of violence and repression, past and present, devoted to fixing and holding borders is plain to see.[5] Indeed, there are good reasons why borders have been termed 'scars of history'.[6]

But a fundamental theoretical inquiry needs to start from the inherent difficulty of discriminating *one identity*, be it that of a state or of anything else, from any other.[7] So we begin with an assumption that discriminations are certain to be made, but nothing can be assumed as to the where or the how. In other words, no one particular border or one particular way that the border is marked is certain. Thus, the amplified difficulties of the present era require a renewed account of the conditions of possibility of states' bordering practices.

THE PROBLEMATIC OF A THEORY OF BORDERING PRACTICES

Borders as a Sub-category of Boundaries

We need first to clarify what borders are. This can effectively be done by considering them as a more formalised and territorialised sub-category of 'boundaries' – a term which, significantly, can be used indifferently about various kinds of entity beside states: territorial, social, personal, etc., both collective and individual.[8]

We then need an abstract definition of a boundary. This we draw from a text by Grahame Thompson[9]:

> Boundaries exist as linked *sites of difference* and local oppositions. Differences and local oppositions are 'connected up'; yoked together to form entities. Thus, boundaries exist 'before' entities. In principle, then, boundaries could exist without entities – they are simply sites of difference, neighborhoods of oppositions. Members and strangers only exist in relationship to boundaries, as several dimensions of difference are linked up, connected to form a boundary. Members are placed 'inside' the entity-to-be, indeed members are made up by the establishment of that boundary.

Thompson himself extrapolates some of the implications of this definition for our goal regarding the nature of borders, and hence for the actions of states. In a border so conceived there is much that is changeable. Any 'point' may disappear, *or* change form or meaning, with implications for the bounded entity of the (political) unit(s) lying on either side. The *mode* of articulation of 'points' in the boundary, or their connectedness may change, increase or fade. Furthermore, a boundary can be sustained or undermined from *either* side, implying that bordering will normally have implications for bounded entities on *both* sides.

In normal usage, all borders are boundaries, but not all boundaries are borders. Boundaries of personal space, for example, would need to be unusually explicit if one was to call them 'borders'. So the key step to make a boundary into a border is that it become more explicit, more evident, more formal, more thing-like. But states specialise in formality: from the grandeur of the monarch and the state buildings; to the legal and constitutional documents (so carefully prepared, revised and announced); to the meticulously drafted inter-state treaties; to the public offices in military, police and state service; to the public finances. All that adds up to the state's 'legitimate right to coercion within its territory'. A fortiori, it is natural that the actions of states should be formalised and territorialised. So, we can say that state borders are particularly explicit and formalised boundaries, and that states are peculiarly well-adapted to engage in border-making that is solider than 'mere' boundary-making.[10]

Bordering Practice

Our theory focuses on theorising *state* 'bordering practices': those activities engaged in by states that constitute, sustain or modify borders between states (principally their own, but effectively others' borders as well – primarily in cooperation with them, but sometimes by imposition). This is not to deny that *non*-state actors are relevant in our conceptualisation. Far from it: state bordering practices are to a large degree performed *in interaction* with other types of non-state actors, processes and organisations.[11] Furthermore, this kind of activity could be initiated from one side of a border or the other. Generally, indeed, such activities are *inter*actions, including actions which entail discursive exchanges. But, even if bordering is in many instances performed by a mix of state and non-state actors, our attention here is primarily on bordering by states.

The term *bordering practices*[12] is especially able to embrace present-day uncertainties. For it poses something *before* any determinate border: namely, the *activities which have the effect* of (in the words of the earlier formulation) 'constituting, sustaining or modifying borders'. 'Practices' necessarily include a range from the most explicit and active to subtler and/or passive activities so as 'to constitute . . .', etc. Thus, 'bordering practices' cover not only actions plainly *intended* to 'border' (e.g., incorporating Jerusalem as the capital of the state of Israel) but also less prominent activities whose side-effects include constituting and/or reconstituting, etc., borders. An instance of the latter would be agreeing on common standards for the railway line running between Germany and France; for this amends the functioning of transit across the formal border between the two countries. Note also that in any particular instance, activities may be more or less *successful* in achieving their pre-set goals, and may, likewise, be more or less *intentionally* pursued by the given actors.

Given the above definitions, we can plot the *range* of instances for what might be included in 'bordering' against levels of 'activeness'. The range is considerable. From concluding a military action so as to clear and fence a border, to its reversal in a treaty of union with the neighbouring state; from meeting those approaching the border with warning signs or threats, to reorganising administration of movements across the border more smoothly – with or without invisible monitoring of vehicles or persons; from amassing troops and defences at the border, to jointly reorganising transit, to opening the border and closing the control posts. All these, and more could be 'bordering practices': that is, practices which 'constitute, sustain or modify borders'. Hence the range embraces 'border-*making*', 'border-*sustaining*' and *de*-bordering actions under the term 'bordering practices', where all may or may not have the character of the border directly in their sights.

The Functions of Borders/Boundaries

Borders are, as we have already observed, a sub-category of 'boundaries'. So, we can determine a lot about the character of borders via the idea of boundaries – hence the slash between the two words in our sub-title. But we must bear in mind that borders would exhibit plainer manifestations than boundaries – such as fences, supervision, official records and so on. Insofar as borders are a sub-category of boundaries, it can safely be assumed that the competent agents' gains or losses are similar for sustaining, etc., boundaries as for sustaining borders. Only more so. For, if the difference is primarily that borders are more manipulable and more manifest, they will be easier *instruments* for the activities of making or modifying boundaries – especially for activities on the part of states. Hence, we can usefully ask: What functions can borders/boundaries fulfil for states and state actors seeking to make, modify or sustain them?

In the post–World War II environment of suspicion for all forms of nationalism, the *positive functions* of borders were rather passed over. The functionalism of Mitrany and the neo-functionalism of Lindberg and Haas, assumed that discriminations between nation-states were fundamentally irrational, and the functional future lay in leaving that kind of thing behind. Karl Deutsch's work in the 1950s likewise found the pursuit of security for individual nations to be *dysfunctional*, so that the future again lay in overcoming the gaps between nations. Taking a historical view on security in the 1980s, Kratochwil realised that state borders may *have been* functional in former times, while holding that they were less and less able to function to ensure security in the post-colonial world. Kratochwil quotes Luhmann approvingly on the principle of the functionality of boundaries, to the effect that borders are functional in themselves, even though they may or may not fulfil the functions accorded to them[13]:

> Boundaries (and *a fortiori,* borders) 'reduce the points with the environment, thus allowing the internal conditioning of various relations with the environment. Only where boundaries do exist, relations between system and environment can increase their complexity, their differentiation and their controlled mutability'.

In spite of the late twentieth-century scepticism on borders, we are entitled to theorise about the positive functions of borders, and their utility to state agents promoting them.

We can first observe that borders help fulfil *epistemological conditions*. Borders produce particular conditions for understanding 'reality'. We who are inside the border are also expected to possess greater knowledge of insiders than of outsiders, which in turn reduces uncertainties regarding our common knowledge on the inside. The border is frequently a bulwark sustaining commonly agreed *measures* of reality (such as national-currency measures for inflation or relative welfare). The border slices the world up into different pieces of reality that we cannot know equally well. That increases as well the *plausibility* of any assertion regarding the circumstances, gains or losses *within* our border. Hence, other things being equal, borders help promote the idea that there are fewer uncertainties in communications between insiders by comparison with communications with those on the outside. This leads to an assumption that we will be able to agree on the terms used to evaluate changes and preferences – even the order of priorities, which is a pre-condition of political decisions. Put in a nutshell, the border provides conditions for greater certainty and agreement for those within it.

Thompson also makes explicit an *ontological* claim for the border/boundary which is implicit in post-structuralism's prioritisation of differences as against commonalities: namely, that '. . . borders exist "before" entities . . .' – that is to say, borders are ontologically prior to specific entities. Borders help constitute the way we conceive the world. This can be demonstrated, inter alia, on the basis of the epistemological claims above. For those epistemological consequences of boundaries provide key *ontological* pre-conditions for the continuity of the given social particular as an integrated entity; and hence also for its identity.[14] The 'fact' of the border helps produce shared understandings of the identities of particulars, both internal *and* external to the particular itself. This includes understandings of *internal* variations and sub-categories (constituencies, classes . . .) *between* insiders/members of the given social particular. The self-identities of members and sub-categories are grounded in, and thus far validated, by seeing those particulars in relation to each other.[15] Likewise, the boundary sustains any determination of the collectivity (the 'nation', or whatever it may be) whose interests may be the basis for decisions and actions on its behalf. This, as Rokkan noted,[16] is especially significant in democratic collectivities, where a large self-aware *demos* is postulated as the ground for decisions that need to accord in some way with the preference of an indeterminable category, the ordinary mass of the people.

The above ontological effects of borders yield yet further consequences. For borders provide *pre-conditions for determinations* of the situation of insiders *relative* to outsiders: claims regarding presumed and/or potential different conditions (be it better or worse) for insiders than for outsiders.[17] The same could be said of any impression of greater/lesser (or potentially greater/lesser) welfare than outsiders. Only with these kinds of claims and impressions in place, can an additional, politically important category of knowledge have meaning: assertions about potential improvements or deteriorations in conditions for the inside.[18] If the existence of the subjects who experience comparative well-being were not given, we would not find meaning in headlines such as 'Danish schools worst on PISA tests'.[19] A fortiori threats which it may be necessary to protect against.

From this last finding, we may further extrapolate that borders help provide *conditions for decisions* as to what is of value. And that is what makes possible 'actorness'. The boundary's epistemological, evaluative and decisional effects are needed for decisions to be made on the part of a collective particular, and hence for actors to act on its behalf – and, a fortiori, for states to be constituted as actors. These decisional frameworks underpin indicators of benefit or dysfunction agreed upon for the inside. They define parameters for actions in relation to others, both inside and outside.[20] Finally, borders and boundaries clarify who may participate in any decision made in the name of the collective whole. In short, boundaries are a precondition for decision and action at the level of the constituted whole – especially where decision-making is undertaken in a 'constitutional*ised*' manner, such as in a constitutional democracy.

We have thus proceeded from a minimal characterisation of the border/boundary to a specification of functions fulfilled by possessing, maintaining or modifying border/boundaries. Those, we deduce, are functions of the border, which underpin the various choices regarding borders, together with bordering practices by states.

The possibility of meeting an 'Other' is always implicit in the activity of inscribing a line of difference. But the ironic corollary of such meetings is that while the Other can be initially experienced as, precisely, 'Other', at the same time he/she/it/they open the question of whether they are indeed *different*, and hence to what extent the given identity determined by the border is stable.[21] Insofar as those on the far side are determined as an 'Other' – independent, different, alien – the border implies the risks and perpetually re-establishes a degree of certainty in relations to what lies outside. But the issue can never be definitively closed. We can see this in migratory border movements, wherever human movements are constructed as a group of 'intruders' with demands, entitlements to charity, alien language, unknown culture, or whatever.[22] As contemporary state borders become more variegated, awareness of such movements must constantly raise the issue of the distinctness of the collective identity which it is the overall function of state bordering practice to resolve.

It would therefore be a mistake to interpret border practices on the part of states as only a 'rational goal' in the sense implied by rational choice theory. That is to suppose that the border/boundary can provide gains which actors can anticipate and will hold desirable, such that they may adopt particular courses of action to attain them. Rather, the border emerges as a *condition of possibility* for being constituted as an entity *or* as an actor capable of formulating desirable outcomes and pursuing them. In other words, the continuity of the boundary is a condition for the continuous identity of the whole whose interest is to be pursued by any 'rational decisions' more narrowly understood. We believe, however, unlike the options for a rational choice as normally understood, action in pursuit of the goal of sustaining or modifying the articulations of the border will feed back upon the very identity of the actor who pursues it. A border of *some* kind is a precondition of being an actor, but in many actions the border itself is in play. So there may be no consistent actor-identity between inception and completion of the course of action undertaken. In this sense, the rational-choice model operates only on the surface of what is happening when activities that regard bordering are decided upon.

The special status of the gains of the border/boundary – as conditions of possibility – means, furthermore, that we cannot formulate a choice for actors *to possess a border or not*. Bordering *in some form* is unavoidable for actors to be actors. Supposed 'gains' postulated for having a border underdetermine the activities of border-making and/or modifying. Borders are conditions of possibility of decisions; because bordering activities underpin conditions where the identity of the social particular is sustained or modified. Social particulars that share knowledge, values, identity and hence interests, rely on their borders/boundaries in order to possess those dimensions, and likewise to be actors (or, for that matter, to be the objects of action by others). Activity, deliberate or otherwise, to modify or reformulate their borders/boundaries will yield the gain of continuous existence in some form or other, even though sometimes modifying its articulations.

INSCRIBING BORDERS

Whether to have some kind of border or not cannot be the choice, as borders for states are precondition for the possibility of choice. Why that should be so thorny for them has been recently articulated with a Derridian insight by Nick Vaughan-Williams.[23] States are perpetually embroiled in *biopolitics* by their efforts to control human persons *through* their domination of territory. Under the heading of 'Alternative border imaginaries', this leads Vaughan-Williams to evince a concept of 'the generalized biopolitical border', primarily in the light of Agamben's account of the fundamental biopolitical nature of state sovereignty. But this is pursued with a take on *all* discriminations, derived from Derrida's early work[24] – that of Agamben included. In Derrida's deconstructivist understanding, no discrimination *of any kind* can be final.

If states are involved in combining government of territory together with government of persons, then they cannot rest content with any established determination of their borders as final. States cannot live *without* borders, but cannot afford to abandon the business of determining and *re*-determining borders. So, rather than looking at any supposed state decision to have borders, we should be looking for variations in *articulations of the borders* that states make. An analytically powerful point of departure would be the *different* materials, physical as well as symbolic, that need to be drawn upon in any determination of borders. In a word, we should study the ways in which states 'inscribe' their borders. We make the categorisation of planes that follows for analytical purposes. This is a limited set of more-or-less independent fields, which need to be examined separately to get a purchase on the different ways that states can 'pick' their borders. These planes, we contend, provide a grid through which we can understand bordering practices by states. In short, a state's choices concern *which* planes to inscribe their borders upon, and *how* to formulate inscriptions that will be 'read' as intended by the various addressees inside and outside.

It is relatively straightforward to draw up a list of familiar fields of state activity which may also be understood as planes for the 'inscription of borders', and which we can go on to use in a grid to observe states' bordering practices. The most obvious is to build on *topography*. A border may be drawn upon the territorial plane: e.g., a mountain ridge or water course that is be modulated from a mere topographic feature to a border. That there is bordering *activity* at work here can be seen from the change in meaning that crossing the given topographic feature then undergoes: from 'trading across' (when a single market is agreed), for example, to 'smuggling' (when a good is declared illegal). In a different register, drawing a boundary around one area of sea together with certain waterways divides zones of *movement* that are subject to different treatment – as, for example, spatial differentiation between Roman commerce and non-Roman zones of barbarism and conflict.[25]

Familiar also, but less straightforward conceptually or politically, is inscription upon *economic relations*. The difficulty here is that these have always been at one and the same time *marked by*, but not fully *subject to* states' border inscriptions – and states themselves have been parties to that. States have long sought to *channel* economic relations around the presupposition of their borders. In doing this, they have accepted (both in practice and in theory) that economic relations have an autonomous dynamic, including the possibility of evading the given state border. The perpetual choice that states have between banning a trade across the border and charging a toll on it illustrates the tension. This is ostensibly the clearest instance of duality arising from the duality of inside with outside. Political issues about what can, or should, be inscribed by states on the plane of economic relations are the stuff of modern liberal states' political and economic debate primarily because the policies arrived, even while softening it, always *mark* the border.[26] Furthermore, it is a border that different kinds of outside will have a hand in: market forces, business elites, foreign powers, border-overstepping social processes of all kinds.

Export and import tolls are payments that *permit* the movement of goods across a *state* border, with a share going to the state. International organisations such as the WTO are established by treaties between *bordered* states which affirm what their borders will or will not restrict movements. Increasingly integrated production and commerce at world and/or regional levels has recently altered the balance between *inscribing divisions* and *managing movement* along state borders; but that has definitely not abolished the state's role.[27] The border does not disappear when international trade is liberalised; properly speaking, it is a condition of trade being '*inter*national'.

The nexus between economic activity and topographic borders brings us face to face with a further duality central to the nature of the border. The border may be *inscribed* territorially, but it is *manifest* in human behaviour. As Foucault puts it in reference to territory, when introducing precisely the layered *complexity* of the relationships involved[28]:

> If it is true that sovereignty is basically inscribed and functions within a territory, and that the idea of sovereignty over an unpopulated territory is not only a juridically and politically acceptable idea, but one that is absolutely accepted and primary, nevertheless the effective, real, daily operations of the actual exercise of sovereignty point to a certain multiplicity, but one which is treated as the multiplicity of subjects, or [as] the multiplicity of a people.

As we extend our list of planes for inscription further, we progress to those where inscription upon their domestic populations by states-as-actors is more and more intangible. That is to say: we meet this tension within the spatiality produced by bordering more and more as we formulate further planes for inscription. Whereas topography operates directly upon territory with corollaries for human beings, many of the planes we describe below operate alone upon human *bodies*, or even human *consciousnesses* with a view to constituting the spatially bounded entity.

Frequently associated with the topographic plane is that inscribed by *coercive force*. For, in effect, that often means to draw a border between one zone where the power of one organised *coercive* force holds sway, and the next zone. Though seemingly close, the topographic and the coercive planes are in fact distinct – as can be seen from the historical evolution in the topologies implicit in the practice of coercive force. To amplify this last point: the armed forces of a modern, Western state are likely to act primarily in concert with those of other states. Each formally belongs in a distinct topographically bounded territory; but they will hardly act to enforce the border *between their territories*. Arranging coercive forces along the national boundary has largely ceased in some areas of the world. Notably, within the European Union where the creation of the 'Schengen border-free zone' has led to the abolition of border control within the Schengen territory. More generally, there has been an evolution over the longer term from 'protecting a national territory' by fixed garrisons of armed personnel; to 'defending the open seas' by a roaming capacity to interdict movements; to 'holding airspace' by an ability to observe and intrude over a zone way beyond the given topographic border.[29]

Normally, à la Weber, formalised statehood is represented on a plane of *legitimised* coercive force. Borders help states to mark the monopoly of the legitimate threat of violence through the *combination* of military/police forces and a plausible claim that its use is 'legitimate'. For Western states, it has been crucial to divide territorially demarcated zones of mutual exclusive legitimate coercion – in other words, to demarcate activities between different state sovereignties.[30] In the eyes of other sovereign states, *effective* coercive control over the domestic population has been a longer standing requirement for formal recognition than legitimacy within the domestic population *themselves*.[31]

That form of inscription of the border interconnects with another: the *jurisdictional framework*, whereby territories and/or activities are deemed to fall within the territorially defined remit of formalised rules and procedures. Again, in essence, this plane is distinct from the previous one. While the territorial-legal is rooted in authority congruent with a bordered space covering all those present and all events within, jurisdiction per se can have other ranges: such as personal (referring to authority over a person, regardless of their location – e.g., in a number of Western countries, sexual relations with minors) and subject-matter jurisdictions (referring to authority over the topic of the matters involved – e.g., torture). It is evident from extra-territorial legislation, as well as from international trade law, that the jurisdictional plane can easily have a range different from a state's effective legitimate coercion.

Linguistic commonalities can clearly mark sites of difference by drawing a border around one group that speaks 'the same' language and the others. This plane has always been more awkward to inscribe any border at all, as linguistic practices easily escape close control from above – as the oddity of the notion of 'incursions' by one language into another indicates. Not that that has prevented states and national-minded intellectuals from making the attempt by formulating correct rules for national languages.[32] The device of a *lingua franca*, or of a sacred language, has frequently provided an alternative plane on which to inscribe a different border – for example, Latin in bordering early Western Christendom from the heathen world.

More recently, the development of rights for linguistic minorities within and across states has re-enforced the idea that linguistic commonalities help constitute borders in a way that is *not* consistent with *state* sovereignty. Language rights have become an issue of contention within several European countries, and as a consequence also between neighbouring states. Disputes have arisen in some countries where the status of the state language has been perceived as threatened in regions where minorities are present in numbers and perhaps also in political life. As part of this process, the Council of Europe adopted The European Charter for Regional or Minority Languages (ECRML) in 1992 to protect and promote historical regional and minority languages in Europe. The Charter protects linguistic minorities and may also function as a way for state authorities to achieve a 'margin of appreciation' – for instance over street names and other topographical indicators.[33] Hence, while linguistic boundaries were earlier an important instrument in the hands of *state* authorities to create national cohesion, the Charter works as a way of qualifying linguistic border-drawing by states.

Cultural proximities constitute a related, yet perhaps more still difficult plane for states to operate upon. 'External intrusion' into supposedly distinct national cultures is so widespread that most national orders exhibit profound difficulty in associating national identities with cultural commonalities.[34] To draw a border around one group such that it has 'the same' cultural reference points (written literature, musical and dance styles, habits of socialising) relative to others has proved difficult since the inception of nations. The unexpected extension of cultural Americanisation under the auspices of 'European' cultural policy is a striking example of the perverse effects on this plane of border inscriptions. It cannot even be seen to have an origin in the will of another, 'external' actor – often referred to in shorthand as 'Hollywood'. As Kroes argues, Americanisation is not simply passive assimilation at the behest of the outsider.[35]

Not only states, but also supranational bodies may seek to take a stake in cultural policy. Notably, the European Union has sought to create European Union citizens with a shared, transnational civic culture, related to their shared rights (such as the all-important right of movement across national borders), and even – more controversially – shared symbols, such as the European Union flag. As Moreira presents it, the cultural policy of the EU is organised around three pillars, which may not be consistent with each other: economic benefits of transnational cooperation; transnational awareness of European heritage; and union citizenship.[36] The ultimate goal of EU cultural policy is to strengthen the sense of belonging to the EU, which is necessarily transnational.

The conundrum of 'local knowledge': Knowledge, a concept which intersects cultural commonalities, can just as clearly mark distinction across a border. Some things are characteristically known amongst those on the inside and not known to those on the outside. The 'conundrum' is this: Whether certain items, or types of knowledge can be said to 'belong' to one or other side of a boundary determined by whoever will most readily acquire it? We comfortably accept that some prior conditions – training, experience, no less than milieu, etc. – can be desirable, *or even necessary* to achieve certain categories of insight, scientific, artistic or otherwise. Conversely, we expect knowledge to be communicable *across* boundaries, ergo *not* confined to one side of any border. Nonetheless, regardless of difficulties it implies for the principle behind our rationalist epistemology, items of knowledge certainly have a place on the list of the planes where borders can be inscribed.

Instances of the difficulties of universal versus national 'knowledge' are seen from international and supra-national bodies, such as the members of the OECD. Again, the OECD's so-called 'PISA'[37] tests offered the example of cross-state, universalised comparisons of national education systems, and of the perverse effects of creating any 'universal' standards for knowledge. Comparing reading, mathematics and science literacy of fifteen-year-old students in thirty-one countries implied the creation universal of items of knowledge. But they have travelled with difficulty – due not only to language barriers, but also to different national traditions and ways of categorising and classifying the world.[38]

A further instance of the ambivalence of bordering knowledge is provided by the ranking system of international journals.[39] The 'universal' rankings became policy-relevant nationally in the 2000s, due to the marketisation of higher education and the increased mobility of students.[40] For administrators and politicians, the quantitative social-scientific information provided by these lists has become an indispensable part of policy-planning. Yet, as tools of symbolic power, ranking-lists reinforce pre-conceived ideas for certain users. For others, university rankings have become part of the global higher education landscape. They present a certain state of affairs as inevitable, shaping reality in the field of higher education. The universal values have contributed to the creation of a new 'status economy', which sets policies in higher education and innovation.[41] Global hierarchies and norms are now reproduced, and further legitimised, by a variety of research institutions specialising in the production of information in terms of these hierarchies. They are funded by nation-states or media corporations. Due to their global coverage and high visibility, these lists are causing significant shifts in national policies to keep up with similar policy scripts and the myth of modernity that is part of its power.[42] With their common norms and beliefs about causality, these symbolic-power tools portray the world in a uniform manner. The figures produced and the perceptions of 'competition' that they communicate tend to lock state policy actors in, leaving little room for policy alternatives.[43]

Disaggregation of Borders/Boundaries

We take this to be a minimal list of different planes for inscribing state borders. At the least, it is enough to take us further to the next claim that our theory of state bordering is founded on. We have been accustomed to group all these distinct planes together without further ado, and expect that specific outcomes at the territorial, economic, coercive, legal, linguistic, cultural and knowledge planes will fall into place alongside each other, corresponding to nation-states' borders. Their comfortable aggregation has indeed been palpable evidence of the solidity of national-state identities. States, in particular, have been accustomed to bundle together distinct planes of bordering, and hence to assign them to one internally coherent set that can comfortably be undertaken by one actor, namely the state itself.

It is vital, however, to repeat that the different planes of inscription of the border are *theoretically* distinct: for that shows that the alignment of the planes cannot be *taken for granted*. In other words, it is *not necessarily* the case that inscribing a border in terms of any one plane (territory enclosed, economic ties sustained, linguistic practices in common, or whatever) will produce a border congruent with that produced on other planes. It follows that over the course of history, we must expect to find many instances where the border in the different planes is not 'aggregated'. And the histories of the welding of territory and population by rising modern states already point to how difficult it has been in the past to achieve something like an aggregation of the border on distinct planes.[44]

Our formulation that 'it is not necessarily the case that inscribing a border in terms of any one plane will produce a border congruent with those produced in other planes' expresses the problematic of state bordering practices in different terms. It also provides an explanatory schema for what indeed appears *prima facie* to be happening. For, the difficulties of the border as expounded in our introduction can be formulated as a *disaggregation* of those 'planes' upon which boundaries may be inscribed. The range of phenomena referred to as our starting point under the titles of 'globalisation' and 'integration' can be seen from the perspective of state bordering activity as inscription. Whereas one agent (one state) on its own could earlier plausibly inscribe a single boundary along different planes that might be aggregated fairly easily; recent developments have progressively magnified the potential for *disaggregation* between the borders on distinct planes upon which borders may be inscribed.

Yet, whilst conditions for bordering may change, the underlying assumptions have remained. The familiar circumstances referred to suggest, then, it is trickier than it formerly was to attain an 'aggregated' border on the different planes. Instances are easy to find – and we have seen some already. Yet, the necessity for states to engage in bordering in the terms set out in the second part remains. We can postulate that state bordering practices continue, but they are exercised in an environment where states themselves are increasingly under pressure to *manoeuvre amongst disaggregated* planes, upon which they may inscribe their borders.

'PICKING AND CHOOSING' SOVEREIGN STATE BORDERS

We have developed an account of how various territorial and functional state borders do not necessarily correspond (do not 'aggregate'), and how the capacity to alter them may lie with various forces and authorities, which can overlap. While the various planes on which state sovereignty is inscribed do not fit neatly on top of each other, states have not surrendered their will or all of their capacity to act on, or manipulate their border inscriptions. Thus we arrive at an account of the arena where states[45] will 'pick and choose' the border: not the *presuppositions*, but the *expressions* of their borders. Given the wider environment, their best option is often to amend the way that their border is *articulated*, that is to make a choice of *how* to inscribe *which* versions of their borders. To complete the picture, two final additions can be made: the historic consequence of this for the dominant concept of state sovereignty; and how states currently adapt inscriptions of the border(s) so as to have them 'read' optimally from the state's point of view – that is, to convey the given states' preferred meaning to the various *addressees* of the inscriptions.

State Sovereignty and 'Disaggregated Planes'

When we talk about the sovereign state and its many planes of bordering, we need to contrast this with received international law definition of the sovereign state as a *territorial* entity:

> A state is an entity that has a defined territory and a permanent population, under the control of its own government, and that engages in, or has the capacity to engage in, formal relations with other such entities.[46]

From this perspective, sovereignty is the *exclusive* right to exercise, within a *specifiable territory*, the functions of a government and be answerable *to no higher authority*. For a state to be a sovereign in this way, it is necessary to specify a territorial border: to inscribe a border on the topographic plane. But sovereign statehood also entails inscribing other types of borders. The requirement of a 'permanent population' thus refers to topological[47] manifestations in a demarcated social group – normally, with bounded economic practices, security expectations, culture, language, knowledge and, in sum, identity. Finally, this ideal requires a 'government', i.e., formal and effective decision-making capacity over that area/population/set of practices – an idea traditionally linked to the Weberian notion of a monopoly of the use of legitimate coercive force. In this conception of the state, the different planes are indeed *assumed* to aggregate, i.e., to be congruent with each other. The demarcation of the population and its practices is expected to fit the territorial border, which will follow the demarcation of formal and political competences and decision-making processes. Thus, the aggregation of border inscriptions appears indispensable for the received idea of the state sovereignty.

Sovereignty is often discussed as a Western construction, an invention, due to European philosophers, kings and jurists. Yet, when viewed from our perspective on state bordering, it is clear that disaggregated borders and authority have a longer history, and that bordering is central to most accounts of political authority across time and space. In Europe, not only did there exist earlier forms of sovereignty,[48] there was a long evolution after this to reach the standard, specifically modern conception of territorial sovereignty. This was intimately associated with the development of specifically modern secularity[49] and identity.[50]

Outside Europe, as anthropologists were the first to bring to our attention, the picture is even more varied.[51] Japanese political history provides an example of this.[52] During the Tokugawa period (1603–1868), Japan was, by Western standards, a nation *without* absolute, fixed borders or clearly defined sovereignty. The emperor in Kyoto was merely a symbolic suzerain; actual governmental power within the main islands was divided between the Tokugawa shogunate (*bakufu*) and about 270 autonomous daimyo domains (*han*), while the peripheries – Hokkaido and its environs to the north, the Ryukyu Islands to the south – were subordinated to the Japanese polity yet not considered to be integral parts of it.

While early modern Japan's borders may appear ambiguous in hindsight, 'at the time they formed a coherent system in which social status ordered groups within the core polity while notions of civilization and barbarism defined identities in the core and periphery'.[53] In a formation that resembles European feudalism, status-, power- and identity-bordering was quite distinctive. Yet this system could express a claim to political borders, making it possible for the Japan of the Tokugawa period to fit in with foreign relations in the modern nation-state system. Borders were inscribed quite differently from what we expect of 'modern' states: linguistic and values borders were uppermost in preserving Japan's isolation from close involvement with Western societies; yet decentralised power could be effective in bringing territorially extended authority over the rural population. Holding this 'Japan' of power-holders together was a demanding culture of dignity for the military elite, which valued the emperor's imprimatur above all.

Even though the border is central to Western state-building, the image of the state as a bordered power container[54] is theoretically problematic and empirically misleading. In the course of the twentieth century, many additional, at first sight aggregated, planes have been even added to the territorial. Bauman describes the resulting structure as a 'tripod of sovereignties', built on the territorial groundwork, which has latterly had to be abandoned.[55] The spatio-temporal construct 'state sovereignty' is elegant and time-honoured, but problematic. Whilst it cannot be wholly dispensed with, it no longer reflects the ways authority and power are organised. At the time of the early modern transition from late feudalism, state sovereignty might have been the answer rulers were looking for. Nowadays, states are intersected by many border-infringing processes.

The non-aggregation of the borders is challenging the received view of the sovereign status of 'sovereign'-state borders. But, we argue, whereas the received view of sovereignty has yet to be fully or formally abandoned, in reality states can nonetheless be expected to adapt the realities of *non-aggregation*. States will manage the circumstances so as to articulate their border differentially and so retain the ability to discriminate, control (or avoid control), and take responsibility (or avoid it), for some of the articulations which are on our earlier list. In the European Union, for example, we see developing forms of picking and choosing when it comes to the idea of force and territory. These activities cash out in cross-border cooperation between national police authorities in the EU member states when they combat drug- and car-smuggling, human trafficking and child pornography.

The abolition of border controls provided for by the Schengen agreement arguably produced a 'security deficit', which enabled 'perpetrators of criminal acts to move as freely as law abiding citizens'. So, the Schengen agreement was amended to allow for 'hot pursuit' across borders (where police are pursuing a criminal who is on the run). This allows police officers from one member state to cross the border and operate inside the territory of another member state, provided that they coordinate their activities with the national police authorities.[56] Today, the EU member states have joint border patrols, joint surveillance operations and joint investigation teams. There is increasing exchange of information and pooling of equipment; national police forces have direct access to other member states' fingerprint, DNA and vehicle registration databases. Within the EU there is no such thing as a 'power container state' when it comes to the use of legitimate force over territory.

In sum, the disaggregation of the planes of bordering does not so much stymie the bordering practices of sovereign states as much as it provides a broader palette for inscription on distinct planes. New kinds of bordering, and more specifically of articulating borders, are an integral part of the contemporary transformation in global and regional authority. Especially in Europe, there is constant jockeying between levels of authority about ways that states may and may not articulate their borders. By examining how states 'pick and choose' their borders, we are now better able to grasp how modern statehood manifests itself and sovereignty is articulated.

Who Conveys What to Whom?: Bordering as a 'Sovereignty Game'

The notion of disaggregated planes redirects sovereignty, and a fortiori state bordering practices, away from claims to the permanent possession of certain qualities. It moves states towards the activities recently characterised as *sovereignty games*: that is to say, the instrumentalisation of claims to legal and political authority by states and other actors in the face of globalisation, regionalisation and international legal regimes.[57] If we consider bordering as inscriptions upon diverse planes, the 'game' consists of picking the optimal modes of inscription of the border that are available. This often implies manipulating domestic and foreign audiences.

Let us first consider who engages in bordering practices. As R. B. J. Walker notes,[58] traditional International Relations theory sees state-players severally or collectively as sovereign bordering actors. Courts, both national and international, may be seen as such bordering actors when it comes both to inscribing and challenging state borders in the legal realm. The EU provides instances of state institutions, notably member states' constitutional courts, defending their national legal order with reasoning that nonetheless points *away from* it, and *towards* the collective decision of all the member states. This has been particularly striking during the 1990s and 2000s where the treaty revisions have become increasingly controversial and politicised.

On 26 November 2008, for example, the Czech Constitutional Court handed down a unanimous opinion finding that the Lisbon Treaty was compatible with the Czech constitutional order.[59] The decision was one of the most significant decisions in the Court's history and had EU-wide implications. Underlining the necessity of European integration in the globalised world, the Court resorted to the concept of 'pooled sovereignty'. The Court noted that

> it is more a linguistic question whether to describe the integration process as a 'loss' of a part of sovereignty, or competences, or, somewhat more fittingly, as, e.g., 'lending, ceding' of part of the competence of a sovereign. . . .
>
> [The] transfer of certain state competences that arises from the free will of the sovereign and will continue to be exercised with the sovereign's participation in a manner that is agreed upon in advance and is reviewable, is not *ex definitionem* a conceptual weakening of the sovereignty of a state, but, on the contrary, it can lead to its strengthening within the joint actions of an integrated whole. The EU's integration process is not taking place in a radical manner that would generally mean the 'loss' of national sovereignty; rather, it is an evolutionary process and, among other things, a reaction to the increasing globalization in the world. (See paras. 104 and 109 of the Judgment)

The decision reflects picking and choosing under circumstance where the planes on which borders are inscribed have become disaggregated. It also harks back to the point made in the Introduction to the effect that bordering is not an action, but an *inter*action. For alongside their endorsement of 'pooled sovereignty', the Court gave voice to a more traditional notion of sovereignty, stressing that the Lisbon Treaty explicitly enables a member state freely to withdraw from the Union.[60]

Indeed, states' bordering practices always involve communicating, often selectively and strategically, to various audiences inside and outside the border. The activity of inscribing a border cannot be seen as complete unless account is taken of the meaning *conveyed* by the inscription. Different constructions with the same border-inscription may be associated with different addressees. No politically intelligent attempt to inscribe a border can be made, therefore, without an awareness that different 'audiences', 'readerships' or 'publics' may interpret the inscription differently. Actors engaging in bordering must therefore seek to control this variable. Thus states will seek to define, or even to keep separate, distinct audiences to whom they intend distinct messages.

This dimension is often evident in what Adler-Nissen refers to as the 'organized hypocrisy' of EU member states vis-à-vis their own publics as against their Brussels colleagues.[61] One of the most radical challenges to the idea of clearly delineated populations is the 'free movement of people', one of the four core freedoms of the EU. Yet unsaying the free mobility of persons across EU borders also helps structure national discourses of bordering. For some states, the Schengen regime (abolishing controls and checks at national borders between EU member states) is so problematic that they have negotiated opt-outs, national treaty exemptions, which at first sight seem to reinstall the border. When the United Kingdom was granted an opt-out from the Schengen agreement this exemption appeared to be absolute. For a significant majority on the British domestic scene, led by Conservatives and other Eurosceptics, the British Schengen protocol appears to constitute a guarantee of the survival of the British nation.[62] However, despite the weight put on the British Schengen exemption, the UK has not opted out at all of the principle of free movement. It is only British border control which has been safeguarded through the treaty protocols. Hence, the UK is just as bound as the other member states to respect the rights granted to EU citizens moving across the border to live in the UK and receive the same social benefits and rights as any British citizen. Articulating a particular form of identity border – i.e., identity demonstrated by differential control of people, and symbolic rehearsal of Britain's status as an island – has protected the image of the British nation. These various bordering practices help to refurbish a useful fiction of national unity, and to fabricate a united identity despite apparent political disagreements over the EU issue. But it has not prevented British and Irish companies from benefiting from the cheap labour forces moving in from Poland and other Eastern European countries, and provided British and Irish citizens with the possibility of enjoying their pensions in Southern Europe.

Another instance of picking and choosing can be found in the field of legal jurisdiction. In the context of European integration, a question often posed concerns how far a state can delegate competencies to international and supranational authorities and still remain a state. This question directs our attention to a crucial element in state bordering practices: the drawing of lines between competences – in itself a major concession to the realities of disaggregation. Regulating the relationship between the competences of national authorities and supranational authorities such as the EU, involves a sort of *constitutional* picking and choosing. This is how one may understand the recent decades' toing-and-froing between national constitutional courts and the European Court of Justice over how to interpret the relationship between the EU treaties and national constitutions. Despite appearances, this is not a zero-sum game, in which the supra-national wins what the national loses, or vice versa.

We can see this in the case of the Czech republic, amongst others. When Czech President Vaclav Klaus refused to sign the Lisbon Treaty (thus prompting the court decision referred to above), he raised the question of whether the Lisbon Treaty is compatible with the limits of Czech legitimate political and legal authority. Apart from making it possible for the Czech Republic to receive extra concessions (e.g., legal guarantees in relation to the Charter on Fundamental Rights securing continued control over ownership of the Czech territory), his opposition served the purpose of asserting for the benefit of the domestic political audience the overall jurisdiction of the Czech Republic within its legal border.[63] President Klaus was re-cycling sovereignty in its traditional form as independence: as an autonomous, fixed capital, capable of annulling decisions that have led to its careless dissipation.[64]

The European integration process provides us with a range of examples where states pick and choose to inscribe their borders on different planes. This can be a more-or-less political exercise. What is more important is the fact that the disaggregation of planes can lead states to become more political in their bordering practices. Although sovereignty games do not fundamentally change the idea of the sovereign state – in fact they may sometimes even strengthen the appearances of it – they indicate a more fluid relationship, as states move to articulate their separate identity in diverse ways, between any state in question and the outside. Practices of bordering – or more particularly practices that imply how the border should be thought of – play a central role when states engage in sovereignty games.

CONCLUSION

States do not choose whether to have a border or not. Yet they have a range of possibilities when it comes to how they inscribe their borders in different materials, or 'planes' (territorial, economic, legal, cultural, etc.). In this article, we have argued that a central corollary of the current degree of 'disaggregation' between planes of bordering is the selective approach to state authority manifested in a will to 'pick and choose the sovereign border'. Consequently, rather than asking to what degree the state is withering away and whether absolute sovereignty is a thing of the past (as globalisation theory might do), a theory of state-bordering practices needs to look at the interplay of the different *functions* of borders which states will seek to fulfil by articulating the border as different *planes* of *inscription*.

We began by arguing that borders should properly be understood as a sub-category of boundaries, which we determined to be pre-conditions for numerous aspects of the existence and continuity of entities – including a fortiori states. We explored the character of the border further by showing how it will fulfil a range of functions – epistemological, ontological and/or decisional – in the existence and continuity of any collective particular. For states, we argued, these functions will be fulfilled by 'inscribing' borders which inhibit or channel movement in terms of some kind of medium, symbolic as well as material. That medium ranges from topology to culture and knowledge. Thus, our theory is primarily interpretative. That is, it identifies what we should be looking for in states' articulations of their borders. While it remains the case – as ever – that states may get to pick and choose the topographical placing of the border, we have presented a case for focussing attention rather on how states articulate border inscriptions to maintain their identities as sovereign.

On different planes, different border inscriptions help constitute a particular topography of each state, a separate social identity for each state, an economic room for manoeuvre, etc. These different inscriptions do not necessarily correspond; indeed, they are semi-autonomous. Thus, what happens to one border inscription on one plane (e.g., economic) does not straightforwardly affect another plane (e.g., cultural). This disaggregation is of course not new. But, we have argued, the ways states articulate their borders has had to become more variegated.

Our final section discusses, primarily in the context of European integration, how those theoretical findings in various sovereign state bordering practices serve not only to uphold sovereign states as a meaningful notion, but also work in more subtle ways to integrate state sovereignty with international organisations and other non-state actors. Seen from the point of view of states, this selective approach to 'the outside' can be instrumentalised in 'sovereignty games'. In some cases, the various border claims constitute symbolic bulwarks against absorption in the Other: rehearsing – despite the dramatic changes taking place – an image of the state with full political and legal authority over its people, territory, money, etc. By focusing on this picking and choosing we understand how states may change as well as how they continue to seem sovereign.

NOTES

1. Michael Mann, 'Nation-States in Europe and Other Continents: Diversifying, Developing, Not Dying', in Gopal Balakrishnan (ed.), *Mapping the Nation* (London: Verso 1996) pp. 281–316.
2. R. B. J. Walker, *After the Globe/Before the World* (London: Routledge 2010) ch. 6.
3. We take topology to cover the science of examining the possibilities latent in shape or the concepts of that science. Topography/topographical, by contrast, refers to the actual indicators which drawn on territory, maps, etc., to determine different segments of space.
4. Michael J. Shapiro 'Moral Geographies and the Ethics of Post-Sovereignty', *Public Culture* 6 (1994) pp. 479–502; Walker, R. B. J. *Inside/Outside: International Relations as Political Theory* (Cambridge: Cambridge University Press 1993).
5. Introduction to Thomas H. Wilson and Donnan Hastings, *Border Identities: Nation and State at International Frontiers* (Cambridge: Cambridge University Press 1998); see article by Antia Mato Bouzas in this issue.
6. Vladimir Kolossov, 'Border Studies: Changing Perspectives and Theoretical Approaches', *Geopolitics* 10/4 (2005) pp. 606–632.
7. John Ruggie, 'Territoriality and Beyond. Problematizing Modernity in International Relations,' *International Organization* 1/1 (1993) pp. 139–174; Yale H. Ferguson and Richard Mansbach, 'Post-Internationalism and IR Theory', *Millennium: Journal of International Studies* 35/3 (Sep. 2007) pp. 548–549; Noel Parker, 'From Borders to Margins: A Deleuzian Ontology for Identities in the Postinternational Environment', *Alternatives* 34/1 (2009) pp. 17–39.
8. For a review of the evolution of border studies, including the variety of meanings applied to the notion of 'border', see Kolossov (note 6).
9. Grahame F. Thompson, 'The Fate of Territorial Engineering: Mechanisms of Territorial Power and Post-Liberal Forms of International Governance', *International Politics* 44/5 (2007) p. 15.
10. By actions of states, we include here actions by officers of the state, presumed representatives of the state, or the state *as such*.
11. To drive this point home, see George Gavrilis, *The Dynamics of Interstate Boundaries* (Cambridge: Cambridge University Press 2008).
12. Nick Vaughan-Williams, *Border Politics: The Limits of Sovereign Power* (Edinburgh: Edinburgh University Press 2009) ch. 1.
13. Friedrich Kratochwil, 'Of Systems, Boundaries, and Territoriality: An Inquiry into the Formation of the State System', *World Politics* 39/1 (1986) pp. 27–52. An instance of this 'controlled mutability' appears in an interesting recent study of the Andes. Even if borders are opened, that does not necessarily imply that persons or goods will flow more easily; new forms of control may be more efficient in *hampering* trans-border flows than those that served closed borders (Anne-Laure Amilhat Szary, 'Are Borders More Easily Crossed Today? The Paradox of Contemporary Trans-Border Mobility in the Andes', *Geopolitics* 12/1 (2007) pp. 1–18).
14. See also David Campbell, *Writing Security: United States Foreign Policy and the Politics of Identity* (Minneapolis: University of Minnesota Press 1998).
15. The entirety of the Hegelian philosophy is characterised by the enterprise of understanding the integrity of the parts and the whole together, which for Hegel is the essence of any ethical justification.
16. Stein Rokkan, *State Formation, Nation-Building, and Mass Politics in Europe: The Theory of Stein Rokkan Based on His Collected Works*, ed. by Peter Flora, Stein Kuhnle, and Derek Urwin (Oxford: Oxford University Press 1999) chs.1 & 2.
17. These gains and losses are of course often differentially distributed between insiders.
18. This formulation is written solely in terms of perceptions regarding outsiders that are articulated and communicated *between insiders*. In reality, such formulations may also be generated (*both* positively and negatively) amongst outsiders or between outsiders and insiders. All these can be arenas for discussion can lend themselves to evaluations of the relative fortune or worth of insiders as against outsiders, together with any threats posed to the well-being of insiders.
19. These were tests organised by the OECD for 15-year-olds in industrialised countries, which caused great heart-searching in Danish political and governmental circles in 2004. See also note 38.
20. Which parts of the collective particular will impact on, or be impacted upon, by the actions under consideration (e.g., deciding to lower duties on a specific product, or to agree on some measure of social protection) has likewise to be understood in the light of that kind of framework.

21. This is the object of analysis for what Kapuscinski calls the 'philosophies of dialogue'; Ryszard Kapuscinski, *The Other* (London: Verso 2008) p. 68f.

22. On illicit flows, see widely differing sources ranging from Jacques Derrida, *On Cosmopolitanism and Forgiveness*, trans. by Simon Critchley and Richard Kearney (London: Routledge 2001) pp. 3–24; to Schendel, Willem van, and Itty Abraham, *Illicit Flows and Criminal Things* (Indiana University Press 2005).

23. Nick Vaughan-Williams, *Border Politics: The Limits of Sovereign Power* (Edinburgh: Edinburgh University Press 2009) especially ch. 5.

24. *Limited Inc.* (1988 – a collection of translations of prior works) and *Positions* (1972) are common points of reference in critiques of political thinking grounded in Derrida's early thought.

25. R. Brian Ferguson and Neil L. Whitehead (eds.), *War in the Tribal Zone: Expanding States and Indigenous Warfare* (Santa Fe, New Mexico: School of American Research Press 1992); Christopher Kelly, *Ruling the Later Roman Empire* (Cambridge, MA: Belknap 2004) ch. 4.

26. Michel Foucault, 'Security, Territory, Population', trans. by Graham Burchell (London: Palgrave 2007) ch.13.

27. Paradoxically, even creating tax havens to provide a particular regime for liquid wealth, amounts to a commercialisation of sovereignty, using the territorial insulation of the given state for the purposes of trans-nationalising capital and *increasing* economic integration across borders; Ronen Palan, *The Offshore World: Sovereign Markets, Virtual Places, and Nomad Millionaires* (Ithaca and London: Cornell University Press 2003).

28. Michel Foucault, *Security, Territory, Population*, trans. by Graham Burchell (London: Palgrave 2007) p. 11.

29. Paul Hirst, *Space and Power: Politics, War and Architecture* (Cambridge: Polity 2005).

30. Clifford Geertz relates a story from a Dutch anthropologist on the attitude in the colonies before the Dutch arrived to impose their conception of a border: 'The Dutch, who wanted, for the usual administrative reasons, to get the boundary between two petty princedoms straight once and for all, called in the princes concerned and asked them where indeed the borders lay. Both agreed that the border of princedom A lay at the farthest point from which a man could still see the swamps, and the border of princedom B lay at the farthest point from which a man could still see the sea. Had they, then, never fought over the land between, from which one could see neither swamp nor sea? "Mijnheer," one of the old princes replied, "we had much better reasons to fight with one another than these shabby hills."' (*Negara: The Theatre State in Nineteenth-Century Bali* (Princeton, NJ: Princeton University Press 1980) pp. 24–25).

31. David Armstrong, *Revolution and the World Order: The Revolutionary State in International Society* (Oxford: Clarendon 1993) chs. 2 & 3.

32. Miroslav Hroch, *The Social Interpretation of Linguistic Demands in European National Movements*, EUI Working Paper No. EUF 94/1 (Florence: European University Institute 1994).

33. See also Gudmundur Alfredsson, 'Frame an Incomplete Painting: Comparison of the Framework Convention for the Protection of National Minorities with International Standards and Monitoring Procedures', *International Journal on Minority and Group Rights* 7 (2000) pp. 291–304.

34. Uffe Østergaard, *Europas Ansigter, Nationale Stater og Politiske Kulturer i en Ny, Gammel Verden* (Copenhagen: Rosinante 1992).

35. Rob Kroes, *If You've Seen One, You've Seen the Mall Europeans and American Mass Culture* (Urbana: University of Illinois Press 1996).

36. Juan M. Delgado Moreira, 'Cohesion and Citizenship in EU Cultural Policy', *Journal of Common Market Policy* 38/3 (2000) pp. 449–470.

37. See note 19 above.

38. Aletta Grisay, 'Translation Procedures in OECD/PISA 2000 International Assessment', *Language Testing* 20/2 (2003) pp. 225–240.

39. In the USA, evaluations of graduate programmes started already in 1920s and a ranking of US colleges was published already in 1983. The university rankings made their way to the UK in the 1990s.

40. Lee Harvey, 'Rankings of Higher Education Institutions: A Critical Review', *Quality in Higher Education* 14/3 (2008) pp. 187–207.

41. Simon Marginson, 'Open Source Knowledge and University Rankings', *Thesis Eleven* 96 (2009) pp. 9–39.

42. John W. Meyer, John Boli, George Thomas, and Fransisco Ramirez, 'World Society and the Nation State', *American Journal of Sociology* 103/1 (1997) pp. 144–181.

43. Tero Erkkilä and Ossi Piironen, 'Politics and Numbers: The Iron Cage of Governance Indices', in Raymond W. Cox III (ed.), *Ethics and Integrity in Public Administration: Concepts and Cases* (Armonk: M.E.Sharpe 2009) pp. 125–145.

44. A classic historical study of how this operated in nineteenth-century France is Eugen Weber, *Peasants Into Frenchmen: The Modernization of Rural France, 1870–1914* (Stanford, CA: Stanford University Press 1976); Peter Sahlins, *Boundaries: The Making of France and Spain in the Pyrenees* (Berkeley and Los Angeles: University of California Press 1989) is another. Apart from the more general Foucault account – referred to earlier – one should also list Malcolm Anderson, *Frontiers: Territory and State Formation in the Modern World* Cambridge: Polity 1996); and Christer Jönsson, Sven Tägil, and Gunnar Törnqvist, *Organizing European Space* (London: Sage 2000).

45. Other bodies can also attempt to do so, either in competition or in cooperation with states; but our topic remains states.

46. *Third Restatement of the Foreign Relation Law of the United States* (Philadelphia: American Law Institute 1986) § 201.

47. See note 3 above.

48. Andreas Osiander, 'Before Sovereignty: Society and Politics in Ancien Régime Europe', *Review of International Studies* 27 (2001) pp. 119–145.

49. Daniel Philpott, 'The Religious Roots of Modern International Relations', *World Politics* 52/2 (Jan. 2000) pp. 206–245.

50. Jens Bartelson, *A Genealogy of Sovereignty* (Cambridge: Cambridge University Press 1995).

51. Two path-breaking anthropologists' studies of other societies' notions of sovereignty and the border, appeared in 'Political Definition: The Sources of Order', in Clifford Geertz (ed.), *Negara: The Theatre State in Nineteenth-Century Bali* (Princeton, NJ: Princeton University Press 1980) pp. 11–25; and Frederik Barth (ed.), *Ethnic Groups and Boundaries* (London: Allen and Unwin 1969).

52. David L. Howell, 'Territoriality and Collective Identity in Tokugawa Japan', *Daedalus* 127/3 (1998) pp. 105–132.

53. Ibid., p. 105.

54. Anthony Giddens, *The Nation-State and Violence* (Berkeley: University of California Press 1987) p. 120.

55. Zygmunt Bauman, 'Europe of Strangers', Seminar Paper, Transnational Communities Programme, 1998. For a historical overview on a larger canvas, see Martin van Creveld, *The Rise and Decline of the State* (Cambridge: Cambridge University Press 1999).

56. Rebecca Adler-Nissen, 'Behind the Scenes of Differentiated Integration: Circumventing National Opt-Outs in Justice and Home Affairs', *Journal of European Public Policy* 16/1 (2009) pp. 62–80.

57. Rebecca Adler-Nissen and Gammeltoft-Hansen Thomas (eds.), *Sovereignty Games: Instrumentalizing State Sovereignty in Europe* (New York: Palgrave 2008).

58. R. B. J. Walker, *Inside/Outside: International Relations as Political Theory* (Cambridge: Cambridge University Press 1993).

59. Decision of 26 Nov. 2008, case No. Pl. ÚS 19/08 (published as No. 446/2008 Coll.). The English translation is available at <http://angl.concourt.cz/angl_verze/doc/pl-19-08.php>.

60. Petr Bříza, 'The Czech Republic: The Constitutional Court on the Lisbon Treaty Decision of 26 November 2008', *European Constitutional Law Review* 5 (2009) pp. 143–164.

61. Rebecca Adler-Nissen, 'Organised Duplicity: When States Opt Out of the European Union', in Rebecca Adler-Nissen and Gammeltoft-Hansen Thomas (eds.), *Sovereignty Games: Instrumentalizing State Sovereignty in Europe* (New York: Palgrave 2008) pp. 81–103.

62. Antje Wiener, 'Forging Flexibility: The British 'No' to Schengen', *European Journal of Migration and Law* 1/4 (1999) pp. 441–463.

63. Along the same lines, the German Constitutional Court continues to argue that despite the surrender of sovereignty and the ECJ's claim that EU law trumps national law, the German Constitutional Court remains the final arbiter in case of conflicts between German constitutional law and EU law. Moreover, the German government remains 'Herren der Verträge' (master of the treaties).

64. Pierre Rosanvallon, *La démocratie inachevée* (Paris: Gallimard 2000) pp. 427–428; Jeanne Morefield, 'States Are Not People: Harold Laski on Unsettling Sovereignty, Rediscovering Democracy', *Political Research Quarterly* 58/4 (2005) pp. 659–669.

Sloterdijk in the House! Dwelling in the Borderscape of Germany and The Netherlands

RUBEN GIELIS[1]
Nijmegen Centre for Border Research, Radboud University Nijmegen, The Netherlands

HENK VAN HOUTUM
University of Bergamo, Italy, and Nijmegen Centre for Border Research, Radboud University Nijmegen, The Netherlands

It is almost a truism to say that people increasingly dwell in a transnational context, that is, in-between societal systems and together with multiple nationalities. Increasingly, people are living in a different nation in which they were born. The nation-states people dwell in cannot be equated with territorial container-boxes anymore, if this ever could. The uniform and straight lines in the sand, that borders once were thought to be, are now better understood as a complex choreography of border lines in multiplied lived spaces. This article zooms in on a specific kind of dwelling with multiple borders. It tries to get a conceptual hold of contemporary dwelling places of short-distance migrants across a EU inner border, in this case the Dutch-German border. In recent years, much facilitated by EU cross-border cohesion policies, a substantial number of Dutch people have bought or built a house just across the border in Germany. This has created an interesting new phenomenon of cross-border dwelling, in which the new location of the house is just across the border and the living largely still goes on in the country of origin. This living in two nations at the same time at such a short distance is what we wish to understand better conceptually in this article. We argue that two fundamentally opposed philosophical dwelling conceptualisations could be distinguished. On the one hand one could distinguish a philosophical view in which dwelling is a form of a Heideggerian nest, where people open a space of being, an intimate and secure bordered place, sheltering themselves for the outside world. On the other hand then, a philosophical view could be distinguished in which dwelling is driven by a Deleuzian need to free oneself from a binding b/order of home, through a constant be-coming and estrangement, hence by constantly othering oneself. We argue that in order to understand the borderscape *dwellings of Dutch migrants in German borderlands, there is a need to relate these two ends of the dwelling continuum. The argument that we bring forward is that a borderline necessarily moves between total (self-)imprisonment and total escapist openness, making borders in an ontological sense intrinsicially and unavoidably always a shifting line in the sand. In our view, Peter Sloterdijk's imaginative* Sphären *(*Spheres*) trilogy could help as a conceptual stimulus to create that much needed bridge between the bordering efforts of nesting and the debordering desire to escape from it. Using Sloterdijk's spherical concepts, the dwelling can be seen as a place which is constantly changing from a secure bubble-like place into a multidimensional foam-like place and back again. With this spherical understanding of the house we argue that this conceptual 'spheric' stimulus could help to rethink the complex and ambivalent character of cross-border dwelling places in an increasingly transnational world.*

Watching the bubbles
rise up through the sand
like ascending souls,
tracing the line of the foam,
drawing our index fingers
along the horizon
pointing home

— People who live, Erica Jong, 1979

INTRODUCTION

Along the Dutch-German border a complex and academically most challenging display of a borderlines dynamic is developing. Since the institutional opening of this border in the light of the unification within the European Union, tens of thousands of Dutch people have decided to buy or build a house just across the border in Germany. Most of these migrants do not move for social or political reasons. The aim of their migration is largely to simply obtain a more spacious and, in most cases, comparatively cheaper house. What makes this particularly interesting is that they are moving house, but to a certain degree the only thing that they are moving is their house.

For, their decision to dwell in another country goes hand in hand with a wish to remain close, also physically, to the country they are coming from. The dwelling places of the Dutch migrants in question are located in a kind of in-between land where the Dutch and German spheres of influence intermingle. So in a sense, these Dutch border migrants keep their homeland on an 'elastic', making the borderline between the two countries diffuse and dispersed.[2]

We argue here that this in-betweenness would fit into the larger process of an emergent transworld.[3] It is almost a truism to argue due to globalisation processes such as the opening of political borders and the developments in communication and transportation technology, the contact with 'strangers', in the sense of people who (used to) live on the other side of (national) borders have increased considerably. In this sense the borderline has become diffused, more fluid. This has persuaded some to argue that we increasingly live in an era of global borders and global borderlands.[4] Seen in this vein then, one could argue that more and more people (both migrants and non-migrants) live in-between (national) cultures nowadays. In this paper we zoom in on this in-betweenness for the case of actual borderlands, the zones alongside national borders. This kind of migration, the emergence of in-between lifeworlds in borderlands is visible along many borders in the world, and is, also due to the active policy stimulation to move and work across the inner EU borders, perhaps most notable along various inner borders of the European Union, such as at the French-Luxembourgian, Dutch-Belgian and Spanish-Portuguese border.

Our quest here concerns how to conceptually take hold of the dwelling practices of transnational migrants in the *borderscapes* alongside the inner borders of the European Union that increasingly question the locational limits of the state.[5] How can we ontologically and epistemologically come to terms with this particular kind of transborder dwelling condition? This quest shares important communalities with the research agenda for critical border studies that was formulated in 2009 in this very journal by a group of border scholars.[6] The argument brought forward here was that borders are increasingly fluctuating, ephemeral and/or impalpable and hence rather than (still) falling in the territorial trap of studying the borderlines as containered states, we need to reflect ontologically on the dynamic and often opportunistic production of shifting lines in the sand. In our case here, we will zoom in on the dynamic interplay of borderlines in the border zone proper, in other words we will study the emerging lines of travelling to, across and from the border, or what could perhaps be called the *choreo*graphy of the transborder dwelling.[7]

To begin to understand this elastic dwelling across borders, this choreographic play with borderlines, we first need to analyse and come to terms with the importance of dwelling in human lives.[8] For our case here, we will argue that two interesting opposing views as ends of a continuum can be distinguished in the philosophical debate about dwelling(s) in the last decades. First, there is the view in which dwelling is principally conceived as a nest-like place where people create an intimate and secure place, as a kind of refuge for the outside world. Typically here the idea of dwelling is closely related to a b/ordered home.[9] The assumption is that people (still or increasingly) need the security and comfort of and identification with a *monadic* homeland and that this is closely related to and made manifest through their compatible b/orderly dwelling practices. In this paper we will analytically tie this dwelling perspective with that of the late Heidegger, and especially his essay *Building Dwelling Thinking*.[10] More on this later. On the other side of the continuum one finds the idea that dwelling principally has to be drastically reconceptualised, namely not in terms of b/ordering but in terms of an endless becoming instead, a dynamic de-bordering. For the purpose of this article we will principally connect this line of thought in this paper with the work of *nomadic* thinkers like Nietzsche and Deleuze and Guattari.[11] Their perspective of dwelling is radically opposed to the Heideggerian perspective. From their perspective, dwelling is about *becoming* instead of (Heideggerian) *being*, which is principally driven by a desire to escape the (re)pressing order of a home(land). In other words, dwelling here is then understood as finding one's routes instead of roots.[12]

Both views, what could be summarised as the monadic and the nomadic,[13] could well be used to analyse the decision to buy or build a house across a national border as a desire to discover new worlds indeed. But at the same time, and this makes it conceptually even more challenging, many of these migrants' houses look like private fortresses, small enclaves in which they withdraw from the German society.[14] This further hints at the idea that contemporary dwelling places are indeed neither merely nests nor nomadic places, but can and often will principally be both depending on the intentions of the migrants in question. What this means is that we have to conceptually think through in a more nuanced way and possibly re-think the dynamic borderlines qualities of this phenomenon of borderscape dwellings that does justice to the complex and ambivalent character of present-day dwelling places.

In this paper we would like to analyse to what extent Peter Sloterdijk's project on *Sphären* (*Spheres*) could be a bridge between Heideggerian and Deleuzian dwelling perspectives. In his thought-provoking, and imaginative *Sphären* trilogy Sloterdijk tries nothing less than to write a new eclectic history of mankind, by showing why and how people live (together) in immune making spatial formations which he calls spheres. His quest is to think through the various 'Innenraums' in which a human being lives during his/her life and how this changed over time. Interestingly, Sloterdijk even argues that the question '*Where* is the human?' goes above all other questions in philosophy. Before we start analysing his work in our context of borderscapes and transworld in more detail, let us, by way of brief introduction spend a few words on introducing his work in more general terms.

In the first part of his 'where'-trilogy, *Bubbles (Blasen)*,[15] Sloterdijk theorises the spatial configuration of human life on a micro-level. He starts with the analysis of the womb, in which the child and his/her mother form a twofoldness of being, resembling the most intact and primary sphere of living. At first therefore the *where* of a human is to be *in* another human. For Sloterdijk the whereabout of a human being is an immanent place which consists of one simple socio-spatial relation, the mother-child relation. The prenatal sphere is thereby understood as a pure inner, comfortable and secure space, completely cut off from the outside world. For him, such a womb-like sphere can also be found in other micro-spheres, in the intimate relationships between human beings, between human beings and the God in them and their personal objects and belonging. Core element in these intimate relations for Sloterdijk is the element of de-distance, 'Entfremdung', which is a state of being in one together, a bi-subjectivity, or, in other words, existence through 'inexisting'. In his second book, *Globes (Globen)*,[16] Sloterdijk theorises further on what it means to live in spheres *after* one is born, after the breaking of the existence through 'inexisting'. He describes, following to some extent the psycho-analyst Lacan's line of thought on the 'lack', that the entering into the globe of the earth, the birth, can be described as a trauma, because man is pulled away from the micro-spherical security of the womb. Famously, for Lacan, alienation in the system of society is what follows after the separation from the co-existing (M)Other. Similarly, Sloterdijk shows how people find substitutes for this uterine security in socio-political macro-spheres such as cities, nations and empires. A close relation with a communal entity or club stands for the replacement of the mother-child dyadic relationship. His third book *Foams (Schäume)*[17] then is an analysis of the current Western world, which in his eyes has become a globe in itself. The high-speed virtualisation and mobilisation of the present-day ('Western') global sphere causes the various communal spheres to no longer exist separately from each other any longer, if they ever did. In a more life-celebrating and less 'traumatic' and troubled way than in the first two books he explains the evolution of the implosion and explosion of bubbles into a multitude of immune-place-productions which he calls foam. He stresses that principally humans largely have become independent from the 'where' of the micro-sphere of the womb, the macro-sphere of gods or the nations. And hence human beings now increasingly have the potential to construct their own, multiple and constantly changing, island-like spheres. In sum, his argument is here that the outer world has entered the inner world, which results in a situation where communal entities like nations no longer have an absolute outside and full spheric enclosure (anymore). In the multiform foamed spheres that he describes there is no absolute inside and outside anymore. Interestingly, following this logic, the result thus is that rather than a place, a human him/herself has become what could be called a topological difference.

Slowly but surely, the potential relevance and meaning of Peter Sloterdijk's work for geographical and geopolitical research is getting recognised. To wit, recently, the journal *Society and Space* opened up Sloterdijk's captivating thinking for geographical research by publishing a special issue which consisted of translations and interpretations of his work.[18] In this paper we would like to seize upon this recent interest in and geographical exploration of Sloterdijk's work and try to elaborate on it, by investigating how his argument on spheres can be used to create a more sophisticated account of the choreography of dwelling places across national borderlines in our what could be called *trans*world.[19] We will argue that his concepts of bubbles, globes and foam are indeed constructive to understand the ambivalences and complexities of these places.

Below, we will first investigate the value of Heideggerian ideas of dwelling for the understanding of present-day dwelling places and relate those ideas to Sloterdijk's spherical concept of the bubble. Next, we will pay attention to the other side of monadism, the nomadism. We investigate the significance of Deleuzian notions of dwelling and relate these notions to Sloterdijk's spherical concept of foam. In the last section, we aim to delineate the either/or discussion and make a continuum between monadism and nomadism instead by focusing on Sloterdijk's conceptions of the dwelling place as being both a bubble-like and foam-like place. Though our attempt to re-think the qualities of dwelling places is principally a philosophical exercise, we will use the dwellings of Dutch migrants in German borderlands to both inspire and ground our thoughts. As the aim of their (international) migration is the moving of their house and not necessarily their lives and belonging, these migrants' houses are interesting laboratories to study the meaning of the dwelling place in a situation where the relation between house, home and homeland is destabilised and shifted.[20] More specifically, the intermezzos from *the borderscape* take place in Kranenburg, a German village near the Dutch city of Nijmegen, which is the city where we both work. As part of his empirical study for his dissertation Ruben conducted ethnographic fieldwork among Dutch migrants in Kranenburg for two years, for which he lived himself in the small German border town of Kranenburg. In this way he was able to intensively study the domestic lives of cross-border dwellers.[21]

DWELLING IN THE SPHERE OF *THE BORDERSCAPE*

So what do the dynamic dwellings of the Dutch migrants look like? To begin with, the spatial in-between lifeworlds, the *borderscapes*, have always existed, both for (Dutch) migrants and non-migrants in some form or another.

Characteristic for present-day *borderscapes* is that perhaps more than before they are the results of what Sloterdijk sees as the explosion of secure national spheres in the worldwide foam. Sloterdijk argues that the nation-state is dominantly seen by many as one of the most important *Globes*. It is a prosthesis for motherly feelings, for the intra-uterine security.[22] In his book *Im Weltinnenraum Des Kapitals*,[23] he eloquently and critically analyses how, under the influence of current social and political globalisation, these separated and stable national spheres have been melted together and into each other in foam-like constellations.

For the Dutch border migrants this world of foam has become anything but abstract. They live in and of the foam as it were. More sharply formulated, the national border is not situated around their lifeworld, but the border cross-cuts and constructs their lifeworlds. The border is their lifeworld. The lifeworld of the migrants who live on the elastic of the national border, in another country, yet, physically and emotionally close, is ontologically defined by the continuous and dynamic interplay between the inside and outside. They are neither here (Germany) nor there (The Netherlands), but always and here and there, hence permanently in-between. They live in a permanent trans-site. For them therefore the border is not (just) a place, but the definition of their own existence. They live and inhabit the ontological difference that is the border.

Characteristic for the borderscape of these migrants is that they enjoy a lot of freedom to arrange their borderscapes the way they see fit. Their transnational lives take shape in a EU context of opened state borders, which gives them in principle the opportunity to cross these borders frequently. And they do, most transmigrants still send their children to school in nearby Dutch villages and towns, go shopping in Dutch supermarkets, and most of them are working in the Netherlands.[24] Freedom also has a social-political meaning for these borderscape migrants, as they have considerable freedom to decide to what extent they want to integrate in the receiving (German) society. Based on the European idea of liberty and equivalence for EU citizens the German government does not (yet) make stringent demands on the integration of Dutch migrants. This implies that the Dutch migrants for instance are allowed to send their children to school in the Netherlands if they want to, and they are not obliged to learn German if they do not want to. This freedom (of obligations) gives migrants a significant amount of independence to manipulate and 'play with' the national borders which cross-cut their lifeworlds. In the current sphere of the Dutch-German border in their practices and identification they can strategically remap and redraw the location of the national border as much and as often as they desire.

Having said that, it is at the same time widely acknowledged that the EU space is still defined by political states and nations, along with their national rivalries and patriotically stressed cultural differences and identities.[25] Such a nationalised European Union is confirmed and reproduced at several places and occasions, ranging from the European political arena in Brussels where in the European Council the heads of the European states still make the most important political decisions, as we have seen in the election of the 'European president' and the recent EURO-crisis, or a still strongly cheered nationalism manifested for instance by European Championships football or the election of members of the European parliament in which still predominantly fellow-nationals are chosen. The result is, as is well-known, that borders between nations are continuously crossed in a physical sense but remain persistently strong in a mental, social and political sense.[26] The lifeworlds of the Dutch border migrants could be characterised as an exemplary projection of this enduring societal duality between rising transnationalism on the one hand and continued nationalism on the other in the European Union.

NESTS OF BEING

I will run for shelter
endless summer lift the curse
it feels like nothing matters
in our private universe

— Private Universe, Crowded House, 1993

How should we then philosophically understand the character of these borderscapes, as dwelling places? To begin to answer this challenging question we need to understand in a more profound way how dwelling is generally understood and conceptualised. Perhaps one of the most famous and important philosophical works on dwelling is that of Martin Heidegger. In his essay *Building Dwelling Thinking* Heidegger argues that humans dwell in relation to the fourfold of earth, sky, mortals and gods. These four elements dwell together all at once, in a simple unity. "To preserve the fourfold, to save the earth, to receive the sky, to await the divinities, to escort the mortals – this fourfold preserving is the simple nature, the presencing, of dwelling".[27] The idea of the fourfold stems from another essay, called *The Thing*, where he argues that practical things (a bridge, a jug, a tree, to name some examples he uses himself) gather the fourfold.[28] Regarding the act of dwelling, people principally build houses to gather this fourfold, according to Heidegger. He analyses etymologically the word dwelling and argues that the original meaning of dwelling is to build. This constructed thing then, the house, holds the gathering together. Gauthier, who has written a dissertation on the dwelling in the works of Heidegger and Levinas interprets this relation between dwelling and the house in the work of Heidegger as follows: "Mortals dwell when they spare the fourfold, and sparing the fourfold is accomplished by building things that enable the fourfold to attain ontological presence".[29] In other words, for Heidegger, principally, the gathering of the fourfold means letting the world be. Constructing a place for him is about opening a space through which we can let (*be-lassen*) a being be. The house then emphasises and binds this being. The border around the house for him is not the end of something, but as something behind which '*begins to be*'. In essence, to dwell therefore implies a peaceful freedom. The house functions as shelter that enables this freedom, a shelter that protects against the outside world.[30] According to Maria Kaika, in her interesting analysis on Heidegger's conceptionalisation of home, it is in the making of a dwelling place that people make a distinction between the own domain, that is, between the social processes which take place within the borders of the house, and the surrounding domain and the social processes which take place outside the dwelling.[31] For Heidegger the borders between the house and the surrounding are principally closed and stable, which makes it possible for people to live a safe, comfortable and secure life in their houses.[32] Hence, Heidegger's ontology of dwelling is based on the immanent idea that the dwelling place houses and encloses man's life,[33] in short, it is a manifestation of 'Interior building'.[34]

In addition, Heidegger also stresses the importance of poetry in dwelling practices. "Poetry is what really lets us dwell".[35] He (and Sloterdijk has followed him in this) most notably refers to the work of Gaston Bachelard, a contemporary of Heidegger, who elaborates this poetics of dwelling by arguing that the house is a nest for dreaming and imagining.[36] However, at the same time these dreams always say something about the house as a place we love.[37] These are nested dreams. The same can be said about the function of poetics in Heidegger's thinking about the dwelling place. For Heidegger, "Poetics is the process by which human beings 'take measure' of their existence within the fourfold", Gauthier argues.[38] Poetry is part of and directed at the fourfold. It is a nested poetry. Principally, for Heidegger the house is a nest-like place, to use Bachelard's words.

In his trilogy on spheres Peter Sloterdijk elaborates further on this Heideggerian concept of the dwelling as an immanent enclosure by theorising further on the social (relational) aspects of the enclosed dwelling. For Sloterdijk the house is a sphere in which people try to create intimate relations with others. His leitmotiv for his analysis on this is Heidegger's famous following argument on nearness: "Im Dasein liegt eine wesenhafte Tendenz auf Nähe".[39] Dwellings then in Sloterdijk's eyes are principally *socially shared* bubbles.[40] So, more than Heidegger, who stressed the nearness to *things*, Sloterdijk stresses the importance of nearness to other people in understanding the persistence of the desire for a dwelling place. It is in houses that people hope to find uncomplicated and stable social relations, so that they truly can call it their home, their private universe (see above quote from Crowded House). This significance of ease and control is confirmed by many of the social-psychologists writings on home. Saunders for instance argues that in their own house people have the agency to control and an unquestioned access to direct intimacy.[41]

Hence, vital for the dwelling as a bubble is that it is a place where people have a feeling of being in control of their own social relations, which is manifested in constantly seeking for the right balance between the inside and the outside of the bubble. In this respect Sloterdijk speaks about people's tendency to immunise and 'isle' their houses.[42] By isolating certain social relations from the outside world they try to build houses which function at the same time as both 'impassioned inner worlds'[43] and immune systems.[44] Sloterdijk uses the modern apartment as a metaphor here.[45] In the often luxurious spheres of apartments people withdraw from society, only having contact with the outside world through the spyhole. For Sloterdijk this refers to people's need to re-create and simulate the perfect bubble: the mother's womb. By creating uncomplicated and impassioned social relations within the bubble of the house, it provides people the uterine security and intimacy they are searching for. So when Heidegger says that "the fundamental character of dwelling is . . . sparing and preserving",[46] then Sloterdijk principally adds that dwelling is also about preserving intimate and simple relations with others.

Following Heidegger's ideas about 'Heimat' Sloterdijk confirms that he also sees a persistently strong relation between house, state and well-being. People (still) try to embed their houses in the secure macro spheres of nation-states, searching for "a unity of hearth and state, house and empire".[47] To this end, Sloterdijk calls the state a 'Thermotopos' ('Thermotop'), which means that it functions as a 'pampering space' ('Verwöhnungsraum') or comfort space. The macro-spherical borders of the state give people's houses inner worlds with extra comfort and security.

A Dwelling in Borderscape I: Castles Across the Border

Walking through the small German border town Kranenburg, around thirteen kilometres from city centre of the large Dutch city Nijmegen, the various new housing estates immediately catch the eye. It is without exaggeration or any moralising undercurrent here that we say, that at these places most Dutch migrants are truly building most comfortable nests. Most houses are rather big semi-detached or detached houses, many have one or more parking spaces adjacent to their houses and some have large lanes and their own gates in front of their houses.[48] The reason most migrants can afford such big houses is that the house and land prices are almost half as high on the German side of the border, compared with the Dutch side of the border. "You get more house for less money", that is how Dutch migrants often answer the question why they move to the German borderlands. For many, it seems that their long-desired dream house can finally be realised now in these German borderlands. Especially the (semi-)detached character of the dwelling seems to be important for the migrants. They want to be detached from the direct surroundings. For many, it is precisely because they are able to build their own protective shelters as little castles in the German borderland that they moved there. Most of them would have stayed in the Netherlands if they could have realised these kinds of places there.

The building or buying of these private paradises across the border is stimulated and facilitated by real estate agents and consultants, who have shot up like mushrooms in recent years. On the internet you can find numerous sites of (mostly Dutch) real estate agents who are specialists in selling houses in the German borderland to Dutch people. And when driving through the German borderland, one cannot miss the references to these 'dream houses' and the agents who make them possible (see Figure 1). A whole new industry of agents and consultants who are making money out of the search of Dutch borderlanders for a hearth across the border has emerged.

Despite the fact that affordable dream houses are sold literally at the doorstep of the Netherlands, it is (still) regarded as peculiar to live on the other side of the border. Ruben experienced that personally in his empirical field research.[49] He often had to explain to Dutch family members, friends and colleagues why he lived in Germany. On the other hand, in Kranenburg he often got the feeling that Germans thought, 'What are you doing here?'. Most probably, the question to explain his move would not have been asked and his feeling of having to defend his move would not have been felt if

FIGURE 1 "Hier entsteht ein Traumhaus" ("Here we build a house of your dreams") (color figure available online).
Source: authors' own collection.

Ruben had moved house within the Netherlands. That the national embeddedness of the house is important also turns out from the fact that most Dutch migrants only live a few kilometres across the border. Though house and land prices are even lower in inland places in Germany (and one can hence build even bigger houses there for the same price), most migrants prefer to live in the borderland, where they are close to the homeland. The real estate agents cleverly take advantage of this need to remain close to the homeland, by using slogans like "A dream house across the border, with the Netherlands as your backyard" (www.landhaus.nl). (See Figure 1.)

Yet, the national embeddedness of their houses means more than just the relatedness of these houses to the territories of the German and/or Dutch state. The Dutch migrants also pull these macro spheres into the micro sphere of their house by what we metaphorically would like to call the building of national cavity walls. Sometimes they do so quite literally, for instance when they hire Dutch construction firms to build (the walls of) their houses. But most of the time, these national cavity walls have a more subtle and symbolic character. To illustrate this, let's take the example of Johanna, who is one of the migrants Ruben intensively studied during his fieldwork in Kranenburg, and is someone who wants to be part of the German society.[50] In many villages in Germany it is considered good custom by many to decorate your house, and especially your front door with attributes which are typical for the season. People place a straw puppet at the front door in autumn, position a pumpkin there around Halloween, put a piece of wood with a painted face of Santa Claus at the front door at Christmastime, etc. Johanna joins in this tradition. "I find it important that my house has a friendly appearance for the people in my daily environment, and those objects create that friendly atmosphere. And, next to it, when you notice that the neighbourhood is doing this kind of things, then you should participate" (interview 18 July 2008). In a way by doing so Johanna copies the attempt to create a sheltered German atmosphere in and around her house. This creation of national refuge in and around the house is what we characterise as the building of national cavity walls. In our view, the building of national cavity walls is a second way in which people try to restore what Sloterdijk calls the unity of hearth and state. The walls of the houses provide a kind of double isolation: they give (personal) privacy and national stability.

NOMADIC DWELLINGS OF BECOMING

This is Major Tom to Ground Control,
I'm stepping through the door.
And I'm floating in a most peculiar way

— Space Oddity, David Bowie, 1969

Heidegger's notion of dwelling in terms of nests and similar conceptualisations of houses in terms of protective, comfortable shelters of being has been criticised by many thinkers for only stressing the desire for enclosure. Influential thinkers like Nietzsche, Foucault, and Deleuze and Guattari have made it their theoretical goal in life to understand and conceptualise the importance of liberating from what they see as the (self)repressive interiority of the protective walls and to emphasise the importance of endless becoming. Perhaps most significantly, it is Nietzsche, who has made a plea for the going beyond of an, by essence, conservative dwelling and to escape from the truth that is constructed by a disciplining, self-denying and nihilising dwelling order.[51] For him it is typically the weak-willed human who borders, suppresses and disciplines himself through an imagined hierarchical (b)order instead of creating himself. As is well-known, Nietzsche therefore argued for transcending oneself through becoming an Übermensch, which principally is an act of de-bordering, self-overcoming, of creative and passionate liberation, the state of being one with oneself. Implicitly following Nietzsche's plea for a desire for self-liberation, in his later works also Michel Foucault theorised on the practice of becoming and de-subjectification, or what he labelled the "aesthetics of existence". And in that same influential period of French philosophy, in an equally compelling way Deleuze and Guattari, theorised on the importance of endless becoming, the escaping from a repressive order.[52] For Deleuze and Guattari, people dwell on change, becoming and consistency, rather than on fixity, being and constancy, as Doel argues.[53]

From a different angle, yet with a similar drive to search for an inclusive otherness, Harrison has recently stated that the defining aspect of dwelling is the (spacing of the) relation between the subject and the other.[54] Besides a shelter and a place of repentance, the house also is a reception room, where the inhabitants of the house have to negotiate about the access of 'the stranger'. Similarly, Varley has argued that the house is the place of *both* the self *and* the other.[55] Hence investigating (the art of) dwelling might help to get a better understanding of the space between us.[56]

Finally, also Sloterdijk argues that there is a need to recognise the desire to break open and go beyond the enclosed sphere of the dwelling. It is in *Foams (Schäume)*,[57] the last book of his *Sphären* trilogy, that Sloterdijk describes how in the current globalised world houses have become multi-spherical places. In their houses people are constantly visited by the outside world, with the result that an absolute outside no longer exists.[58]

Yet at the same time, Sloterdijk stresses, thereby implicitly following perhaps the nomadic thought of thinkers like Deleuze and Guattari, people's ability and wish to escape the order of the house. This escapism clearly has an important mental side, something which is of crucial importance in the psycho-analytical writings of Deleuze and Guattari, but Sloterdijk merely develops the technological side of it. For Sloterdijk the moving spirit behind the transformation and interconnecting dwelling places is the virtual revolution, in which the internet and various telecommunication means give the inhabitants of the house the possibility to discover new outside worlds. For Sloterdijk, people are increasingly linked up with a network of virtual neighbourhoods in their own houses.[59] Home-based technology for him brings people and processes from all over the world to and into the house, which makes houses increasingly important receivers of messages from the extraordinary.[60] On a whole, one could argue that Sloterdijk thinks quite positively about these technological developments and their impact on and consequences for the domestic sphere. This is radically different from the way some other influential thinkers have theorised on that. In Anthony Giddens' perception for instance, communication means creating huge social-psychological risks and instability, and therefore he has argued that finding ontological security (in the house), a home, has become a real struggle in contemporary society.[61] Also according to Heidegger technology has a negative influence on people's being at home. He argued that people become homeless in their homes due to technology, because it pulls people away from the (holy) *here*.[62] Where technology leads to homelessness in Heidegger's view, for Sloterdijk it is an intrinsic part of people's frivolous act of dwelling.[63]

Because of mental and virtual nomadism and the incoming of the Other, for Sloterdijk contemporary houses are *foamed* places: multi-relational and multi-local spheres which are constantly changing in form and content. The foaming of spheres occurs in two ways, and consequently, in his view, foam has two important manifestations. First, foam arises from the explosion of bubbles. In this situation the walls of the bubble explode, which means that the bubble gets related to other bubbles and hence becomes part of a larger foamed sphere. For the house this means that it is not (just) an enclosed sphere where people isolate themselves from the environment, rather is (also) embedded in and influenced by other houses (and other kinds of bubbles). Second, foam arises from the implosion of bubbles. In this situation bubbles move into each other.[64] The individual bubble gets complicated from within and turns into foam itself. For the house this means that it no longer (just) accommodates a simple social relation, rather has (also) become a socially complex place. It would even be possible that houses get so many characteristics from places and people 'outside' that its inhabitants almost transcend these houses. In that respect Sloterdijk speaks about 'floating houses'[65] and 'houses as vehicles'.[66]

A Dwelling in Borderscape II: Escapist Places Across the Border

The dwellings of the Dutch migrants are not only new protective shelters, they could also be seen as escapist places at the same time. The very act of moving to the other side of the border suggests a desire to look beyond the national (b)order and to discover new worlds. For many, the nation one is born in is seen as the self-evident place to live in. The dominant pattern on this planet still is immobility, not cross-border mobility. To actually buy a house, a home, in a foreign country is seen as an adventurous act by many, a flight into the unknown. Telling for this is that most migrants still strongly connect themselves to people and societal processes in the Netherlands from their house, for instance by following the news via Dutch newspapers and television channels, shopping and working in the Netherland and by staying in close (e-mail) contact with people in the Netherlands. In these situations they live in mental and, what Sloterdijk calls, virtual, neighbourhoods which do not necessarily coincide with the physical neighbourhood of their houses which are located in Germany. And yet, migrants often still used words like 'we' and 'here' when talking about these 'Dutch' spheres.[67]

And so one could argue that the spatial materiality of their lives takes place between two national spheres, making the connecting between what they see as their house and as their home a rather complex one. The Dutch migrants often make use of this in-between location of their houses also in a cognitive dissonance reductive way. Leon, who is one of the migrants Ruben intensively studied during his fieldwork in Kranenburg, is an example of someone who creatively plays with the border in that sense. For instance, when we talk about the high taxes and social insurance contributions in the Netherlands or when he mentions the, in his perception, negative social climate in the Netherlands, he states that he is "happy not to be part of this country any longer". On the other hand, he also admits that when he is addressed as someone who lives in Germany, he sometimes tends to refute that because "I have got the feeling that I still live in the Netherlands" (interview 28 April 2008, see Gielis, 2011).

Apparently, in their houses, Dutch migrants have to deal with as well as can play with the foaming of the Dutch and German national spheres (see Figure 2). This is something Sloterdijk does not pay attention to so much, at least not explicitly. For Sloterdijk the foaming of the house is primarily related to the explosion and implosion of the walls of the house. In our view the foaming of the house is not just about the collapsing local walls of the house. Rather it takes place in a context where the walls of the nations, the societal systems in which the houses are embedded, are ex- and imploding as well (see Figure 2). So, in our view there is a double ex- and implosion of the house.[68] The foaming of the national macro spheres is particularly tangible for Dutch transmigrants, because they live on the borders of these ex- and imploding national globes.

THE DWELLING AS BUBBLE AND FOAM

Considering the above intermezzos, we would argue that borderscape dwellings could and perhaps should be seen as both nests *and* nomadic

FIGURE 2 The foaming of spheres, expressed by the many bilingual road signs in the German border town Kranenburg. 'Durchgangsverkehr' and 'Doorgaand verkeer' is German and Dutch respectively for 'through traffic' or 'ring road' (color figure available online).
Source: authors' own collection.

places. In our view, the philosophical debate on the cross-border dwelling should not restrict itself to an either/or discussion (Heideggerian monadic nests on the one hand and Deleuzian nomadic places on the other). What we would propose instead, is to understand this form of dwelling as a continuum between the monadic tendency to build orderly and comfortable shelters on the one hand and liberating, permanently temporal living conditions on the other.[69] We think that Sloterdijk's recent theorisations on (the) dwelling could be a useful continuum-maker in that respect. In his work on *Sphären* he covers the whole spectrum of dwelling, as his idea of bubbles is largely based on similar ideas of Heidegger and his idea of foam shares important Deleuzian similarities. In our view, therefore, Sloterdijk's spherical concepts are suitable to develop an idea of the dwelling place which does justice to both ends of the continuum, and hence does justice to the subtleties and complexities of contemporary dwelling places across borderlines.

For Sloterdijk the house is an ambivalent place. On the one hand, it is a place that generates a protective feeling of being at home, an inner world that allows and enables people to live with the total immensity of the globe. It is important and striking to say for the purpose of this article that in this explanation of the dwelling place as an immune system, he indeed significantly draws on the work of Heidegger. But at the same time, apart from being an immune system, a bubble, for Sloterdijk the dwelling is also a place where people are involved in complex multidimensional relationships with others. Hence, the house is also a vehicle or foam. Houses are always both immune systems and vehicles at the same time. It is this paradox of people's wish to protect themselves against the world outside and their wish to re-create this world in miniature which makes the house such a complex and sophisticated place. According to Sloterdijk, contemporary houses have blind windows on which people paint scenes from the outside world.[70] Hence, houses are places where people experience 'weltferner Weltoffenheit'.[71]

In our view, Sloterdijk's work is most useful for our work here where he shows that the two poles, the house as immune system and as a vehicle, do not exist separated from each other but are related. This means that when we experience the house as a bubble, we also have to take into account that it is also a foamed place. Sloterdijk takes the walls of apartments as a metaphor to prove his point. These walls on the one hand isolate the occupants of the dwelling from their neighbours and others and give them a bubble-like privacy and security. But at the same time the occupants have to realise that they share these walls with their neighbours; hence the apartment walls also indicate that people dwell in relation with others (outsiders). So, occupants of apartments live in connected isolations,[72] in a co-immunity as it were. But it is also the other way around. When people experience the house as a (internally) foamed place, they can still find simple social relations there as well. For instance, by chatting with friends on the home-based computer we create a foamed house, but at the same time this virtual seemingly borderless network can feel like a bubble in which we can lose ourselves.

In Sloterdijk's spatial ontology of mankind, man can only be understood medially. He denies the existence of man as merely a subject; rather, he claims that man is a medium or an in-between in itself.[73] Following from this ontological position, the spheres in which people live are *inter*subjective spaces, or what Sloterdijk calls 'in ecstasies'.[74] And when these spheres have the character of bubbles, the intersubjectivity has a simple nature, and when these spheres have a foamed character the intersubjectivity is more complex. So, for Sloterdijk the difference between bubbles and foams is not so much a fundamental one, it rather concerns the degree of social complexity these two forms of spheres contain. Bubbles and foams easily and smoothly disappear and overflow into each other by means of the constant 'airquaking' ('Luftbeben') which is going on in spheres.[75] In our view, the same 'airquaking' is to some extent also taking place in our contemporary houses. Due to the need to enclose our lives in our houses on the one hand, and our opposite need to escape this domestic order and the social reality that strangers knock on our front door on the other hand, our houses are constantly changing from bubbles into foams and vice versa.[76]

(ANTI)CLOSURE

In this paper we have argued that Peter Sloterdijk's work on *Sphären* can serve as an interesting bridge between Heideggerian dwelling approaches which argue for the conception of dwellings as nests, and Deleuzian approaches which wish to argue for dwellings as open and escapist places. We believe conceptually building this bridge is of crucial importance when one wishes to understand the increasingly dynamic choreography of dwelling places in the current globalised and transnational world, where people increasingly live in a *borderscape*, hence in-between societal systems and together with strangers.[77] The houses of Dutch migrants in German borderlands are in effect ambivalently b/ordered places. The borderline should thus be understood as elastic here, as a constant moving fabricated target that is strategically used in the case of short-distance transmigrants in the European Union borderlands of Germany and the Netherlands. Houses are both nests, hence places where people try to withdraw from the outside world, and open and escapist places where this outside world (gets invited to) come(s) in and where people try to escape to other places. The search for a home and the moving away from that same home are two contradictory processes which are at play in the houses of the Dutch migrants simultaneously. The case of the Dutch migrants particularly shows that the role of the nation in cross-border dwellings seems to be ambivalent. On the one hand people (still) seem to need the nation to create a secure and nest-like dwelling place. They try to embed their house in a larger national territory, and also try to nationalise the local place of their house by what we have called the building of national cavity walls. On the other hand people feel the need to go beyond this order of the nation.

So, following Sloterdijk's work on this point, on the one hand, people try to turn their houses into bubbles: intimate and enclosed places with simple social relations, which are embedded in safe national globes. On the other hand, bubble-like houses constantly implode or explode into socially complex foams, because its inhabitants feel the need to look beyond the social order of their houses (and nation) and others sometimes enter our houses, be it friends, neighbours or construction workers. So, in our view, the various Sloterdijkian spheres are present simultaneously in contemporary houses.[78] From this, we could conclude that there is a constant dialogue between isolation and connection, immobility and mobility, closeness and openness, within contemporary transborder dwelling places. We hope to think that this conceptual analysis feeds and hopefully pushes further the research agenda presented on critical borders studies as was presented earlier in this journal.[79] Our conceptual exploration has also learned that perhaps we should not see the movement between b/ordered and debordered as a tension as is sometimes done by populists but rather as a relation, because, and reasoning in line with Sloterdijk, each bubble can easily become foam or part of foam by imploding or exploding walls, and each foam consists of individual bubbles and also can easily become a bubble again. In our view, this relational approach of the house stirringly shows us that the desire to enclose the dwelling often will lead to the opposite desire to move away from this place and vice versa.

Unlike Heidegger then, whose dwelling approach is based on gravity, Sloterdijk pleads for a frivolous philosophy of the dwelling place. In *Foams*, the third part of his *Sphären* trilogy, he argues that we should deal with the constant 'airquaking' of spheres in a frivolous and flexible way. "Perhaps every happy life is a commuting between 'exorealism' ('Exorealismus') and 'endorealism' ('Endorealismus')", he argues.[80]

For us, a challenging question for the future then is whether people are able to find or create a kind of ontological security within this flexible and ambivalent sphere of their houses. Is it possible to feel at home in a house which constantly changes from a bubble-like sphere into a foamed sphere and back again? How do we strike a comfortable balance? And how can we construct a geopolitical space that uses these notions? Many questions to answer still. There surely is an interesting world to discover between the 'private universe' of Crowded House and the nomadic 'floating in a most peculiar way' of Bowie's Major Tom.

NOTES

1. The order of the authors is alphabetical.
2. Henk van Houtum and Ruben Gielis, 'Elastic migration: the case of Dutch short-distance transmigrants in Belgian and German borderlands', *Tijdschrift voor Economische en Sociale Geografie* 97 (2006) pp. 195–202.
3. Huib Ernste, Henk van Houtum and Annelies Zoomers, 'Trans-world: debating the place and borders of places in the age of transnationalism', *Tijdschrift voor Economische en Sociale Geografie* 100 (2009) pp. 577–586; Homi Bhabha, *Nation and Narration* (London: Routledge 1990).
4. e.g. Zygmunt Bauman, *Society under Siege* (Cambridge: Polity Press 2002).
5. See Arjun Appadurai, *Modernity at Large. Cultural Dimensions of Globalization* (University of Minnesota Press 1996); Prem Kumar Rajaram and Carl Grundy-Warr (eds.), *Borderscapes, Hidden Geographies and Politics at Territory's Edge* (University of Minnesota Press 2007).
6. See Noel Parker and Nick Vaughan-Williams et al., 'Lines in the Sand? Towards an Agenda for Critical Border Studies', *Geopolitics* 14 (2009) pp. 582–587.
7. See also Henk van Houtum, 'Mapping Transversal Borders: towards a Choreography of Space', in Chiara Brambilla and Bruno Riccio (eds.), *Transnational Migrations and Dis-located Borders* (Rimini: Guaraldi Publishers 2010) pp. 119–138.
8. See Jon May, 'Of nomads and vagrants: single homelessness and narratives of home as place', *Environment and Planning D: Society and Space* 18 (2000) pp. 737–759; Shelley Mallett, 'Understanding home: a critical review of the literature', *The Sociological Review* 52 (2004) pp. 62–89; Alison Blunt and Robyn Dowling, *Home* (New York: Routledge 2006); Paul Harrison, 'The space between us: opening remarks on the concept of dwelling', *Environment and Planning D: Society and Space* 25 (2007) pp. 625–647.
9. Henk van Houtum and Ton van Naerssen, 'Bordering, ordering and othering', *Tijdschrift voor Economische en Sociale Geografie* 93/2 (2002) pp. 125–136.

10. Martin Heidegger, *Poetry, Language, Thought*, translated by A Hofstadter (New York: HarperCollins Publishers 2001 [1971]).

11. Gilles Deleuze and Félix Guattari, *Anti-Oedipus*, translated by R Hurley, M Seem, HR Lane (London/New York: Continuum 2004a [1972]); Gilles Deleuze and Félix Guattari, *A Thousand Plateaus*, translated by B Massumi (London/New York: Continuum 2004b [1980]).

12. See also Joris Schapendonk, *Turbulent Trajectories: Sub-Saharan African Migrants Heading North*, Dissertation, Radboud University Nijmegen (2011); James Clifford, *Routes: Travel and Translation in the Late Twentieth Century* (Cambridge/London: Harvard University Press 1997).

13. See also Henk van Houtum, 'Waiting before the Law, Kafka on the border', *Social and Legal Studies* 19 (2010a) pp. 285–297; Henk van Houtum, 'The mask of the border', in Doris Wastl-Walter (ed.) *Ashgate research companion to border studies* (Ashgate 2010b) pp. 49–62.

14. See also Ruben Gielis, 'The value of single-site ethnography in the global era: studying transnational experiences in the migrant house', *Area* 43/3 (2011) pp. 257–263.

15. Peter Sloterdijk, *Sphären I: Blasen, Mikrosphärologie* (Frankfurt am Main: Suhrkamp 1998).

16. Peter Sloterdijk, *Sphären II: Globen, Makrosphärologie* (Frankfurt am Main: Suhrkamp 1999).

17. Peter Sloterdijk, *Sphären III: Schäume, Plurale Sphärologie* (Frankfurt am Main: Suhrkamp 2004).

18. Stuart Elden and Eduardo Mendieta, 'Being-with as making worlds: the "second coming" of Peter Sloterdijk', *Environment and Planning D: Society and Space* 27 (2009) pp. 1–11.

19. See Ernste et al. (note 3); Bhabha (note 3).

20. See also Gielis (note 14).

21. For an extensive and precise reconstruction and evaluation of this ethnographical study, see Gielis (note 14).

22. Sloterdijk (note 17) p. 803.

23. Peter Sloterdijk, *Im Weltinnenraum des Kapitals* (Frankfurt am Main: Suhrkamp 2005).

24. See for a more extensive analysis of the empirical behavioural patterns of these short-distance transmigrants, e.g., Van Houtum and Gielis (note 2) and Gielis (note 14).

25. See e.g. Adrian Favell, *Eurostars and Eurocities: free movement and mobility in an integrating Europe* (Oxford: Blackwell Publishing 2008).

26. See e.g. Van Houtum (2010b, note 13).

27. Heidegger (note 10) pp. 158–159.

28. Ibid, p. 161.

29. David Gauthier, Martin Heidegger, Emmanuel Levinas, and the politics of dwelling, PhD dissertation, Department of Political Sciences, Louisiana State University, New Orleans 2004, p. 137.

30. Heidegger (note 10) p. 145.

31. Maria Kaika, 'Interrogating the Geographies of the Familiar: Domesticating Nature and Constructing the Autonomy of the Modern Home', *International Journal of Urban and Regional Research* 28 (2004) pp. 265–286.

32. See Harrison (note 8).

33. Heidegger (note 10) p. 158; see also Harrison (note 8) p. 633.

34. Marie-Eve Morin, 'Cohabitating in the globalised world: Peter Sloterdijk's global foams and Bruno Latour's cosmopolitics', *Environment and Planning D: Society and Space* 27 (2009) pp. 58–72.

35. Heidegger (note 10) p. 215.

36. Gaston Bachelard, *The poetics of space*, translated by M Jolas (Boston: Beacon Press 1994 [1958]) p. viii.

37. Bachelard (note 36) p. xxxv.

38. Gauthier (note 29) p. 138.

39. See Sloterdijk (note 16) p. 206.

40. See also Elden and Mendieta (note 18) p. 6.

41. Peter Saunders, *A Nation of Home Owners* (London: Unwin Hyman 1990); see also Ann Dupuis and David Thorns, 'Home, home ownership and the search for ontological security', *The Sociological Review* 46 (1998) pp. 24–47; Ade Kearns et al., '"Beyond Four Walls". The Psychosocial Benefits of Home: Evidence from West Central Scotland', *Housing Studies* 15 (2000) pp. 387–410.

42. 'Insulierungen', Sloterdijk (note 17) p. 309; see also René ten Bos, 'Towards an amphibious anthropology: water and Peter Sloterdijk', *Environment and Planning D: Society and Space* 27 (2009) pp. 73–86.

43. 'Beseelte Binnenwelten', Sloterdijk (note 17) p. 310.

44. Sloterdijk (note 17) p. 534.

45. Sloterdijk (note 17) p. 56 and 568.
46. Heidegger (note 10) p. 149.
47. Sloterdijk (note 17) p. 400.
48. See also Gielis (note 14).
49. Ibid.
50. Ibid.
51. Friedrich Nietzsche, *De geboorte van de tragedie* (translation of Die Geburt der Tragödie) (Amsterdam: International Theatre Bookshop 1987 [1872]).
52. Deleuze and Guattari (note 11).
53. Marcus Doel, 'A hundred thousand lines of flight: a machinic introduction to the nomad thought and scrumpled geography of Gilles Deleuze and Félix Guattari', *Environment and Planning D: Society and Space* 14 (1996) p. 430.
54. Harrison (note 8).
55. Ann Varley, 'A place like this? Stories of dementia, home, and the self', *Environment and Planning D: Society and Space* 26 (2008) p. 50.
56. Harrison (note 8) p. 643.
57. Sloterdijk (note 17).
58. See Sjoerd van Tuinen, *Sloterdijk: Binnenstebuiten denken* (Kampen: Uitgeverij Klement 2004) pp. 168–173.
59. Sloterdijk (note 17) pp. 259–260; see also Van Tuinen (note 58) p. 80.
60. Sloterdijk (note 17) p. 516.
61. Anthony Giddens, *The Consequences of Modernity* (Stanford: Stanford University Press 1990); Anthony Giddens, *Modernity and Self-Identity: Self and Society in the Late Modern Age* (Stanford: Stanford University Press 1991).
62. See Gauthier (note 29) pp. 119–120.
63. Sloterdijk (note 17) pp. 724–725.
64. Ibid, p. 24.
65. 'Das schwebende Haus', *Sloterdijk* (note 17) p. 554.
66. 'Häuser als Fahrzeuge', *Sloterdijk* (note 17) p. 549. In our view, for Sloterdijk explosion and implosion are equally important for understanding the foaming of spheres. However, this is not always recognised by scholars discussing Sloterdijk's foams. These scholars usually seem to focus on the explosion of bubbles, and tend to overlook (Morin (note 34) p. 67) or underestimate (Nigel Thrift, 'Different atmospheres: of Sloterdijk, China, and site', *Environment and Planning D: Society and Space* 27 (2009) pp. 125–126) the importance of the idea of imploding bubbles.
67. See Gielis (note 14). As the Dutch migrants pull these Dutch spheres into their house, these virtual and mental neighbourhoods could also be interpreted as ways to build a Dutch cavity wall around their houses.
68. Or perhaps there is even a triple ex- and implosion, as also the national cavity walls of the house ex- and implode.
69. See also Van Houtum (note 13).
70. Sloterdijk (note 17) p. 59.
71. Sloterdijk (note 17).
72. Ibid, pp. 576–577.
73. Peter Sloterdijk, *Selbstversuch: Ein Gespräch mit Carlos Oliveira* (München: Carl Hanser Verlag 1996) p. 32; paraphrased in Van Tuinen (note 58) p. 110.
74. Sloterdijk (note 73) p. 70.
75. Sloterdijk (note 17).
76. Van Houtum (2010a, note 13).
77. See Ernste et al. (note 3); Van Houtum (note 7).
78. Which shows once more, and which is also stressed by others (Morin (note 34); Van Tuinen (note 58)), that Sloterdijk's Sphären trilogy is perhaps not just a historical project, but also an anthropology of the current world.
79. Parker and Vaughan-Williams et al. (note 6).
80. Sloterdijk (note 17) p. 742.

Cartopolitics, Geopolitics and Boundaries in the Arctic

JEPPE STRANDSBJERG
Department of Business and Politics, Copenhagen Business School, Frederiksberg, Denmark

Critical Border Studies emphasise how distinct political spaces are produced by borders. In this article I suggest that the order of this relationship should be reversed. I argue that space precedes and conditions the manifestation of borders. The argument is based on an understanding of cartography as a practice that mediates the relationship between space and borders. Drawing on Bruno Latour, I introduce the notion of cartopolitics to describe the process where questions pertaining to sovereign control over space are decided through cartography and law. In analysing current border practices in the Arctic, the term cartopolitics captures how the relationship between the United Nations Convention on the Law of the Sea and cartography is shaping the attempts by Arctic states to expand sovereign rights into the sea. The key is the continental shelf and how it is defined in law. In this process cartographic practices work to establish a particular spatial reality that subsequently serve as a basis for border making.

In this contemporary clash of scientific knowledges, legal regimes and offshore technologies, the uncertain spatialities of the Circumpolar Region are being reconfigured.[1]

Geographical knowledge clears the path for commercial enterprise, and commercial enterprise has been in most lands the beginning of civilization.[2]

INTRODUCTION

Issues of boundaries are contested and currently subject to much attention in the Arctic region. The increased accessibility of the Arctic caused by climate change exacerbates the significance of unsettled borders between Arctic states. Norway and Russia have only recently signed an agreement on a maritime border in the Barents Sea; Denmark and Canada disagree on control over Hans Island; and Canada and the US disagree on the border north of Alaska. The diminishing ice cap is, in effect, a withdrawal of a boundary for commercial enterprise as both shipping, oil, and mining companies direct their attention to new Arctic spaces. In addition, indigenous people have shown concern for the development of the future governance architecture of the Arctic with regard to questions of defining the very nature of the Arctic as a new political space. And the problem for settling these disagreements over borders is tied to a lack of a clear spatial foundation for borders.[3]

While border studies typically emphasise that – and how – borders create particular spaces; and as such stress the significance of border practices for our understanding of political spaces, practices in the Arctic demonstrate a reversal of this relationship. This is to say that the effectuation of particular border imaginations not only produces spaces, but also depends on a particular spatiality. To exemplify, it is obvious that the establishment of legal boundaries between sovereign states produce different (yet similar) political spaces, and that legal boundaries between sovereign jurisdiction and the high seas create two different spatialities: sovereign spaces and international spaces.[4] Yet, I argue that the ability to establish such legal boundaries in the first place depends on a particular spatiality, and, as such, boundaries do not produce space – it is space that decides how boundaries can be drawn and practiced. Hannes Gerhardt et al. have argued "that ongoing contestation of sovereignty in the Arctic is rooted in the region's indeterminate and unstable geographical characteristics".[5] This suggests that sovereign borders somehow depend on a stable and determinate spatiality; and, by implication, it suggests a need to investigate how space as a historical and social, yet material, phenomenon is established. Drawing on the science studies of Bruno Latour and the political geography of Stuart Elden, I suggest that space should be seen as a historicised assemblage of people's relationship to land; and that space precedes and conditions boundaries.[6]

The growing political and commercial concern with the Arctic has raised the spectre of geopolitics, at least in public discourse. Yet, in this article I argue that the term cartopolitics[7] is a more apt description of current border practices in the Arctic[8] than a conventional understanding of geopolitics signifying strategic concerns with control over places of military or economic significance. I introduce cartopolitics to describe the process where questions pertaining to sovereign control over space are decided through cartography and law.[9] The term is not employed to suggest that there is an unproblematic or disinterested relationship between the two; on the contrary, the term describes the attempt to let geography speak to sovereignty through cartography. The United Nations Convention on the Law of the Sea (UNCLOS) is instrumental in the efforts of Arctic states to expand their sovereign rights over the continental shelves. It describes particular geological conditions that serve as the basis for the expansion of a territorial logic into the sea. The borders that are established on this basis not only delineate particular spaces but, rather, they demarcate sovereign maritime spaces from maritime zones common to humankind. The practices that lead to such a division are, initially, concerned less with specific border practices than with cartographic attempts to map the seabed in general, and the continental shelves in particular. As such, these practices are concerned more with providing a cartographic reality of space that subsequently determines or conditions the way in which borders can be drawn.[10]

Despite the ongoing development of Critical Border Studies scholarship, as reflected in the 'Lines in the Sand' Agenda and this special section more generally, such work has yet to comment substantively on the empirical context of Arctic Geopolitics. From a critical geopolitics perspective, more broadly, Sanjay Chaturvedi, Klaus Dodds, Phil Steinberg, Hannes Gerhardt, and Richard Powel have studied the Arctic.[11] The notion of cartopolitics clearly draws from the aspirations of critical geopolitics in order to make a contribution to critical border studies. Yet, while critical geopolitics tends to discourse analysis of representational practices, cartopolitics suggests a more narrow focus on cartographic practices as space making questioning more openly the relationship between 'science' and 'politics' rather than assuming that geography necessarily lends itself to statecraft.[12] This does not mean that there is no politics or interest behind cartopolitics; of course there is. However, a cartopolitical view on boundary-making emphasises the controversies that emerge in the attempt to let cartography decide questions of sovereignty and the tensions between different spatialities that arise through this process. As such, the overall contribution of this article is to show how a particular engagement with cartographic practice allows critical border studies not only to investigate how borders create spaces but also, on a more general level, how the assemblage of particular spatialities condition and decide the establishment of sovereign borders.[13]

THE ARCTIC AS A NEW ARENA OF GEOPOLITICS

What is considered to be geopolitical depends on the eyes that see something as a geopolitical concern or not. During the Cold War the Arctic was central to the nuclear strategies of the US and USSR.[14] Today, most of the Arctic states have renewed their political strategies in preparation to boost their presence in the region. Norway has explicitly prioritised 'the High North' as their main strategic interest since 2005; Stephen Harper's government in Canada has made repeated claims to their Arctic presence; and Russia prioritises the Arctic as their future source of energy.[15] Yet for the indigenous peoples in the Arctic, geopolitics has historically been a constant aspect of their encounter with colonising states with regard to issues such as land rights, housing and residence patterns, and national spatial planning more generally.[16] Despite this, the Arctic received little attention from a global public prior to the 2000s. Now, as discussed subsequently, for the media the Arctic has provided a new arena for geopolitics witnessed by the amount of somewhat sensationalist articles published in recent years dealing with competition for resources, maritime spaces and influence.

At least three factors have fuelled the contemporary concern with the Arctic: a shrinking ice cap which, in turn, increases accessibility to resources and potential shipping routes; technological developments facilitating extraction of resources from deep seas; and the legal, political and technical processes relating to the ratification of UNCLOS, which allow countries to extend their sovereign rights in maritime areas. In 2008, US Geological Survey published an estimate of undiscovered oil and gas north of the Arctic Circle suggesting that the "extensive Arctic continental shelves may constitute the geographically largest unexplored prospective area for petroleum remaining on Earth".[17] In 2010, for the first time, a bulk carrier sailing under a flag other than that of Russia used the Northern Sea Route (the North East Passage) as a transit trade lane carrying iron ore from Norway to China suggesting the viability of this shorter and safer route for commercial shipping.[18] Oil has been exploited in the Canadian and US Arctic and just recently, Cairn Energy published hopeful results for potential off-shore oil drilling west of Greenland.[19] In sum, these developments will increase the level and range of human activity in the Arctic, and this is likely to change the geopolitical significance of the region from a closed militarised strategic space to a commercial space increasingly accessible for outsiders due to climate change. As a consequence, many states realise that they are Arctic powers[20] and increase their efforts to get their share of the potential wealth of the region.

The third factor mentioned above concerns the way in which UNCLOS defines the conditions under which states can claim a larger maritime jurisdiction. This lends itself to an image of states in mutual competition for the North Pole and surrounding areas. While this does not reflect the actual processes relating to UNCLOS, the uncertainty surrounding the distribution of sovereignty and the prospective wealth has caught the attention of the media positing the process as a potential conflict scenario. The image of the melting ice cap increasing the accessibility to a hitherto mental 'white blank' on the map (for most southerners), supposedly containing considerable wealth in terms of natural resources, has reinvigorated fantasies of exploration and expansion into *'terra nullius'*, and a new (black) gold rush. Headlines such as 'Canada joins rush to the Arctic' and 'The Scramble for the seabed' clearly echo imperial histories of European expansion and a particular set of geographical imaginaries.[21] The sensationalist discourse was fuelled by Russia's spectacular planting of a Russian flag on the seabed of the North Pole symbolically suggesting the Arctic as Russian during their *Arktika* expedition in 2007. And indeed the submarine event triggered newspaper articles showing large parts of the Arctic Regions under a Russian flag[22] and spurned a general concern over increasing militarisation and hostility between Arctic states.

This fear seems overstated. It is true, though, that most of the Arctic countries are in the process of either upgrading or reforming their military presence,[23] and several commentators have warned against the danger of armed conflict.[24] Military restructuring plans have been accompanied by somewhat confrontational statements among leading policymakers. In particular, Canada's prime minister Stephen Harper has been very assertive with regard to the Arctic: "Canada has a choice when it comes to defending our sovereignty in the Arctic; either we use it or we lose it, [and] make no mistake this government intends to use it. Because Canada's Arctic is central to our identity as a northern nation. It is part of our history and it represents the tremendous potential of our future".[25] In addition, Russian policymakers have made very assertive statements on the Arctic,[26] and among the NATO countries of the Arctic there has been a sceptical attitude towards Russia's intentions. Speaking against the militarisation thesis, however, defence analyst Kristian Åtland argues that even if Russia is upgrading its military capacity it is still far from the level of the Cold War. And further, the sections within Russia that are pushing for an opening and commercialisation of the Russian Arctic seem more influential than those seeking a closed and securitised Arctic.[27] Meanwhile Canada's often-cited plan to construct a number of naval vessels with ice-breaking capacity has been postponed indefinitely.[28] Furthermore, it has been suggested that the assertive attitude of the Harper government primarily addresses a domestic audience[29] and, as such, there is little evidence to support the scenario of a heavily militarised Arctic.[30]

For many it appears paradoxical that a decrease in ice cover caused by a warmer climate has increased access to fossil fuels, which is likely to contribute to a yet warmer climate. This concern dovetails with the fear that natural resources, particularly oil, exploitation will impact negatively on a unique Arctic ecosystem. In order to protect the Arctic environment and prevent militarisation some observers have suggested a specific Arctic treaty.[31] The idea behind this is to create a particular and binding legal regime for the Arctic region mirroring the Antarctic Treaty System establishing a legal regime to govern the area as a shared space between potential claimants. However, there are obvious differences. Whereas Antarctica is a continent, mostly occupied by penguins, governed by an international treaty and surrounded by sea; the Arctic is a mediterranean sea covered by ice and surrounded by land occupied by people falling under the sovereign jurisdiction of a state.[32] In effect, they are almost mirror opposites and the legal concerns with boundaries are also different. Compared to Antarctica, the legal and spatial conditions for border practices are very different in the Arctic.[33] The land areas of the Arctic are inhabited and they are already divided between sovereign states. The central area of dispute – the Arctic Ocean – is a maritime area and as such governed by UNCLOS which represents the general international legal framework in maritime areas.

In response to the concerns over a conflict-ridden Arctic future and the media emphasis on the competition for resources, the Danish government launched an initiative that led to the signing of the Ilulissat Declaration. In May 2008, the so-called Arctic-5 states (Canada, US, Denmark-Greenland, Russia, and Norway) agreed that

> notably, the law of the sea provides for important rights and obligations concerning the delineation of the outer limits of the continental shelf, the protection of the marine environment, including ice-covered areas, freedom of navigation, marine scientific research, and other uses of the sea. We remain committed to this legal framework and to the orderly settlement of any possible overlapping claims. . . . The five coastal states currently cooperate closely in the Arctic Ocean with each other and with other interested parties. This cooperation includes the collection of scientific data concerning the continental shelf, the protection of the marine environment and other scientific research. We will work to strengthen this cooperation, which is based on mutual trust and transparency, inter alia, through timely exchange of data and analyses.[34]

With this, the five Arctic Sea coastal states not only promise to solve any conflict through existing law and cooperate widely in terms of settling any sovereignty issue; they also reject the idea that it should be necessary to establish an Arctic Treaty or a similar legal instrument for governing the Arctic. On the contrary, they state that there is nothing special about the Arctic; that it is a place like any other in the world governed by established international law, and in particular there is no pressing need to involve outsiders in Arctic governance.[35] The cooperative tone between Arctic states was recently confirmed when the Arctic Council ministers signed the 'Nuuk Declaration May 2011' that involves a search and rescue agreement in the Arctic. This was deemed important for political reasons because it represents the first legally binding agreement negotiated under the auspices of the Arctic Council.[36] As such, this agreement confirms that this forum represents an important governance institution.

In sum, whereas militaristic echoes of imperial geopolitics from the past have surfaced in the media the issues surrounding sovereignty, resources, and shipping appear much less controversial on the ground. Instead, what is more interesting concerning the situation in the Arctic is the way in which the law of the sea defines the criteria for border extension. As I will discuss, the legal framework is somewhat unclear given that the wording of the Ilulissat Declaration refers to custom law as well as the 1958 Conventions of the Law of the Sea and the 1982 UNCLOS. This is partly due to the fact that the US is still not part to UNCLOS and cannot therefore make any claims under the convention. Despite the absence of the US from the list of UNCLOS signatories, the key issue remains the way in which UNCLOS defines a set of geomorphological conditions which give a country the right to expand its 'marine territory'. That is, that the distribution of sovereignty is, in the first place, determined by scientific measurement; i.e., cartography. It is on this basis that I suggest that the Arctic represents a theatre for cartopolitics rather than conventional geopolitics. In sequence, this demonstrates how it is necessary to establish a particular spatiality in order to establish political boundaries.

THE SPATIAL CONDITIONS OF BOUNDARIES

In a recent publication in this journal, Noel Parker and Nick Vaughan-Williams outlined an agenda for critical border studies.[37] In an attempt to interrogate critically the notion of boundaries and shift the attention to the social *practices* of boundaries, they introduced the metaphor of 'Lines in the Sand'. Border studies in general, and the 'Lines in the Sand' project in particular, have done much to change the perception of the border from a territorially fixed static line to think in terms of actors and sets of social practices. Yet, this literature tends to prioritise borders over space in that the production of various socio-political spaces is seen to be the result of border imaginations and practices. Reversing this order, I will argue that borders are also conditioned by distinct spatialities established within particular historical contexts. The notion of 'Lines in the Sand' bears upon connotations of fluidity and transformation and describes well the ephemeral character of boundaries. Yet, without a stronger emphasis on space we are poorly equipped to grasp the tension between the ontological sandiness of borders and the apparent scientific-juridical fixity of state borders. It is exactly the ability to fixate space through cartography that provides a relatively stable spatial foundation for borders.

For a long time, International Relations theory has had an uneasy relationship with space. The spatial determinism of the geopolitical tradition of Ratzel, Haushofer, and Mackinder made spatial arguments dubious within the discipline even if geopolitical thinking remained a significant contribution to strategic planning by states during the Cold War.[38] With the critical constructivist turn in the late 1980s attempts were made to deal with hidden spatial assumptions of the discipline.[39] Attempts to question the spatial order (both politically and theoretically) were fuelled by the end of the Cold War and the notion of globalisation widening discussions about the status of territory in global politics.[40] In the effort to question a particular spatial order and at the same time avoiding spatial determinism, critical scholars have turned the attention to how various border practices and patterns of inclusion/exclusion have generated particular spaces of control, power, and so forth.

The problem with emphasising boundaries, however, is that they tend to assume or demand a particular spatiality. And if this spatiality is not interrogated, it will – logically – have to be assumed. Unless we think that boundaries can be effectuated in a vacuum, there will necessarily be spatial conditions for boundaries. As political geographer Stuart Elden has argued on a number of occasions, "It is the understanding of political space that is fundamental and the idea of boundaries a secondary aspect, dependent on the first."[41] Hence, I propose that in discussions of territory where the emphasis is on borders, a notion of a natural – or otherwise given – space remains assumed as a background against which borders can be drawn or practiced. Through the demarcation of such borders, socio-political spaces are being defined on top of that given reality of space.

In consequence, approaches that see political space solely as an outcome of border practices by implication assume the *a priori* unity of space. This is the case both with scientific realist approaches, maintaining a notion of reality independent of social processes and knowledge production, but it is, indeed, also the case with much social constructivist work concerning boundaries and political space. Yet, if space is not taken as a given background to social practices then it should become obvious why space-formation necessarily precedes border-practices and conditions the way in which boundaries can be established. Bruno Latour has somewhat controversially suggested that the most significant impact of 'the West' in the history of the world is the 'insertion of a unified nature' behind cultural differences.[42] By this he means that the division between what is considered the world as a unitary nature and what is culture as human diversity has allowed for debates over cultural difference and identity but all this has taken place within a given spatial frame of a global space. This makes conflicts over space simply social or cultural affairs while leaving 'the unified space of nature' as an undisputed settlement. Yet, if we do not accept a notion of given space as the backbone of social and political theory, then space has to be analysed and historicised as a social construction. In consequence, this is a suggestion to push the constructivist impulse to cover the reality, or materiality, of space. The question is, of course, how to do this.

I have already noted that Critical Geopolitics generally lends itself to discursive analyses of space. As noted by Nigel Thrift, who calls for greater attention to specific material practices such as census taking and map making, the reading of texts "producing the world as discursive construction . . . has problematic consequences for understanding *how* (and therefore why) geopower is actually practiced".[43] Not unrelated to the general sentiments of Critical Geopolitics, a series of writings on calculable territory has emerged in recent years.[44] In Elden's contribution, he emphasises how it was a particular ability to calculate and measure that conditioned the emergence of 'space' as a category that came to inform possible ways of thinking territory.[45] With that, modern territory and border practices depend on the emergence of calculable space. When I wish to introduce a notion of cartopolitics in order to emphasise the significance of cartography for the distribution of sovereignty, it obviously draws on both critical geopolitics and the 'calculation of space' argument, but there is still a sentiment within this literature that the technologies of calculation are acting on space; on the landscape. Instead, with cartopolitics, I draw on Latour, and the notion that space is assembled in networks of calculation in which 'ideas of space' and the 'materiality of space' in common social science parlance interact. This means that cartopolitics is not about representing or acting *on* space but rather, it emphasises how space is assembled *in* networks between surveying, calculation and the objects of the environment. In brief where the notion of calculability develops a Foucauldian understanding of political space, cartopolitics owes more to a Latourian understanding of space.

To illustrate how the cartopolitical take on space affects border studies, it is useful to take a historical example. Prior to the European Renaissance, there were no general, or standardised, measures of space. Generally, distance-space were measured in travel time; use-space such as agricultural land, was measured in functional measures such as the time it took to work the land (carrucates) or the amount of seed required to sow the land (barrels), and so forth. In terms of representing territory, there were no uniform or universal cartographic standards that would bring unity to space. As a consequence, territorial boundaries were often unclear zones and the constitution of the territory did not take place as a result of border making but rather as a result of social ties of allegiance which would tie the land-holding nobility and the church to a sovereign. The territory of the sovereign then would, in principle, vary with the allegiance of landholding subjects. As such border making was secondary to the assemblage of territory through social networks and there were no uniform measures of space that would allow for boundaries to be drawn or defined in accurate terms.[46]

Hence, the way in which space is made real through cartographic, or knowledge, practices of space conditions the way in which boundaries can be demarcated. And, the notion of a unified spatial reality requires some notion of abstraction from social practice and the immediate experience of the landscape. With a cartography informed by geometry in the European Renaissance a system was set up which allowed space to be measured and mapped with reference only to measurement and calculations based on geometry. The same cartographic principles gradually came to be applied whether maps were global, territorial or of household or private property. As the globe was conquered and surveyed, Europeans gradually produced a cartographic image representing an abstract assemblage of global space.

With the abstract knowledge of space provided by the geometric map it became possible to make decisions about spatial partitions and boundaries simply based on a visual representation of space. Without such knowledge it would be necessary to make specific references to known features of the landscape or it would be necessary to travel through the landscape and mark the border directly on the ground.[47] Translated into the geopolitics of border making this means that the political organisation of space is as much about defining a particular spatial reality as it is a question of enclosing, territorialising, controlling or otherwise partitioning space.

CARTOPOLITICS

The notion of cartopolitics implies a process where politics is made to correspond with a cartographically constructed reality of space, and by implication, that it is cartography that conditions the way in which sovereignty can be tied to a certain understanding of territory. Whereas it is a widespread belief that maps are representations of existing spaces, the literature on the social power of cartography has stressed that map-making plays a performative role in the constitution of political space.[48] On a general level cartography, as a specific cultural form mediating space and society, plays a conditioning role for the way in which space is conceived and territory can be produced. With Latour we can understand cartography as a space-assembling practice. This means practices of surveying, measurement and calculation intermediates the human relationship with the environment. This implies that different cartographies establish different spatialities which, in turn, provide different conditions for thinking and practicing boundaries. In consequence, cartopolitics, understood as processes where sovereign control over space is decided through cartography and law, is not necessarily a contemporary phenomenon. It requires, though, a cartography that allows sovereignty and law, more generally, to speak or relate to the landscape. As described above, this was not possible in medieval Europe where sovereignty was a relationship between rulers and subjects.

Early developments in 'scientific cartography' in Renaissance Europe allowed state sovereignty to be defined in spatial terms by abstracting the notion of territorial space from the people inhabiting this space.[49] The reasoning behind this claim is that when the knowledge and understanding of space is abstracted from its social functionality it becomes possible to conceive of space as an autonomous category that exists by virtue of itself. To exemplify this, political territories in Medieval Europe were, as a rule, constituted through personal networks of loyalty that brought the possession of various lords within the realm of a territorial ruler. In this system it was near impossible to think of the territory independently of this social network. With the advent of so-called modern cartography, it became possible to represent space as autonomous and hereby territory took on a more defining role in terms of the boundaries of the state and society.

Crucially, this allowed territorial divisions of areas that were unknown; that is, it enabled a division of territories to be. This was the case with the Treaty of Tordesillas which, in 1494, divided the world into a Spanish and a Portuguese sphere and determined legitimate sovereignty claims of lands to be discovered between them. The Tordesillas Treaty set up a system in which territorial claims were based on and legitimised by cartography. The treaty was established in order to find a negotiated settlement between the expanding empires of Spain and Portugal in order to avoid large scale conflict over the issues of control and legitimate possessions in the new colonies. The treaty divided the world according to a longitudinal boundary in purely abstract terms meaning that nobody knew exactly where the boundary was running nor what existed on either side of the boundary; but these were issues that were, in principle, going to be solved through cartography. It was only when the Atlantic and Americas were explored further by the Iberian powers that they realised what lands had come into their legitimate – from their point of view – possession through this treaty. It was, for example, due to the Tordesillas treaty that Brazil became Portuguese because it was located on the Eastern side of the boundary.

The Treaty of Tordesillas can be said to have institutionalised the primacy of cartography for territorial settlements between competing states. While there is no linear history in the development of the relationship between mapping and politics, Tordesillas stands as a striking historical example of how politics of spatial control came to be mediated through a specific, geometrically based, cartographic regime which turned rightful possession into a question of science and measurement. As such, Tordesillas stands as a historical parallel to the current UNCLOS regime, which also prescribes mapping as a way to legitimise claims to *terra nullius*. In the historical cases of disagreements between Spain and Portugal, it was common to set up 'juntas' (small scientific committees) from both sides and then meet and discuss the various claims.[50] As such it was a matter of negotiation to reach a settlement, but the legal terms of the negotiation were to a large extent defined by the bull *Inter Caetera* issued by the Pope in 1493 to settle the dispute between the Iberian powers.[51] As such the Tordesillas regime can be described as a universal authority (the Pope) issuing directions for how to solve disputes over territory through cartography.

Now, whereas land boundaries could be established based on practical knowledge of the landscape, and thus without an abstracted knowledge of space, it is clear, however, how the abstract knowledge of space presented by the geometric map allows boundaries to be described and enforced as simple coordinates referring to a spatial reality mediated by the map. In practice, boundaries have been described through a combination of spatial features of the landscape and abstract spatial coordinates. In the border documents drafted in Paris 1921 describing the Danish-German border, a combination of spatial points described in longitude and latitude is combined with references to features in the landscape such as *Vesterskov Mølle* (a mill), or a bridge located west of *skomagerhuset* (a house).[52] Boundaries at sea, however, are an altogether different issue. Maritime boundaries cannot be marked by erecting stones and the like, and there are no mills, bridges, or mountains which can serve as a reference point. Philip Steinberg has argued how social factors of production, use, regulation and representation has constructed the different historical conceptions of ocean space across the globe[53]. In contrast, I would emphasise the degree to which a particular knowledge of space conditions the possibility of drawing boundaries.

While boundaries at land have typically been concerned with the divisions of jurisdiction, passage, taxation rights, language, religion, and identity between different rulers and societies, boundaries at sea have also been about dividing a common sphere from a sovereign, or territorial sphere. It is problematic to talk about territory in the context of the sea but to an extent the notion of 'territorial sea' can be seen as an idea of extending the sovereignty over territory into the adjacent sea. Up through the seventeenth century, the notion developed in European 'international law' that a state could claim sovereign rights over the territorial sea, which was defined in terms of the range of a cannon ball. The Dutch jurist, Cornelius von Bynkershoek, for example, suggested in 1702 that the sea was common to all except along the coast where dominion could be claimed by a state as far as a cannon could shoot.[54] This way of demarcating and measuring a spatial relation resonates with previous practices on land, as discussed before, where spatial measures were conceptualised in terms of functionality. In that respect it mattered less that the range of cannon balls would vary according to technology and increase over time. It was only with a shift in cartographic and calculation abilities that boundaries, at sea as well as at land, could be turned into fixed lines.

ASSEMBLING MARITIME SPACE

In the Grotian legal system, the sea was divided into a territorial and a common zone. However, particularly since World War II, there have been increasing attempts by states to claim ownership over resources such as oil, gas, and fish stocks, beyond a narrow breadth of the territorial sea. These attempts to expand sovereign rights created a need for new legal norms and standards. With the ratification of UNCLOS, which has been called a legal constitution for the ocean,[56] the two main principles for extending sovereign rights are the Exclusive Economic Zone (EEZ) and the Continental Shelf (CS).

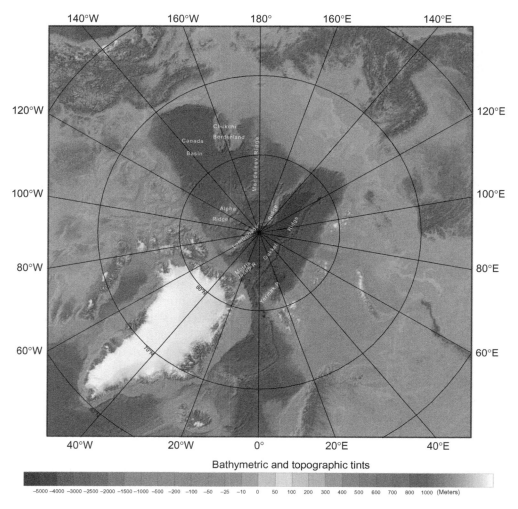

FIGURE 1 The 'International Bathymetric Chart of the Arctic Ocean (IBCAO)' is a result of an initiative to develop a digital database that contains all available bathymetric data north of 64 degrees North, for use by mapmakers, researchers, and others whose work requires a detailed and accurate knowledge of the depth and the shape of the Arctic seabed.[55] (color figure available online).

Within the EEZ a state has rights to all living and non-living resources, and it can be extended to a maximum distance of 200 nautical miles (nm) from baseline (i.e., the juridical coastline of a state). The EEZ was an invention of UNCLOS and was related to previous practices of establishing fishing zones in particular.[57] The concerns with the CS have been related to the exploitation of natural resources of the seabed. Geologically, the continental shelf is the extension of the landmass into the sea, and in legal terms, then, this continuation of the land constitutes an extension of sovereign territory into the sea. In consequence, the border between sovereign and common international spaces is tied to a geological phenomenon, the continental shelf.

In the second part of the twentieth century, the desire to expand sovereign rights to the resources of the seabed was linked to technological development that made it possible for states to exploit the seabed where it was hitherto not possible. The 1958 Convention of the Continental Shelf defined the CS in terms of its exploitability. In the light of the discussion in the previous section, the definition of the CS as legal space was tied to a notion of functionality.[58] This has been superseded by the definition in §76 of UNCLOS where the CS takes a peculiar form combining a juridical and geological definition. On one hand, the CS is a purely juridical concept that is defined as a zone extending 200 nautical miles from baseline (same distance as the EEZ). This means that all states have a 200 nm zone where they have exclusive rights over resources.[59] At the same time, however, in cases where the 'natural' continental shelf extends beyond the 200 nm defined by 'the juridical CS', the natural continental shelf can serve as the foundation for extending the sovereign rights of a state beyond the 200 nm. The rights claimable by states in the extended CS area are less than within the 200 nm zone. For example, states have to pay a contribution based on the resources exploited in the extended zone to the International Seabed Authority. Nevertheless, what concerns me here is the way in which §76 defines the conditions under which states can extend their sovereign rights in the extended CS zone.[60] By defining the extended CS in geological terms, UNCLOS turns the extension of sovereign rights, in principle, into a question of cartography (see Figure 2).

The idea of basing boundaries on natural features in the landscape has a long history. It was particularly during the seventeenth and eighteenth centuries that the notion of natural boundaries became widespread in Europe. Rivers were often used as boundaries and in a famous case the Pyrenees were positioned as a natural boundary between France and Spain.[61] While the submarine continental shelf is not 'visible' in the immediate encounter with the landscape the notion that it is somehow possible to rely on natural, objective, features to decide the location of boundaries remains the same. By letting nature determine boundaries, the decision of border demarcation is dislocated from the immediate 'political decision' to the contours of the landscape. The problem is, of course, how it is possible to relate the border to the landscape. The solution historically, within the Treaty of Tordesillas regime, discussed above, was through cartography and surveying. Similarly, today, UNCLOS turns the political decision of demarcating sovereign spheres from common ones into a question of science and measurement. A state that wishes to claim an extended continental shelf zone must provide the necessary data confirming the extension of the CS to a UN body, the Commission on the Limits of the Continental Shelf (CLCS).

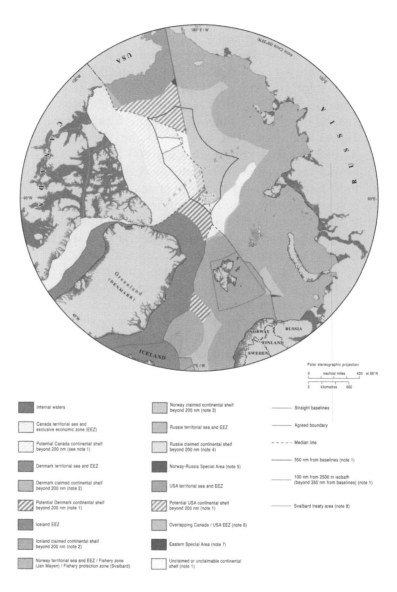

FIGURE 2 Map of maritime jurisdiction and boundaries in the Arctic region showing the potential claims of the relevant states. By courtesy of the 'International Boundaries Research Unit' Durham, available at <http://www.durham.ac.uk/ibru/resources/arctic> (color figure available online).

The CLCS will then make recommendations to the member states based on their material, and: "The limits of the shelf established by a coastal State on the basis of these recommendations shall be final and binding."[62]

Hence, UNCLOS identifies geographical features as the legitimate boundaries between sovereign and common jurisdictions. Paradoxically, though, the geography that the convention refers to is not present. In other words, §76 presupposes a particular spatial reality and concordantly a particular way of producing knowledge of space. For this to work, seen from the perspective of this legal-science nexus, nature must be made to speak with 'one voice'. If nature – or space – is settled, then the drawing of the line demarcating sovereign from common spaces is made straightforward. The problem is, however, that nature is not immediately present to serve this function. There is, as discussed, never a given spatial foundation for the law and for politics, and this is recognised by scientists and lawyers as well. An editorial in *Nature Geoscience*, for example, acknowledges that geology has been politicised, and the suggested response is that only "if the science that underlies its recommendations stands the test of time will the shelves' outer limits established under UNCLOS be globally respected as the one and only valid demarcation line".[63] And in a classic textbook on international law, it is equally recognised that there is an element of social construction of geography: "The way in which the geographical situation is described may suggest particular solutions, so that the seemingly objective process of geographical identification may indeed constitute a crucial element in the adoption of any particular juridical answer".[64]

There is an intentional ambiguity in the way that I have presented the notion of cartopolitics. On the one hand, cartography can support the interest of a particular state in terms of extending its claim to sovereignty. In that sense, the term would be associated with a historical notion of natural boundaries and later developments in geopolitics that justified the attempt to control specific national spaces or legitimised a natural quest for *lebensraum*. This fuelled a particular politics of space where certain geographical features or domains were seen as natural goals for the particular state to obtain. On the other hand, cartography provides a general spatiality against which various sovereignty claims can be negotiated. It is the latter understanding of the term that seems particularly significant for Arctic politics. UNCLOS provides a legal framework that binds all states (subject to the convention) to the same legal framework, and as such, provides an objective measure of border delineation. The science informing claims to sovereignty must present itself as universal and be accepted by the CLCS. In that sense, UNCLOS leads to a replacement of geopolitics with cartopolitics but this does not reject the possibility that cartography in these processes serves particular interests.

In practice, though, the Arctic Ocean states cooperate widely on their projects establishing a maritime spatial reality in order to settle the UNCLOS definition of the continental shelf. Norway has to a large extent settled its claims, Russia is gathering more data after its first claims were rejected in 2001. The US is cooperating widely with Canada in the effort to map the continental shelf north of Alaska, and Canada is cooperating in a formalised manner with Denmark about the areas north of Greenland. But Denmark does not only work with Canada. In the area north of Greenland, there have been five expeditions all conducted in cooperation with Canada. In 2007, the LOMROG I expedition was established in cooperation with the Swedish Polar Research Secretariat using a Swedish icebreaker with support from the nuclear-powered Russian icebreaker let Pobedy. In 2009, the LOMROG II expedition continued the measurement and data collection of the seabed north of Greenland, again in cooperation with Sweden, using the same icebreaking vessel. This time a Russian sea surveyor participated as well.[65] What appears from these mapping expeditions is that there is a high degree of cooperation between countries with potentially antagonistic interests.

There is a limit, as well, to the extent that cartography can serve particular interests within the regime. Cartography is a not a question of imposing an ideology on space but rather about a technology that allows for the assemblage of a particular spatial reality. In that, 'objects have agency too'[66] which means that the contours of the seabed obviously will affect the cartographic assemblage. It is in the encounter between the objects and contours of the seabed and mapping expeditions with surveying and measuring equipments and software that a new maritime space is in the process of being assembled (see Figure 1). With the Latourian understanding of space, this maritime spatial reality is of course a social construction in the sense that there is no objective given in the way that the continental shelf, or any of the other spatio-legal terms that are employed in maritime law, is being defined. On the contrary, it is the legal text that decides the way in which the CS should be defined and subsequently how it should be mapped. But the mapping itself engages in an interaction between these social constructs and the rocks, sediments, ridges and other features of the seabed. The maritime spatial reality that will serve as a basis for the subsequent drawing of political demarcation lines emerges, therefore, as an assemblage of objects, ideas, and practices of measurement and calculation that draws together the disparate elements in the attempt to establish a stable spatial foundation for sovereignty.

Discussing the impact of science on society, Bruno Latour paraphrases Clausewitz's famous dictum: "Science is politics pursued by other means."[67] The question, now, is what kind of politics. Asked directly about this, the leader of the Greenland part of the Continental Shelf Project of the Kingdom of Denmark states that scientists will seek to interpret the data in a way that is as beneficial as possible for extended Continental Shelf claims while staying within what is scientifically credible.[68] While it is impossible to predict how data will be treated, this suggests a somewhat pragmatic course among scientists with a desire to establish data that will generally be acceptable to the CLCS and a wider scientific community even if the data collection (or production) is unavoidably being politicised. It also illustrates that the ability of cartography to make nature speak with one voice is not only a question of measurement and data but also a question of a commitment among scientists and policymakers across the involved countries to achieve this. However, based on current evidence and political commitment made by the signing of the Ilulissat Declaration, there is no indication that this task will not be successful in the sense that the five countries involved will establish a stable maritime cartographic space which can serve as the basis for the distribution of sovereignty.

As a final reflection on the settlement of the spatial foundation for Arctic boundaries, there are a number of remaining uncertainties surrounding the wording and context of UNCLOS that might reopen the door for more formalised political disputes. First, it has been pointed out that the wording of §76 is ambiguous and will lead to potential conflicting interpretations between member states and CLCS.[69] However, if the states and scientists can overcome the general conflicting interests stated above, there is no reason why they should not be able to deal with this issue of uncertainty as well. Second, as long as the US stands outside UNCLOS there will be uncertainty about the general commitment to the process of all the states. While this is true, there is also a stated commitment by the administration to the continuing effort to make the senate accede to the convention.[70]

Finally, the UNCLOS regime only deals with the border between sovereign and common maritime spaces; potential overlapping claims will still have to be dealt with between states within the established practice of international law (re. UNCLOS §83). And equally significant for the problematique of this article, is the question of the reliance on a 'given natural space' in order to achieve a peaceful distribution of maritime space in the region. The reliance on science ignores that any spatial assemblage – reality of space – is always a social construction. And therefore, space is never a natural given but always something that has to be assembled according to various conventions and ideas about what space is. In this case, UNCLOS presupposes a spatial reality that is empty and abstract; one that can be partitioned and made a subject to state jurisdiction independently of the people living in, using, and constructing Arctic sea space in a manner that does not necessarily fit with the cartographic reality of space required by §76.

CONCLUSION: CARTOPOLITICS, GEOPOLITICS, AND CRITICAL BORDER STUDIES

In the 1880s, Henry Morton Stanley emphasised how the study of geography was intimately linked with the growth of the British Empire: "Geographical knowledge clears the path for commercial enterprise, and commercial enterprise has been in most lands the beginning of civilization."[71] He was convinced that the previous "white blank in the old maps" had been proved to contain "unexampled fertility, watered by mighty rivers, which have their perennial sources in deep woody recesses on the flanks of the mountain barriers."[72] His inaugural address to the Scottish Geographical Society, from which these quotes are taken, was delivered during what is known as the 'scramble for Africa' and the quest to control the resources and trade routes of the world by European colonial states. It was also the time of the quest to reach the North and South Poles representing the last frontiers yet unexplored by 'Western civilization'.[73] And just as the 'blanks' of the African map were considered to contain vast resources, the yet uncharted continental shelves of the Arctic are deemed to contain significant riches. And just like Stanley's geography was paving the way for civilisation and commerce, so too the contemporary charting of the Arctic will likely pave the way for commerce, and it could be argued, a civilising of geopolitical conflict.[74]

Adhering to a combination of a universal legal framework and a scientific cartography would allow states to deal with questions of jurisdiction through negotiation and spatial measures. Within a state logic this is an appealing proposition that could prevent militarisation and lead to a 'civilised settlement' of border issues. Even if UNCLOS does not provide explicit guidelines for the settlement of overlapping claims and therefore leaves space for a militarised geopolitics, the Arctic Ocean states have signed the Ilulissat Declaration. While this only expresses a political commitment to legal and peaceful settlement of border issues, events such as the treaty between Norway and Russia on the Barents Sea border could be seen as a confirmation of this commitment.[75] Yet, what is more crucial in the context of this article is that the settlements of ensuing issues of overlapping claims are likely to be based on the particular spatial reality that is currently being established through the cartographic projects by Arctic states.

Independently of how one looks at the issue of civility in the discussion of geopolitics, it is a historically troubled term. Not only was Stanley promoting self-interested practices and policies but the epistemic consequences of the role of science for the colonised people have been a central concern of postcolonial scholarship. Sounding almost like a parody, Lord Curzon was adamant about the service of geography to the imperial state in the early twentieth century:

> From the cloistered alleys and the hallowed groves of Oxford, true to her old traditions, but widened in her activities and scope, let there come forth the invincible spirit and the unexhausted moral fibre of our race. Let the advance guard of Empire march forth, strong in faith of their ancestors, imbued with a sober virtue, and above all, on fire with a definite purpose. The empire calls, as loudly as it ever did, for serious instruments of serious work.[76]

As argued above, cartography in the Arctic today is less explicitly serving an individual state, but this might only serve to make the power of the particular spatiality they seek to establish all the more opaque. Its strength and apparent solidity, I suggest, arises exactly from its particular networked relationship between surveyors, cartographic technologies and the maritime landscape. Yet, it is nevertheless a particular reality of space derived through cartography that presents itself as being universal.

Challenging the nexus between scientific cartography and law, the indigenous people have challenged the quest to decide ownership of Arctic space under international law. Addressing the question of who owns the Arctic, who can traverse the Arctic, and who has rights to develop Arctic resources, the Inuit Circumpolar Council (ICC) published a declaration on sovereignty in 2009 that came as a response to the Ilulissat Declaration. Among other thing the ICC declaration states that

> "sovereignty" is a term that has often been used to refer to the absolute and independent authority of a community or nation both internally and externally. Sovereignty is a contested concept, however, and does not have a fixed meaning. Old ideas of sovereignty are breaking down as different governance models, such as the European Union, evolve. Sovereignties overlap and are frequently divided within federations in creative ways to recognize the right of peoples.[77]

Central to the declaration is that the Inuit are recognised as an indigenous people and therefore have a right to self-determination even if they live across the boundaries of four recognised states. Whereas the current regime of territoriality arising in Western Europe during the fifteenth century considers land as territory, and the sea as a space to traverse across, as a navigable space, or a source of resources to support the way of life on land, the Inuit have claimed a different conceptualisation, use, and practice of space.

> Life in the Arctic is dependent on movement, and that sea ice is integral to this movement. The Inuit have been a nomadic people living in the Arctic since ancient times: their entire culture and identity is based on free movement on the land. Inuit rely on free movement in order to eat, to obtain supplies for traditional clothing and art, and generally to keep their rich cultural heritage alive. Inuit temporarily move out from settlements to harvest resources that are sometimes bartered or traded. This movement takes place on the sea ice that surrounds and connects Inuit communities.[78]

Not only does this emphasise the importance of movement vis-à-vis the notion of parcelling space out into sovereign jurisdictions, it also questions the central division between land space and sea space that informs the current distinction between territorial and maritime boundaries. Especially with regard to the status of ice, which in international law is considered a maritime space but for many constitutes a very material space which is used to travel across, as a hunting space, and appears to play a somewhat hybrid role in between the dogmatic distinction between land space and maritime space.[79]

All this serves to illustrate that to bring a particular spatial reality to bear upon international law will always have political implications. In this case the controversy is not so much about particular attempts to draw borderlines but rather a dispute of the cartopolitical practices in the Arctic. Competing cartographies establish competing spatialities which, in turn, support different ways of organising space politically. This also illustrates the need for critical border studies to scrutinise not only how border imaginaries and practices produce different spaces but also how the construction of different spatialities – in this case through cartography – support and condition different kinds of border practices. Maritime boundaries that are not defined in terms of a social functionality can only exist on a map and subsequently be enforced at sea through positioning systems that determine the location of a particular activity in relation to the said border. Again, both the border and its policing are conditioned by a particular spatiality.

In the introduction, I discussed the relationship between the unsettled borders in the Arctic and the absence of a clear spatiality that could serve as their foundation. I have made an attempt to argue that cartopolitics is a more precise description of the distribution of sovereignty in the Arctic than a conventional – or even critical – use of the term geopolitics. The particular focus on cartography emphasises its mediating role between the law and the landscape in order to establish a particular assemblage of apparently fixed sovereign space. Maritime boundaries will remain ambiguous in the absence of an unambiguous spatiality, and in that sense, cartopolitics is concerned with an extension of a territorial logic into remote maritime zones. As noted in the 'Lines in the Sand' agenda, many borders are becoming increasingly invisible and ephemeral; yet reversing this somewhat, border practices in the Arctic seems more concerned with making borders visible and tangible. And this might exactly be due to the ephemeral quality not only of the border but also the absence of a spatial foundation. Analysing the epistemology and spatiality of the border, critical border studies would do well to focus more on how ontologically unsettled spatialities are stabilised and solidified through cartographic practices in order to provide a foundation for subsequent border practices.

ACKNOWLEDGEMENTS

Previous versions of this paper have been presented at the AAG Annual Meeting April 2010, Washington DC; at a workshop at the Danish Institute of

International Studies titled 'Sovereignty, Territory and Emerging Geopolitics'; and at a Work in Progress Seminar at the Department for Business and Politics, Copenhagen Business School, September 2011. I would like to thank all the participants at these events for their constructive comments. Furthermore, the three anonymous reviewers provided really excellent and constructive feedback for the improvement of the manuscript. For this I am grateful. Finally, I would like to thank the editors of this special section for their time and effort, and particularly their engagement with the manuscript at various stages. A previous version of this paper was published as a working paper under the title 'Cartography and Geopolitics in the Arctic' (DIIS Working Paper 2010: 20). The present paper has been significantly expanded, revised, and corrected. Duncan Wigan and Gurminder K. Bhambra read through the entire paper at the final stages: You are stars. The research of this paper is generously funded by the Danish Research Agency as part of a project called *Territorial Expansion and Contraction*.

NOTES

1. R. C. Powell, 'Configuring an 'Arctic Commons'?', *Political Geography* 27/8 (2008) p. 827.

2. H. M. Stanley, 'Inaugural Address – Delivered before the Scottish Geographical Society at Edinburgh, 3rd December 1884', *The Scottish Geographical Magazine* 1 (1885) p. 4.

3. Spatial foundation in this context should, as will be explicated subsequently, be thought of as a historical social assemblage and does not, therefore, refer to a notion of a stable natural geography – whatever this might mean.

4. For the history of this distinction, see J. Kish, *The Law of International Spaces* (Leiden: A.W. Sijthoff 1973).

5. H. Gerhardt, P. E. Steinberg, J. Tasch, S. J. Fabiano, and R. Shields, 'Contested Sovereignty in a Changing Arctic', *Annals of the association of American Geographers* 100/4 (2010) p. 993.

6. It is difficult to find a neutral term referring to the material environment. Denis Cosgrove, for example, has written excellent accounts of the emergence and effect of the idea of landscape in 'Prospect, Perspective and the Evolution of the Landscape Idea', *Transactions of the Institute of British Geographers* 10/1 (1985) pp. 45–62. Despite such difficulties, I will use the terms landscape and environment interchangeably with reference to what is often considered as the natural geography or natural space. As I will explain subsequently, I use the term assemblage to emphasise how space emerge in the encounter between the non-human (rocks, soil, capes, lakes, etc.) and the human (imaginaries, mobilities, technologies, calculation, etc.).

7. The term cartopolitics appeared the first time, to my knowledge, in a conference announcement for 'Border Management in an Insecure World', 5–7 April 2006, in *Borderlines*, the newsletter from the International Boundary Research Unit, University of Durham, Issue 5, Jan. 2005. The only other published use of the term, that I know of, appeared very recently in an online essay on networks by G. Lovink and N. Rossiter: 'Understanding Cartopolitics: The Logic of Networks, from Visualization to Organization', available at <http://nedrossiter.org/?p=215>, accessed 27 Oct. 2011.

8. In this article I refer to the Arctic and Arctic region interchangeably. I limit the analysis to the five states adjacent to the Arctic Ocean: Norway, Denmark, Russia, Canada, and the US.

9. Related terms drawing on cartography are cartographic violence (M. Neocleous, 'Off the Map: On Violence and Cartography', *European Journal of Social Theory* 6/4 (2003); C. Brun and T. Jazeel, *Spatialising Politics: Culture and Geography in Postcolonial Sri Lanka* (Los Angeles: Sage 2009)) and cartographic aggression (B. K. Nijim, 'A Case Of Cartographic Aggression', *The Professional Geographer* 33/2 (1981) p. 251). I am grateful to Morten Ougaard for making me aware of the latter term.

10. This argument is based on a series of interviews with people involved in the process, national strategy papers, legal texts, as well as general news sources.

11. S. Chaturvedi, *The Polar Regions: A Political Geography* (Chichester: Wiley in association with the Scott Polar Research Institute 1996); K. Dodds, 'Flag Planting and Finger Pointing: The Law of the Sea, the Arctic and the Political Geographies of The Outer Continental Shelf', *Political Geography* 29/2 (2010); Powell (note 1); Gerhardt et al. (note 5).

12. G. Ó Tuathail, *Critical Geopolitics* (London: Routledge 1996) p. 18.

13. In the article I abstain from analysing the different interests behind the various sections in UNCLOS. Also, I pay little attention to the background of the different interest of the Arctic states, as well as the interests of non-Arctic states and organisations. While relevant for the general geopolitical theatre of the Arctic, they add less to the overall argument concerning cartopolitics that I present in this paper.

14. J. S. Roucek, 'The Geopolitics of the Arctic', *American Journal of Economics and Sociology* 42/4 (1983) p. 463.

15. Utenriksdepartementet, 'Nordområdesatsingen – Status oktober 2010', Oslo (2010). For quick access to the Arctic Strategies of relevant countries, see the Norwegian research project, 'GeoPolitics in the High North', available at <http://www.geopoliticsnorth.org/index.php?option=com_content&view=article&id=159&Itemid=69>, accessed 16 Nov. 2011.

16. This point was emphasised during an interview with Corinne Gray, Executive Director of the Inuit Circumpolar COuncil (ICC), Canada, March 2011, when I asked about Inuit perspectives on Arctic Geopolitics.

17. K. J. Bird, R. R. Charpentier, D. L. Gautier, D. W. Houseknecht, T. R. Klett, J. K. Pitman, and T. E. Moore, *Circum-Arctic Resource Appraisal; Estimates of Undiscovered Oil and Gas North of the Arctic Circle* (U.S. Geological Survey 2008) p. 1, available at <http://pubs.usgs.gov/fs/2008/3049/>.

18. For more on this, see <http://www.nordicbulkcarriers.com/nsr-project>, accessed 10 Nov. 2011.

19. Cairn Energy PLC, *Greenland Operational Update*, 8 Nov. 2011.

20. B. S. Zellen, *On Thin Ice: The Inuit, the State, and the Challenge of Arctic Sovereignty* (Plymouth: Lexington Books 2009).

21. *Financial Times*, 9 Aug. 2007; *Economist*, 16 May 2009.

22. A. Proelss, 'Governing the Arctic Ocean', *Nature Geoscience* 2 (May 2009).

23. For Canada, see for example, 'Backgrounders: Arctic/Offshore Patrol Ships', available at <http://www.navy.forces.gc.ca/cms/3/3-a_eng.asp?id=617>, accessed 26 Sep. 2010. For Russian military plans and capacities, see K. Åtland, 'Russia's Armed Forces and the Arctic: All Quiet on the Northern Front?', *Contemporary Security Policy* 32/2 (2011) pp. 267–285.

24. For example, S. G. Borgerson, 'Arctic Meltdown: The Economic and Security Implications of Global Warming', *Foreign Affairs* 87 (2008) pp. 63–77.

25. Quoted from 'Harper on Arctic: "Use it or lose it"', available at <http://www.canada.com/topics/news/story.html?id=7ca93d97-3b26-4dd1-8d92-8568f9b7cc2a>, accessed 23 Nov. 2010.

26. This has also led to concerns among academics, see for example, N. Petersen, 'The Arctic as a New Arena for Danish Foreign Policy: The Ilulissat Initiative and its Implications', N. Hvidt and H. Mouritzen, *Danish Foreign Policy Yearbook* (Copenhagen: Danish Institute of International Studies 2009) pp. 35–78.

27. Åtland (note 23).

28. <http://www.casr.ca/doc-dnd-icebreaker.htm>, accessed 10 Nov. 2011.

29. J. Manicom, 'Maritime Boundary Disputes in East Asia: Lessons for the Arctic', *International Studies Perspectives* 12/3 (2011) pp. 327–340.

30. A similar assessment is made by O. R. Young, 'Whither the Arctic? Conflict or Cooperation in the Circumpolar North', *Polar Record* 45/01 (2009) pp. 73–82.

31. Ibid., p. 75; Powell (note 1).

32. G. Osherenko and O. R. Young, *The Age of the Arctic: Hot Conflicts and Cold Realities* (Cambridge: CUP 1989) p. 12.

33. For an in-depth comparison between the polar regions with regard to international law, see D. Rothwell, *The Polar Regions and the Development of International Law* (Cambridge: Cambridge University Press 1996). He maintains that despite the noted differences, the two regions also share common feats through a combination of geography, environment and political factors.

34. Ilulissat Declaration, Arctic Ocean Conference, Ilulissat, Greenland, 27–29 May 2008.

35. M. Breum, *Når isen forsvinder: Danmark som stormagt i Arktis, olien i Grønland og kampen om Nordpolen* (Copenhagen: Gyldendal 2011).

36. Arctic Council, *Nuuk Declaration, on the occasion of the Seventh Ministerial Meeting of the Arctic Council*, 12 May 2011, Nuuk, Greenland.

37. N. Parker, L. Bialasiewicz, S. Bulmer, B. Carver, R. Durie, J. Heathershaw, H. Van Houtum, et al., 'Lines in the Sand? Towards an Agenda for Critical Border Studies', *Geopolitics* 14/3 (2009) pp. 582–587.

38. I discuss this in more detail in J. Strandsbjerg, *Territory, Globalisation and International Relations: The Cartographic Reality of Space* (Basingstoke: Palgrave 2010) pp. 21–30.

39. J. Agnew, 'The Territorial Trap: The Geographical Assumptions of International Relations Theory', *Review of International Political Economy* 1/1 (1994) pp. 53–80.

40. F. Kratochwill, 'Of Systems, Boundaries, and Territoriality', *World Politics* 39/1 (1986) pp. 27–52; J. G. Ruggie, 'Territoriality and Beyond – Problematizing Modernity in International-Relations', *International Organization* 47/1 (Winter 1993) pp. 139–174; M. Albert, D. Jacobson, and Y. Lapid *Identities, Borders, Orders: Rethinking International Relations Theory* (Minneapolis: University of Minnesota Press 2001).

41. S. Elden, 'Missing the Point: Globalization, Deterritorialization and the Space of the World', *Transactions of the Institute of British Geographers* 30/1 (2005) p. 11.

42. B. Latour, *War of the Worlds: What About Peace?* (Chicago: Prickly Paradigm Press 2002) pp. 11–12.

43. N. Thrift, 'It's the Little Things', in K. Dodds and D. Atkinson (eds.), *Geopolitical Traditions: A Century of Geopolitical Thought* (London: Routledge 2000) p. 380.

44. J. W. Crampton, 'The Cartographic Calculation of Space: Race Mapping and the Balkans at the Paris Peace Conference of 1919', *Social & Cultural Geography* 7/5 (2006) pp. 731–752; J. W. Crampton, 'Cartographic Calculations of Territory', *Progress in Human Geography* 35/1 (2011) pp. 92–103; S. Elden, 'Land, Terrain, Territory', *Progress in Human Geography*, doi:0309132510362603; M. G. Hannah, 'Calculable Territory and the West German Census Boycott Movements of the 1980s', *Political Geography* 28/1 (2009) 66–75.

45. Elden, 'Missing the Point' (note 41); for a similar argument, see J. Bartelson, *A Genealogy of Sovereignty* (Cambridge: Cambridge University Press 1995).

46. J. Strandsbjerg, 'The Cartographic Production of Territorial Space: Mapping and State Formation in Early Modern Denmark', *Geopolitics* 13/2 (2008).

47. This argument is developed in more detail in Strandsbjerg, *Territory* (note 38).

48. D. Wood, *The Power of Maps* (New York: The Guilford Press 1992); J. B. Harley and P. Laxton, *The New Nature of Maps: Essays in the History of Cartography* (Baltimore, MD: Johns Hopkins University Press 2001); J. Pickles, *A History of Spaces: Cartographic Reason, Mapping, and the Geo-Coded World* (London: Routledge 2004).

49. Strandsbjerg, *Territory* (note 38).

50. U. S. Lamb, 'The Spanish Cosmographic Juntas of the Sixteenth Century', *Terrae Incognitae* VI (1974).

51. For the relationship between the bulls issued by the pope and the Treaty of Tordesillas, see P. Steinberg, *The Social Construction of the Ocean* (Cambridge: CUP 2001) pp. 75–86.

52. Department of State, USA, *Denmark – Germany Boundary – International Boundary Study* (Washington, DC: The Geographer Office of the Geographer Bureau of Intelligence and Research 1968) pp. 3–7.

53. Steinberg (note 51).

54. W. McFee, *The Law of the Sea* (New York: J.B. Lippincott 1950) pp. 139–140; H. S. K. Kent, 'The Historical Origins of the Three-Mile Limit', *The American Journal of International Law* 48/4 (1954).

55. M. Jakobsson, R. Macnab, L. Mayer, R. Anderson, M. Edwards, J. Hatzky, H. Werner Schenke, and P. Johnson, *An Improved Bathymetric Portrayal of the Arctic Ocean: Implications for Ocean Modeling and Geological, Geophysical and Oceanographic Analyses*, v. 35, L07602 (2008), Geophysical Research Letters, doi:10.1029/2008GL033520, available at <http://www.ngdc.noaa.gov/mgg/bathymetry/arctic/>, accessed 20 Nov. 2011.

56. S. Nandan, 'A Constitution for the Ocean: The 1982 UN Law of the Sea Convention', *Marine Policy Reports* 1 (1989) pp. 1–12. UNCLOS entered into force 16 November 1994 (M. N. Shaw, *International Law* (Cambridge: Cambridge University Press 2003) p. 492).

57. Shaw (note 56) p. 517; R. R. Churchill and G. Ulfstein, *Marine Management in Disputed Areas: The Case of the Barents Sea* (London: Routledge 1992) pp. 18–20.

58. Shaw (note 56) pp. 521–522.

59. 'The United Nations Convention on the Law of the Sea' (1982) § 76.1, available at <http://www.un.org/depts/los/convention_agreements/convention_overview_convention.htm>, accessed 10 Nov. 2011.

60. As such, I will abstain from a detailed discussion of the different rights attributed to each zone.

61. D. Buisseret, 'The Cartographic Definition of France's Eastern Boundary in the Early Seventeenth Century', *Imago Mundi* 36 (1984); P. Sahlins, *Boundaries: The Making of France and Spain in the Pyrenees* (Berkeley: University of California Press 1989).

62. UNCLOS (note 59) §76.8. See Dodds (note 11) for a more detailed discussion of the process relating to the submissions and the CLCS. For general treatments of international law and the Polar Regions, see A. G. Oude Elferink and D. R. Rothwell, *The Law of the Sea and Polar Maritime Delimitation and Jurisdiction* (The Hague: Nijhoff 2001); and Rothwell (note 33).

63. Editorial comment, *Nature Geoscience* 2 (May 2009) p. 309.

64. Shaw (note 56) p. 534.

65. These sections rely on information from the website of the Continental Shelf Project, <http://a76.dk/lng_uk/main.html>, and an interview with project leader Christian Marcussen, 20 Sep. 2010.

66. This is discussed in several places by Latour; see for example, B. Latour, *Reassembling the Social: An Introduction to Actor-Network-Theory* (Oxford: University Press 2005) pp. 63–86.

67. B. Latour, 'Give Me a Laboratory and I Will Raise the World . . .', in M. Biagioli (ed.), *The Science Studies Reader* (London: Routledge) p. 273.

68. Interview with Marcussen (note 65). There is an important distinction here between Denmark and the Kingdom of Denmark, where the latter includes Greenland and the Faroese Islands. The continental shelf project is joint within the Kingdom.

69. R. Macnab, 'Submarine Elevations and Ridges: Wild Cards in the Poker Game of UNCLOS article 76', *Ocean Development and International Law* 39 (2008) pp. 223–234; T. Potts and C. Schofield, 'Current Legal Developments: the Arctic', *The International Journal of Marine and Coastal Law* 23 (2008) pp. 151–176.

70. Council on Foreign Relations, *National Security/Homeland Security Presidential Directive on Arctic Region Policy*, National Security Presidential Directive/NSPD 66; Homeland Security Presidential Directive/HSPD 25 (9 Jan. 2009), available at <http://www.fas.org/irp/offdocs/nspd/nspd-66.htm>, accessed 11 Nov. 2011.

71. Stanley (note 2) p. 4.

72. Ibid., p. 15.

73. The British commenced systematic exploration of the Arctic after the Napoleonic Wars where they fielded a surplus naval capacity and were anxious to counter Russian expansion in the icy region. Later in the nineteenth century the US and Scandinavian countries entered the stage of polar exploration (K. Hastrup, *Vinterens Hjerte: Knud Rasmussen og hans tid* (Copenhagen: Gads Forlag 2010) pp. 37–53).

74. I owe this formulation to Janus Hansen.

75. This was expressed by Thomas Winkler, Under-Secretary for Legal Affairs, Ministry of Foreign Affairs Denmark, in a conversation, 14 Nov. 2011.

76. L. Curzon of Kedleston, *The Romanes Lecture 1907: Frontiers* (Oxford: Clarendon Press 1908) pp. 57–58.

77. ICC, *A Circumpolar Inuit Declaration on Sovereignty in the Arctic*, available at <www.iccalaska.org/servlet/download?id=15>, accessed 13 Nov. 2011. For a discussion of the concept of Inuit sovereignty, see J. Shadian, 'From States to Polities: Reconceptualising Sovereignty through Inuit Governance', *European Journal of International Relations* (2010), doi:1354066109346887.

78. Inuit Circumpolar Council, Canada, *The Sea Ice is Our Highway: An Inuit Perspective on Transportation in the Arctic* (2008) p. i.

79. Ice has an ambiguous status in international law but according to Christopher C. Joyner sea should be considered as a maritime space in legal terms; in C. C. Joyner, 'Ice-Covered Regions in International Law', *Natural Resources Journal* 31 (1991) p. 213.

Off-shoring and Out-sourcing the Borders of EUrope: Libya and EU Border Work in the Mediterranean

LUIZA BIALASIEWICZ
Department of European Studies, University of Amsterdam, The Netherlands

The article examines some of the novel ways in which the European Union carries out its 'border-work'– border-work that stretches far beyond the external borders of the current Union. It highlights, in particular, the role of EUrope's neighbours in new strategies of securitisation, drawing attention to some of the actors, sites and mechanisms that make the Union's border-work possible. The emphasis in the paper is on the Mediterranean, long the premier laboratory for creative solutions to the policing of EU borders. The discussion focuses predominantly on a difficult neighbour turned 'friend' – Libya – and its role in the EUropean archipelago of border-work.

INTRODUCTION: BORDERS BEYOND 'LINES IN THE SAND'

This paper attempts to answer, in small part at least, the call issued in the collectively authored piece entitled 'Lines in the Sand: Towards an Agenda for Critical Border Studies' published in this journal in 2009.[1] The motivation for the piece came from the strong feeling on the part of many of us that the study of borders – in political geography as well as in political science and international relations – was increasingly lagging behind the amazing sophistication and complexity of bordering practices themselves. The manifesto thus called for critical understandings able to in some way dissociate the study of borders from their traditional 'territorial trap'. Equally importantly, it also argued that the political and ethical implications of this transformation of bordering practices continue to be under-theorised. The focus of this paper is precisely on some of these political and ethical implications and, in particular, what these entail for the EU's self-professed geopolitical identity as a 'normative' or 'civil' power. My comments here rely in great part on the work done by a number of NGOs and volunteer organisations dedicated to exposing the workings of the EU border-regime, most notably those working with/in the MIGREUROP network. It is these organisations that have provided some of the most sustained and perceptive studies of the on-the-ground practices – and effects – of the externalisation of EUropean borders and I would like to acknowledge my debt to them.

Although the focus of this paper will be on the European Union, many of the points regarding the changing nature and function of borders could certainly be made about other parts of the world as well. The United States, for one, has been actively 'de-bordering' its borders since 9/11 and many of the border management techniques discussed here in the European context have been in place in North America for quite some time now: from a general blurring of traditional distinctions between 'external' and 'internal' security, to the 'thickening' of border defences through the creation of 'buffer zones', to the notion of 'smart borders' able to 'filter' rather than simply block out flows of people and goods, and the increasing use of military technologies for border enforcement, as well as 'layered' border inspection/policing approaches that move customs and immigration inspection activities away from the actual territorial border.[2]

Despite these similarities, I will argue that the European Union is quite unique in other ways – if only for the under (or un-)stated ways in which it carries out what Chris Rumford terms its 'border-work'[3] – border-work that stretches far beyond the external borders of the current Union. French political sociologist Zaki Laidi[4] argued some time ago that it is at EUrope's borders that we can best discern 'the distinct aesthetics of European power', where we can best perceive that which Peter Sloterdijk has called the uniquely European process of *translatio imperii*.[5] It is at/through borders that the European space is constituted and selectively 'stretched' – or, to use Sloterdijk's terms, 'translated'.[6] EUrope's borders, in all their different manifestations, are no longer merely the 'shores of politics but . . . the space of the political itself', as the 'Lines in the Sand' manifesto argued, invoking Etienne Balibar.[7]

For a political geographer, what is particularly interesting are not only the new forms that EU border-work takes, or new border-sites, but also the very peculiar 'nature of the beast', as James Sidaway has put it.[8] For it is a very difficult beast to grasp: the EU's border-work (unlike the North American case, for instance) proceeds through a fluid assemblage of functions, mechanisms, and actors; a series of loose institutional arrangements, recomposed in variable geometries 'as necessary'. Some commentators (Didier Bigo most prominently) have referred to the Union's bordering practices (and its security architecture more generally) as 'virtual', since there appears to be 'no there there'; no single institution, no single set of actors that can be identified as the bordering 'State' (no European Department of Homeland Security in other words).[9]

Even FRONTEX, the Union's agency for external borders created in 2005 (its formal name is 'the European Agency for the Management of Operational Co-operation at the External Borders of the Member States of the European Union'), is (on paper at least) simply a 'regulatory agency', responsible for the exchange of information and co-operation between member states on issues related to border control, the gathering of intelligence and the carrying out of 'risk analyses', and the provision, 'when necessary', of training and 'operational support'. As the most visible actor in the Union's increasingly exclusionary border-work, FRONTEX has been the target of countless protests: the re-worked FRONTEX logo (defined as the Union Deportation Agency) in Figure 1 comes from a Polish No Borders activist group that offers a different take on the Warsaw-based agency's real slogan, *Libertas, Securitas, Justitia*, here rendered as 'Slavery', 'Intolerance' and 'Injustice'. Yet FRONTEX is part of a much wider group of inter-governmental organisations engaged in formulating policies for 'managing migration' on behalf of/for the European Union, including the International Organization for Migration (IOM) and the International Centre for Migration Policy Development (ICMPD) – agencies whose work is much more invisible to the public eye, yet whose contribution to both shaping the terms of the 'illegal migration' debate, as well as the very notion of EU 'border (in)security' has been fundamental.[10] What is more, many of the instances of EU border-work that I will cite in the paper have been implemented without the formal engagement (even in a consultative capacity) of FRONTEX, relying rather on a variety of bi-lateral agreements between EU Member States and third countries that often do not have migration control as their explicit focus.

At the same time, it is also important to emphasize that border-work is not simply about the policing of migration. EUrope's border-work is, indeed, part of a broader attempt to 'secure the external', a process that has been taking place at the Union's Southern and Eastern borders for quite some time now. As numerous authors have argued, the preoccupation with 'securing the external' has driven EU relations with its immediate 'Neighbourhood' for almost a decade now.[11] One of its most visible expressions has certainly been the EU's engagement in state-making in the Balkans: in Montenegro in 2006

FIGURE 1 Re-fashioned FRONTEX logo (color figure available online).

(where European institutions set the conditions of the referendum that sanctioned the new state's independence from Serbia), and in Kosovo in 2008, where the EU specified the legal conditions for state-making.[12] The motivation (beyond the lofty goals of promoting democracy and peace) has been, of course, the stabilisation – and (norm)alisation – of a region that lies just too close for European comfort. The main remit of the 2,000-strong EULEX force (made up of judges, police, border guards and a variety of civil servants and administrators) that was sent in to support KFOR's military presence in the newly independent Kosovo was declaredly 'pacification and stabilisation' but also – and above all – (norm)alisation, to be read as the incorporation of this region into the (EU)ropean normative and legal/regulatory space.[13]

In this process of (norm)alisation, the question of border-control has been paramount. All through the past decade, the EU has provided specialist training to border guards in Bosnia and Croatia. So too in Kosovo, seen by the EU as a potential conduit to all sorts of illicit flows heading for European shores.[14] The Kosovo example provides a useful mirror to the political geographies of EU influence in its 'Neighbourhood' and the 'incorporation by law' through which countries are brought into Europe's orbit. Jan Zielonka has termed it 'Empire by Example': the creation of what he terms '(semi)protectorates whose sovereignty is not denied but 'creatively constrained'[15] – but we can also usefully understand such interventions as part of broader attempts on the part of the Union at the externalisation or extra-territorialisation of governance (also termed by scholars 'governance at a distance', or 'remote control' governance).[16]

The European Neighbourhood Policy, launched in 2003 with the explicit aim of fostering 'stability and peace' at the Union's external borders by creating a 'ring of friends' has, in recent years, shifted its rhetoric from that of collaboration and 'friendly' exchange to an explicitly security-led agenda, rendered in the phraseology of 'preventative security'.[17] In the past couple of years in particular, that focus has become increasingly blunt: speaking at an European Commission sponsored conference on 'Climate Change and International Security' in March 2008, then-EU foreign policy chief Javier Solana argued for

> a key role for the ENP as well as the EU-Africa Strategy and the Union's Middle East and Black Sea policies in preventative security and in countering climate change based security risks. These include the challenges posed by climate change induced migration, threats to energy security, but also the possibility of major changes in landmass leading to territorial disputes [and] political radicalisation [at Europe's borders]. In the face of uncertain and de-territorialised threats, the EU must develop new regional security scenarios.[18]

Such a shift in rhetoric – from democratisation and collaboration to securitisation – has been matched by funding flows: a 2009 report by the EU Court of Auditors uncovered that 90% of all EU aid to the Neighbourhood partner countries of the Ukraine, Belarus and Moldova was spent on 'border management'.

EUrope's neighbours are, in other words, becoming EUrope's policemen. As Elspeth Guild noted in her study for the Observatory of the Centre for European Policy Studies,

> When the [European] Neighbourhood Policy was developed, it was inspired by an expansive spirit of inclusion of the neighbours in the benefits of the internal market including free movement of persons. By the time a process was established to develop the neighbourhood policy, the approach towards persons appears to have changed substantially. . . . the emphasis is on placing obligations on the neighbours to act as the buffer between the EU and other third countries as regards irregular migration. Exchanges of information, monitoring irregular migration flows, readmission agreements, these are the staples of the ENP in this area. The consequences of this approach are likely to be to harm the neighbours relations with their neighbours beyond the EU as our neighbours will be required to take coercive action against the nationals of their neighbours. Instead of reinforcing solidarity in the region such an approach is likely to create tensions and instability.[19]

This new – and increasingly explicit – role envisioned for EUrope's neighbours in its border-work foregrounds, once more, the need to consider the EU's bordering activities as part of a broader attempt to 'translate' the EUropean space by re-making the world beyond it. Writing about the emergence of a distinct EU 'anti-illegal immigration policy', William Walters argues, in fact, that we must locate any analysis of the EU's border-work 'squarely within the realm of geopolitics',

> embedded within the 'combat' against illegal immigration is a political imagination in which Europe is cast as a bounded, self-contained region distinct from and confronted by an external world of similarly bounded but far less well-governed political entities. Illegal immigration is at once a major symptom of this asymmetry in governance capacity, and a source of justification for Europe to involve itself in attempts to remake the world beyond it in the image of the well-governed, territorial state. In short, anti-illegal immigration activity is more than a branch of migration management. It is nothing less than state-making in a new form'.[20]

EU BORDER-WORK IN THE MEDITERRANEAN

The Mediterranean has long been the premier site for the 'translation' of the EU space and the externalisation of EUropean governance – as well as the premier laboratory for experimenting creative solutions to the policing of EU borders. The Mediterranean has also become Europe's graveyard: there have been over 10,000 documented deaths along the EU's maritime frontiers in the past ten years – a figure that would swell further if we added those missing at sea, or those who did not even make it to the boats supposed to ferry them to their European Dream; those who died along the way, somewhere in the Niger or Algerian desert. UNITED, the European Network Against Nationalism, Racism, Fascism and in Support of Migrants and Refugees, has since 1993 been keeping a 'List of Deaths'. The List includes all reported deaths that have occurred as a consequence of European immigration policy, due to clandestine journeys to Europe, border militarisation, detention conditions and deportation procedures. On June 20 2010, International Refugee Day, their estimate stood at 13, 824, but as UNITED's press release on the day noted

> it is impossible to know the real death count and experts estimate it is likely to be three times higher. The 'List of Deaths' is compiled using news sources, reports, testimonies, artwork and documents produced by NGOs, research institutes, journalists, governmental sources, artists and film-makers among others. These 13,824 are not only statistics, each one is a human life with its own personal history, background, reasons for fear and hopes for the future. The EU failed to protect each one.[21]

The highly publicised map from 2005 in Figure 2 traces the routes taken by migrants across the African deserts. The map, produced by FRONTEX, also shows the areas of deployment of joint EU border patrols, focussed on the principal sites for the departure of vessels ferrying migrants to Europe's shores. Naturally, as patrols have intensified in recent years, the traffickers have simply re-located: crossings that a few years prior departed from the shores of Morocco and Tunisia have now moved further south, bringing ever higher risks for those attempting the journey, with the deployment of EU-led maritime patrols extending as far south as the shores of Mauritania and Senegal. Figure 3 (also produced by FRONTEX) illustrates the re-location of the principal migratory flows in the Mediterranean in 2009.[22]

Such maps powerfully illustrate to the European public both the supposed scale of these migration flows – and of the attempts to contain them. Nonetheless, this 'spectacle of militarised border enforcement' (to cite Nicholas de Genova) is just the most visible part of the story, for the EU's border-work extends far beyond the gun boats off Africa's shores.[23] The visible 'off-shoring' of EUropean migration controls has also been accompanied by the 'out-sourcing' of migration management to African states themselves. When the Lome Convention (specifying the terms of trade and aid between the EU and 77 African, Caribbean and Pacific (ACP) countries) was up for revision, the EU demanded the insertion of a clause on re-admission and re-patriation. When the new convention was signed in 2000 – now called

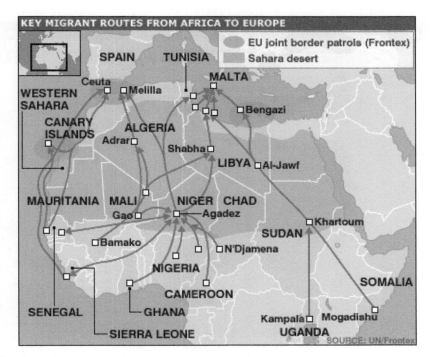

FIGURE 2 FRONTEX map with migration flows across Africa and the Mediterranean (color figure available online).

Source: FRONTEX.

the Cotonou Agreement – it required ACP states to 'accept the return and readmission of any of its nationals illegally present in EU territory' (and to pay for such return and readmission). The ACP states were also now bound to deter illegal migrants from leaving, as well as facilitating the work of European Immigration Liaison Officers (ILOs) in assessing asylum and immigration claims in situ (i.e., before would-be-migrants' departure). Although there were no explicit retaliatory clauses in the Agreement itself, a number of subsequent declarations hinted at 'measures' against countries that would refuse to cooperate in 'preventing and combating these phenomena'.

On June 22, 2010, representatives of the EU and the ACP states met to deliberate on the second revision to the Cotonou Agreement in Ouagadougou. The meeting was highly contested and while a revised Agreement was signed, the parties failed to reach consensus on revisions to Article 13 – the migration provision. In the preceding months, the EU had been pressuring ACP states to agree to changes in the existing Agreement which would make it easier for EU member states to return illegal or irregular migrants from the EU to their home countries. The ACP states resisted incorporating such a provision into the revised Agreement, requesting to deal with re-admission issues on a bi-lateral basis. Failing to reach agreement, the two

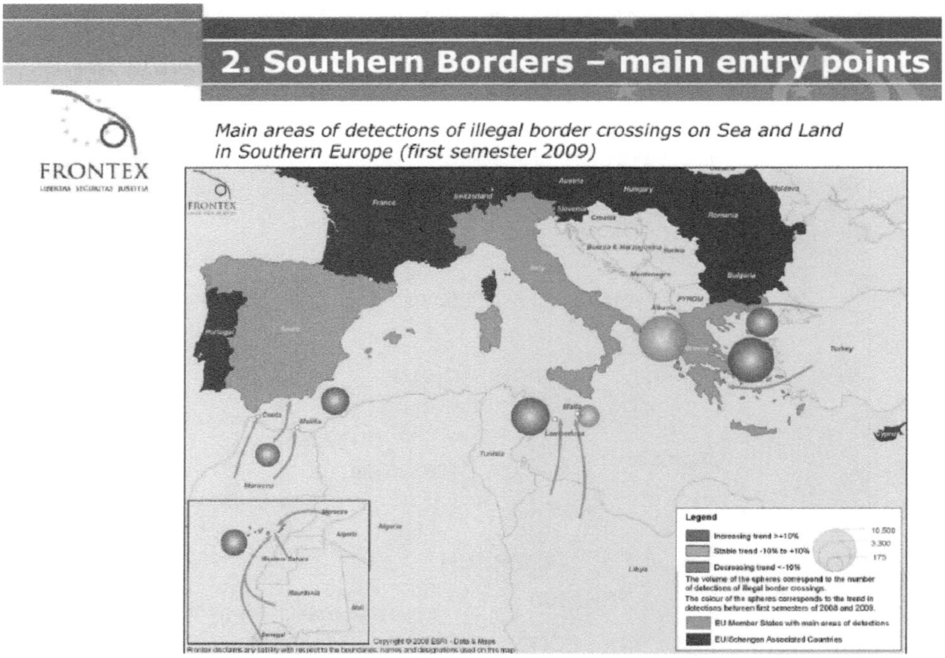

FIGURE 3 FRONTEX map showing shifts in main migratory flows (color figure available online).

Source: FRONTEX, Presentation to the European Parliament LIBE Committee, 11 Jan. 2010.

sides produced a Joint Declaration, signed in conjunction with the revised Cotonou Agreement, pledging that

> The Parties agree to strengthen and deepen their dialogue and cooperation in the area of migration, building on the following three pillars of a comprehensive and balanced approach to migration: 1. Migration and Development, including issues relating to diasporas, brain drain and remittances; 2. Legal migration, including admission, mobility and movement of skills and services; and 3. Illegal migration, including smuggling and trafficking of human beings and border management, as well as readmission.[24]

The EU's push for the readmission clause in the Cotonou Agreement to become self-executive and binding for all ACP countries without needing complementary bilateral agreements had been strongly criticised not only by representatives of the ACP states themselves but also by numerous European NGOs and human rights organisations. CONCORD, the European NGO Confederation for Relief and Development, in a briefing paper for European Parliamentarians on the negotiations, warned that should the obligatory readmission clause go into effect, this would imply unmanageable obligations for many countries and hence an increased risk of migrants' rights violations throughout the process of readmission. Moreover, CONCORD argued:

> in no way should EU and individual Member States' ODA [n.b. Official Development Assistance] be dependent on the signature of readmission agreements (whether bi-lateral or multi-lateral). By making development aid conditional on cooperation on border control, *the EU is turning development aid into a tool for implementing restrictive and security-driven immigration policies* which are at odds with its commitment to make migration work for development.[25]

Beyond the current question of how to manage re-admission and re-patriation, however, the original 2000 Cotonou Agreement *already* contained a number of quite revolutionary – from a political geographic *and* legal point of view – provisions detailing the role of ACP countries in migration management 'in collaboration with' (though perhaps more appropriately 'for') Europe. These included the role of ILOs (mentioned above) and the 'in situ' processing of asylum claims and visa requests.

Such proposals for the 'off-shoring' of migration management were given important impetus with proposals first advanced by the UK Home Office in early 2003 to create 'external asylum processing centres' that would, again, 'assess claims in situ', before migrants undertook their perilous journeys and that would provide 'protection in the region' for refugees and asylum seekers.[26] The Home Office proposal envisaged the establishment of 'transit processing centres' in third countries on major transit routes to the EU. Asylum seekers arriving spontaneously in the EU (or those intercepted en-route) would be sent back to such centres for 'status determination'; those whose requests were approved would be resettled within the EU or the region, while the others would be returned to their country of origin under 'new and strengthened re-admission agreements'.[27]

As Gammeltoft-Hansen notes in his discussion of these proposals, although the scheme was originally vetoed by Germany and Sweden at the June 2003 Thessaloniki European Council, it served to frame subsequent and ongoing initiatives to dissolve the traditional link between the provision of protection and asylum processing and the territory of the State undertaking these functions.[28] But, he argues, subsequent EU initiatives have adhered to a somewhat different logic than the simple 'out-sourcing' and 'off-shoring' of asylum processing imagined by the proposals for 'external processing centres':

> Rather than merely deflecting the responsibility on to third States or neglecting it altogether, current initiatives to off-shore asylum processing and outsource protection all presuppose some sort of responsibility on the part of the externalising State, ranging from the formal assertion of authority to merely providing financial assistance or compensation.[29]

Indeed, since 2003–2004, the externalisation of asylum has been seen by the EU as part of the broader externalisation of EUropean governance and (in words at least) presented as part of the projection of EUropean norms and standards into its Neighbourhood – highlighting, once more, the place of migration management in wider geopolitical strategies and 'state-making' at a distance.

Yet while – in rhetoric at least – the EU's border-work may be presented as part of a wider strategy of 'governance at a distance' and phrased in a managerial language of cooperation and partnership, stressing 'technical know-how' and 'best practice' as well as the key role of norms, standards and regulations, the on-the-ground management of migration in the Mediterranean in recent years tells a rather different story. In the remainder of the paper, I would like to focus on a country that has fulfilled this function 'for' EUrope in recent years: Libya. Libya is a particularly interesting example of the 'out-sourcing' and 'off-shoring' of EUrope's border-work for its then-government officially denied the presence of refugees on its territory, and did not recognise the very institution of asylum. My discussion here focuses largely on the period 2009–2010, with just a brief comment on the opening weeks of the 'Libyan Revolution' of Spring 2011 in the closing 'addendum' to the paper. In my conclusions, I note how EUrope's reaction to the Libyan crisis foregrounds, once again, the links between migration management and geopolitics.

DOING EUROPE'S BORDER WORK

> There are 1.5 million foreigners in Libya. . . . We don't know if they are political refugees, we just know that they are here. . . . Are we expected to give them all Libyan citizenship?
> — Abdul Ati al-Obeidi, Secretary of European Affairs at the General People's Committee for Foreign Liaison and International Cooperation, Tripoli, Libya, May 2009

> Political asylum is out of place [in Africa]. These people [n.b. African migrants] come from the forest and the desert and most of them don't even have an individual sense of self.
> — Colonel M'uammar Al-Gaddafi, on the occasion of his visit to Rome in June 2009, responding to critiques regarding Libya's treatment of refugees[30]

Following the first FRONTEX 'Technical Assistance' mission to Libya in June of 2007, in December 2007, Italy and Libya signed a series of bi-lateral agreements creating joint patrols on the Libyan coasts so Italian coast guard vessels would now be allowed to operate in Libyan waters. The agreement also specified the provision of surveillance equipment for the monitoring Libya's land and sea borders – to be funded by the European Union. It was announced to great fanfare that Libya – on its path to 're-joining the international community' – would help 'share the burden' of migration control in the Mediterranean.

In August 2008, Italy and Libya signed The Treaty of Friendship, Partnership and Co-operation.[31] The Treaty, hailed as a historic step towards reconciliation between Italy and its ex-colony, agreed Italian compensation to Libya for its occupation of the country between 1911 and 1943 and included a 5 billion euro package for construction projects, student grants and pensions for Libyan soldiers who served with Italian forces during the Second World War. It also included, however, provisions for bilateral efforts to combat illegal migration, facilitated by the joint sea patrols already launched in December 2007. Libya agreed, among other things, to tighten control of its territorial waters and accept disembarkation on its soil of individuals intercepted at sea by Italian vessels. Italy undertook to provide 'the necessary resources', including technology, to control migrant flows through the southern borders of Libya.

In May of 2009, on the heels of an anti-immigration crusade by the Berlusconi government, the Italian parliament approved legislation that made irregular immigration illegal, punishable by a fine of up to 10,000 euro and detention. It also authorised the direct deportation of migrants through a new 'push-back' policy: from May on, migrants intercepted in international waters by Italian coast guard vessels would be ferried to Libya directly, before assessing their rights/claims to asylum.

The first incident occurred in the very first week of the implementation of this new policy: on May 6, distress calls were sent from three vessels with an estimated 230 third-country nationals on board. Italian coast guard vessels were the first to intervene, but transported the individuals directly to Tripoli, without stopping in an Italian port and without checking whether any individuals on board were in need of international protection or basic humanitarian assistance. In the last week of that same month, over 500 African migrants – some of whom had actually already *reached* Italian shores – were 'pushed back' to Libya. Further interceptions and returns occurred in the subsequent months: according to official information from the Italian Ambassador to Libya, between 6 May and 3 September 2009, over 1,000 individuals were returned to Libya, including nationals from Eritrea, Somalia and other sub-Saharan African countries. Commenting three months on, Italian Minister of the Interior Roberto Maroni referred to the scale of the returns as 'an historic achievement after one year of bi-lateral negotiations with Libya'.[32]

The United Nations High Commissioner for Refugees (UNHCR) and Italian and European human rights organisations provided a different reading. That same May, UNHCR spokesperson, Ron Redmond, expressed serious concerns about the returns procedures, noting that Italy's new 'push-back' policy gravely undermined access to asylum for individuals potentially in need of international protection and risked violating the principle of *non-refoulement*, which prohibits the return of any person in any manner whatsoever to a situation where he or she would be at risk of torture or other serious human rights violations. The principle of *non-refoulement* is a fundamental obligation of all signatories of the 1951 Convention on the Status of Refugees which states that

> No Contracting State shall expel or return ("*refouler*") a refugee in any manner whatsoever to the frontiers of territories where his [or her] life or freedom would be threatened on account of his [or her] race, religion, nationality, membership of a particular social group or political opinion.

This obligation is also enshrined in the European Convention on Human Rights to which all EU member states are signatories.

Libya at the time was not a state party to the 1951 Convention and, moreover, did not possess a national asylum policy (as the citations at the outset of this section attest). Libyan officials, in fact, consistently denied the presence of any 'asylum-seekers' or 'refugees' in Libya.[33] During Amnesty International's fact-finding visit to Libya in May 2009, officials from the General People's Committee for Foreign Liaison and International Cooperation said that there were no refugees or asylum-seekers in Libya, 'only economic migrants'. The Director of the Misratah Detention Centre, some 200 km from Tripoli, which at the time held more than 400 Eritrean and about 50 Somali nationals, stressed to Amnesty International delegates on 20 May 2009 that there were no refugees in Misratah. As the Amnesty Report stresses, also at the highest level of the state, 'there [was] a belief that all foreign nationals in Libya are there solely for economic reasons'.[34]

Libyan authorities have been documented to regularly deport migrants directly to their countries of origin, regardless of their conditions or right to asylum. In many cases, citing lack of resources (or where states of origin have not been forthcoming with the funds or vessels/planes for repatriation), migrants have been accompanied directly to the southern border with Niger, creating a new line of business for the people smugglers who now wait to accompany migrants back across the desert. Many of the expelled migrants become stranded in places like Agadez (Niger), out of money and at the mercy of the smugglers and local officials, working in slave-like conditions to simply assure their survival; unable to reach Europe, but also unable to return home.[35] Enrica Rigo has written extensively on this phenomenon, not only in the case of Libya, noting how transnational migratory paths are increasingly also becoming what she terms 'transnational corridors of expulsion'.[36] In Libya, such mass expulsions had been ongoing: European Commission figures estimate that 43,000 and 54,000 migrants were deported from Libya already in 2003 and 2004, respectively; in 2005, the figure reached 7,000 expelled migrants per month; in 2006 the reported annual figure was 64,330. In 2008, the Libyan authorities claimed to have expelled around one million illegal immigrants.

Those who were not deported faced the brutal conditions of Libya's detention centres, not only with no legal guarantees but where forced labour, rapes and beatings were a constant, as numerous UNHCR and Amnesty International reports have documented.[37] It is interesting, then, how Libyan officials were quick to take up the notions of 'protection in the region' and 'preventative measures' promoted by EU agencies such as FRONTEX. Between 2009 and 2010, detention facilities for suspected irregular migrants were officially re-named 'care centres', designed to 'ensure the physical integrity of irregular migrants, particularly as they expose themselves to dangerous situations, such as crossing the desert or the Mediterranean' (to cite Maha Omar Othman, Director of Consular Affairs in the Secretariat of Expatriates and Migration).[38]

Speaking with UNHCR representatives in 2010, Othman explained that in implementing Libya's policy of preventing irregular migrants from travelling further, the authorities felt it necessary to place them in temporary 'care centres' in order to identify their country of origin and repatriate them as soon as possible. The stated reason behind prolonged detention was the difficulty in identifying irregular migrants' countries of origin when they destroyed their travel documents. Enquiries by UNHCR and other NGOs have documented that individuals suspected of being irregular migrants were being held in detention for months and sometimes even years, particularly in the cases of Eritrean and Somali nationals.

FLEXING EU NORMS

Facing international criticism following the implementation of Italy's new 'push-back' policy in May of 2009, Italian Foreign Minister Franco Frattini (until that month, Vice-President of the European Commission, responsible among other things for migration policy) declared that 'it is a complex legal issue to which there is no easy answer. It is not black and white'.

The institutional (and practical) arrangements guiding the deportations and the 'out-sourcing' of the assessment of asylum claims to the Libyan authorities were, indeed, far from 'black and white'. And it is precisely in this ambiguity that they found their space of possibility – using bi-lateral agreements (and, in the case of Italy and Libya, also *informal* agreements) to circumvent existing EU legislation, while 'getting the job done'; that is, protecting EUropean shores.

The new Italian policy relied on a highly articulated interpretation – and implementation – of international legislation on migration control. The push-back policy was to be implemented by two forces: the *Guardia di Finanza* and the Italian Navy.

> The *Guardia di Finanza* is in charge when the vessel carrying the migrants is intercepted between 12 and 24 nautical miles from the Italian coast; the Navy intervenes when such interception takes place beyond 24 nautical miles. If the vessel is intercepted in Italy's territorial waters (within 12 nautical miles from the coast) the migrants who are intercepted are brought to land, where they benefit from the legal and procedural safeguards provided under Italian and EU law as regards reception and access to asylum procedures. . . . When a vessel believed to transport migrants is sighted, the *Guardia di Finanza* or the Navy, whichever is competent, intercepts the boat and transfers the migrants onto the Italian vessel. The Coast Guard is also dispatched and coordinates rescue operations and first aid provided by medical personnel present on its vessels. Should the medical personnel deem it necessary to hospitalise any of the migrants, the Coast Guard ensures the transfer of the persons concerned to Lampedusa [n.b. where the Italian *Centro di Permanenza Temporanea* is located] The remaining migrants are returned to Libya by the Italian intercepting vessel, or transferred onto a Libyan vessel which returns the migrants to Libya.[39]

In July 2009, the Council of Europe's Committee for the Prevention of Torture sent a fact-finding mission to Italy and Libya, whose report was made public on 28 April 2010. The Committee's report noted with some surprise that

> The Italian authorities have acknowledged officially that they do not proceed with the formal identification of migrants who are intercepted at sea and pushed back. . . . The Italian Government has affirmed that no migrant has ever expressed his/her intention to apply for asylum and that, consequently, there has been no need to identify these persons and establish their nationality.[40]

The report remarked, however, that 'even if what is affirmed were to correspond to reality, it must be borne in mind that persons surviving a sea voyage are often not in a condition in which they should be expected to declare immediately their wish to apply for asylum'. What is more,

> information gathered through interviews held by the delegation would indicate that, even if a migrant were to request protection whilst aboard an Italian vessel, there is no procedure in place capable of referring him/her to a protection mechanism; nor have the competent authorities been instructed on how to identify and screen migrants. It should be noted, in this context, that intercepted migrants do not have access to linguistic or legal assistance on board the intercepting vessels, in order to express their needs. Indeed, representatives of both the Navy and the

Coast Guard with whom the delegation spoke, clearly stated that they are not responsible in any way for the identification of migrants, the provision of information on how to apply for asylum, or the treatment of asylum requests; nor have they been instructed by the Ministry of the Interior in relation to these issues.[41]

How is this possible in Italy, an EU state, bound both by the 1951 Convention as well as the European Convention of Human Rights that extends the principle of *non-refoulement* to 'all persons who may be exposed to a real risk of torture, inhuman or degrading treatment or punishment should they be returned to a particular country'? Under the terms of the ECHR, the prohibition of *refoulement* to a danger of persecution is, indeed, seen as applicable to 'any form of forcible removal, including deportation, expulsion, extradition, informal transfer or renditions, and non-admission at the border'. Moreover, the principle applies not only in respect of return to the country of origin or, in the case of a stateless person, the country of former habitual residence, but also to any other country to which removal is to be effected or any other country to which the person may subsequently be removed. EU member states are, therefore, also obliged to examine whether a relevant risk would be incurred through 'chain deportation' or indirect *refoulement*.

In recent years, the European Court of Human Rights has recognised a number of specific situations which may also give rise to an 'extraterritorial' application of ECHR obligations and EU states' responsibility in this respect. Recent rulings have noted that a state's 'extraterritorial jurisdiction' may be based, in particular, on (a) the activities of the State's diplomatic or consular agents abroad and on board craft and vessels registered in, or flying the flag of, that State; (b) the State's effective control of an area outside its national territory; or (c) the State's exercise of authority over persons or property through its agents operating on the territory of another State or in international territory/waters.[42] The 'push-back' activities of Italian seaforces (*Guardia di Finanza*, Navy and Coast Guard) as well as those of their Libyan counterparts (using vessels donated by Italy and registered in Italy) were thus – in theory at least – covered by such obligations.

But the returns policy remained in place regardless. In June 2010, the UNHCR estimated a decrease of between 50 and 95% in summer arrivals on Italian shores compared to the same period the preceding year. The IOM has similarly estimated that there was a 90% drop in arrivals on Italian shores from over 37,000 in 2008 – before the policy went into practice – to just 4,300 in 2010. The 'job', in other words, was getting done, with Italian authorities continuing to claim that no laws were being violated. The argument of the Ministry of the Interior was that the capture and 'push-back' of migrants conformed to the UN Convention against Transnational Organized Crime, and the Protocol against the Smuggling of Migrants by Land, Sea and Air. The question, then, was not refugee flows but tackling organised crime and people-smugglers. Indeed, the 2007 and 2009 bi-lateral treaties and 'technical protocols' signed by Libya and Italy were explicitly focussed on 'collaboration in the fight against terrorism, organised crime and irregular migration', with no mention of the regulation of asylum, or any sort of 'out-sourcing' of migration controls. This rhetorical strategy is, of course, not unique to dealings between Italy and Libya: as for a variety of anti-illegal immigration measures implemented by other European states post 9/11, the stated focus on 'terrorism' and 'organised crime' readily identifies 'bad things' that doubtless must be 'combatted'.[43]

The (willing) ambiguity that has characterised Italian-Libyan relations is mirrored in Libya's relations with international organisations such as the UNHCR, as well as with the EU itself. When the EU lifted its embargo against the country in 2004, one of the conditions was Libya's ratification of the 1951 Convention. In 2010, there were still no signs that this was forthcoming: as the citations that open this section indicate, Libyan authorities have stuck to the line that all migrants in Libya are 'economic migrants' and that the question of asylum policy is a 'European obsession'. Libya has also avoided signing a Memorandum of Understanding with UNHCR, preferring to interact with the UNHCR mission on an ad hoc basis. Indeed, although it was included in the EU/UNHCR plan to set up an EU-directed asylum system in the five Maghreb countries by 2010, the Libyans have explicitly preferred informal cooperation and have refused to officially commit to any agreement with the EU or the UNHCR.

In the years prior to 2010, an 'unofficial' UNHCR mission had provided food, health care and shelter when it has been able to do so, and has delivered certificates and letters attesting refugee status, a status which has been variably respected by the Libyan authorities. UNHCR has progressively won the right to enter detention facilities in Tripoli, and has tried to organise refugee resettlement. In April 2009, a three-year project attempting to put together an asylum system in Libya was launched after the Libyan government eventually concluded an agreement on 'mixed migration flows' with UNHCR, the Libyan NGO IOPCR (International Organisation for Peace, Care and Relief), the Italian NGO CIR (*Consiglio Italiano per i Rifugiati*) and ICMPD (International Center for Migration Policy Development). Following this agreement, UNHCR was allowed to visit several migrants' detention camps in order to identify refugees.

On 8 June 2010, however, the Libyan authorities unilaterally shut down the UNHCR office and expelled its staff of 26. All those that were in some way being assisted by the mission were left, literally, stranded. Nine thousand refugees and 3,700 asylum-seekers were registered with UNHCR in Libya at that time; the majority were Palestinians, Iraqis, Sudanese, Somalis, Eritreans, Liberians or Ethiopians.[44] The reaction to this event on the part of European institutions was surprisingly muted. The spokeswoman for Catherine Ashton, the EU's High Representative for Foreign Affairs, on the day following the news of the mission's closure, noted: 'We are concerned about the negative impact of this decision [but] it is one more reason to engage in productive dialogue [with the Libyan authorities]'. The carefully measured response may have been linked to the fact that the Commission was at that very moment in the process of negotiating an Association Agreement with Libya in order to

> set the relations with Libya into a clear and comprehensive legal framework. It is envisaged that this agreement will establish mechanisms for political dialogue and cooperation on economic issues [including] provisions for a free trade area. The agreement is expected also to foresee close cooperation on Justice, Freedom and Security issues [including] support to border control and the fight against illegal immigration.[45]

A formal Agreement, under negotiation in late 2010, was never signed as Libya spiralled into civil war in early 2011. Nonetheless – and despite the lack of any formal provisions – EU Member States contributed in significant fashion to the securitisation of Libya's frontiers ever since the lifting of the embargo in 2004.

Beyond the 5 billion euro package pledged to Libya by Italy under the terms of the Friendship Treaty, Libya has been the recipient of millions of euro in aid and contracts both directly from EU institutions and other Member States. Italy has certainly been the key player, providing helicopters, maritime surveillance aircraft and naval patrol vessels to the Gaddafi regime, together with support for the training of pilots and operators. In October 2009, an Italian company, Selex Sistemi Integrati (a subsidiary of the part-state-owned conglomerate Finmeccanica), won the bid to construct an electronic 'security barrier' to be put into place along Libya's southern borders. This electronic 'wall' was estimated to cost 300 million euro, 50% to be financed by the EU, and 50% by the Italian state. The barrier would include a remote 'operations and monitoring centre' (presumably in Italy), on-the-ground mobile detection devices (such as truck-mounted radar and infrared scanners) but also blimp-like patrol drones.[46] Although Italian military equipment sales to Libya have accounted for over a third of all EU sales (between 2008 and 2009, 205 million euro, out of a total of 595 million in arms sales), it is certainly not the only Member State that has done a brisk business in securitising Gaddafi's Libya's land and sea borders. French sales have accounted for 143 million (mainly in aviation), but Germany (57 million) and Great Britain (53 million) have also been relevant players. Tragically, much of this equipment was in action in the early weeks of the 'Libyan Revolution' in February 2011 – albeit deployed not to protect Libya's borders but rather to violently pacify the streets of Benghazi, Tobruk and other Libyan cities.[47]

Returning to late 2010, however, it is notable how the EU's preoccupation with 'normalising' and 'legalising' relations with Libya, in particular on questions of migration control, did not appear to extend to the potential dangers of the associated militarisation of Libya's frontiers (financed with EU money, no less). Indeed, a curious 'geographical' justification was provided in arguing for Libya's unique challenges in facing migratory flows through and from its territory – and thus its inability to conform to European standards. The conclusions of the report of the first Frontex Technical Assistance Mission to Libya put it succinctly:

> As a result of the visit to the desert southern regions of Libya, the mission members were able to appreciate both the diversity and the vastness of the desert, which bears no comparison to any geographical region in the EU. *Border control and management of such a vast and inaccessible area cannot be achieved by applying existing EU standards, and there is a clear need for a fresh approach to determine how best some form of improved control could be implemented.*[48]

What such a 'fresh' approach was to entail was never specified, so the actual practices of 'improved control' simply developed in the gaps consented by bi-lateral agreements (such as those with Italy), supported by military hardware furnished also by other Member States.

How can we relate the Libyan case to EUrope's attempts at 'rule at a distance', to its attempts to 'translate' EU spaces through the diffusion of specific norms, values, regulations, the 'Empire by Example' that Zielonka writes about?[49] Surely EUrope's 'normative power' wanes once flexible norms, flexible standards are applied – or, as in Libya, suspended altogether? In her perceptive analyses of migration and deportation flows between Libya and Italy, Rutvica Andrijasevic has argued that it is more accurate to understand the Italian push-back and deportation arrangements as 'a retraction of the right of asylum rather than its externalisation'.[50] She notes that although 'it is tempting to identify the collective expulsions [to Libya] in terms of the externalisation of asylum' and thus see them as part of the broader trend towards the de-territorialisation and 'off-shoring' and 'out-sourcing' of EU border security,

> the idea of externalisation presupposes however that asylum seekers and refugees are relocated to facilities where they are granted protection and where they can access the asylum determination process. Since the external processing centres do not yet exist and since Libya in practice has no refugee policy, Italy's expulsion of third-country nationals to Libya constitutes a *retraction* of the right to asylum rather than its *externalisation*.[51]

As I noted at the outset of the paper, much of the recent literature on EUropean migration and border policies has, quite rightly, focussed on the increasingly 'managerial' aspects of these latter as distinct political/ geo-political technologies based within a host of calculative and administrative practices including auditing and accounting mechanisms such as 'best practice' indicators. In a recent paper focused on the work of the IOM engaging with such studies, Andrijasevic and William Walters write about how borders are increasingly constituted as a 'problem of management' and note the emergence of 'new forms of authority and expertise' in border management, in particular what they refer to as 'the constitutive work of technical norms, standards and regulations'. They also note 'particular ethicalized stylings of government', such as 'the partnership' and 'the dialogue' that dominate the EU's understandings of 'globalised' border management.[52] In his work on the European Union's Border Assistance Mission to Moldova and the Ukraine (EUBAM) (held up by the EU as a 'model' example of its new style of 'externalised' border management) Adam Levy similarly points to the powerful rhetoric of 'European standards' and 'best practice' that underpins the EUBAM's activities – and how the language of partnership masks EUropean attempts at the securitisation of its Neighbourhoods, East as well as South.[53]

The Libyan case brings to the fore a somewhat different strategy. Here, it is no longer the case (as in Moldova, for instance) of the EU 'teaching' proper migration management, with securitisation couched in the language of 'partnership' and 'best practice'. What we see, rather, is the full-scale *suspension* of presumed EUropean norms and standards. Here, we are faced with what Nick-Vaughan Williams in his work on the 'generalised biopolitical border' identifies as the production of 'a global archipelago of zones of juridico-political indistinction'[54] – 'off-shore' black holes where European norms, standards and regulations simply do not apply, legitimised through bi-lateral agreements declaredly aimed at combating readily recognisable 'evils' such as criminal networks and international terrorism.

ADDENDUM: THE 'LIBYAN REVOLUTION', THE END OF THE STORY?

The 'Libyan Revolution' in Spring 2011 threw into even starker relief many of the ambiguities that have characterised the EU's relations with the North African country and, more broadly, the Union's geopolitical role in its southern 'Neighbourhood'. Remarking upon the EU's staggering delay in responding to the massacres taking place on the streets of Libyan cities, the title of an editorial on Spanish daily *El Pais* in February 2011 said it all – 'The infamy of the Europeans' – proceeding to outline the ways in which 'Europe shrinks back in the face of the revolutions taking place on its southern shores'. In *El Pais*' words, EU Foreign Affairs Representative Catherine Ashton's much-critiqued call for 'restraint' was simply infamous:

'When a tyrant unleashes his tanks and aviation against citizens demanding his departure, and when the death toll is already in the hundreds, it is simply infamy to call for restraint'.[55] The comments on *El Pais* were echoed by other European newspapers, all noting one and the same thing: faced with the brutal killings of hundreds, perhaps thousands of people, EUrope's main concern appeared to be 'keeping the Libyans within their borders'.[56]

The reticence with which EU leaders and the governments of individual European Member States reacted to the Libyan atrocities was truly surprising. The justifications given for the delay in any form of immediate intervention – from the freezing of Libyan assets, to sanctions, to direct 'humanitarian' intervention – were focussed chiefly on the need to 'get our people out first', not an un-important concern to be sure, considering the thousands of European (and non-) citizens working in the country. But as Libyan diplomats in various European capitals began to defect, one by one, and call on the UN and the EU for decisive action, this reticence became even more surprising. Also because there were clear signals on the part of the United States that this was a 'European matter', and that it was European governments, because of their well-developed political and economic relations with Libya, that were best placed to act.

On 21 February, as Gaddafi's planes were bombing demonstrators, Franco Frattini (Italian Foreign Minister and former EU Commissioner) announced that 'we cannot give the wrong impression to appear to wish to interfere [in internal Libyan affairs]. We need to favour peaceful reconciliation'. That same day, Frattini, together with his Maltese counterpart, had argued at a meeting of European Foreign Ministers for including in the final statement of the Council on the Libyan situation a statement 'fully recognising Libya's sovereignty and its territorial integrity'.[57]

Why the concern for recognising Libya's sovereignty? The answer was given a few days later by Frattini's colleague, Defence Minister Ignazio La Russa, announcing at a news conference that the Treaty governing bilateral relations between the two states was suspended with immediate effect since it was 'no longer operational' as 'the other party was no longer able to assure full sovereign control and thus its operability'. La Russa's comments were relevant for they came just days after an official communiqué by Frattini that Italy feared a wave of between 200 and 300,000 migrants fleeing the unrest in Libya: in his words, 'a biblical exodus' ten times that of the Albanian exodus of the 1990s.

The real peril of the revolutions in North Africa, therefore, was that by undermining dictatorial regimes (of Ben Ali first, now Gaddafi) they would unleash a flood of migrants of 'apocalyptic proportions' on Europe's shores – a fear in part realised as boatloads of migrants fleeing Tunisia began appearing on the Italian island of Lampedusa the week prior. Frattini's words were echoed by European Commission officials who spoke of a possible 1.5 million migrants ready to flee the North African country. Although the International Organisation for Migration had estimated that approximately 1.7 million foreigners were present in Libya in 2010, almost 30% of the population, responding to Frattini's and the Commission's comments, Jean-Philippe Chauvy, spokesperson for the IOM, rejected such alarmist assessments as 'irresponsible', suggesting that the EU and Italy should, rather, be concerned about the fate of these migrants within Libya.[58]

As Gaddafi's hold on power began to wane – and with the danger of a full-blown civil war sweeping the country – the ability of the Libyan state to honour its obligations in retaining its migrant masses appeared seriously compromised. And yet, just a day following Italy's official suspension of its bi-lateral agreements with Libya, in the midst of the massacres, another EU state attempted to 'push-back' unwanted migrants back to Libya. Twice, on February 23 and 24, as EU governments were desperately trying to 'get their people out', French border police at Roissy Airport tried to repatriate a Senegalese man back to Tripoli, as the validity of his residence permit was in dispute. The man had changed planes in Tripoli on his way back from a visit home and Libya was thus deemed his last place of provenance. It was only with the emergency intervention of the European Court of Human Rights that the repatriation procedures were interrupted.[59]

What sort of formal agreements regarding the 'New Libya's' participation in EU border management in the Mediterranean will be put into place is as yet unclear, but it is illustrative that the first discussions between EU representatives and the Transitional National Council in Benghazi in May 2011 focussed also on questions of border control.[60] Nevertheless, if the 'Privileged Partnership' agreements elaborated between the EU and the new Tunisian government in September 2011 are anything to go by, it is highly likely that the 'management of mobility' will continue to be a key pillar in shaping relations between the Union and the North African state.[61]

NOTES

1. N. Parker, Luiza Bialasiewicz, Sarah Bulmer, Ben Carver, Robin Durie, John Heathershaw, Henk Van Houtum, et al., 'Lines in the Sand: Towards an Agenda for Critical Border Studies', *Geopolitics* 14/3 (2009) pp. 582–587.

2. For an overview, see among others P. Andreas and T. Biersteker (eds.), *The Rebordering of North America: Integration and Exclusion in a New Security Context* (London: Routledge 2003); D. Bigo and A. Tsoukala (eds.), *Terror, Insecurity and Liberty: Illiberal Practices of Liberal Regimes after 9/11* (London: Routledge 2008); N. Vaughan-Williams, *Border Politics: The Limits of Sovereign Power* (Edinburgh: Edinburgh University Press 2009).

3. C. Rumford, *Citizens and Borderwork in Contemporary Europe* (London: Routledge 2008).

4. Z. Laïdi, *La Norme Sans la Force* (Paris: Presses de la Fondation Nationale des Sciences Politiques 2005).

5. P. Sloterdijk, *Falls Europa erwacht* (Frankfurt am Main: Suhrkamp Verlag 1994).

6. Ibid.; see also A. Somek, 'Constitutional *Erinnerungsarbeit*: Ambivalence and Translation', *German Law Journal* 6 (2005) pp. 357–370.

7. E. Balibar, 'The Borders of Europe', in P. Cheah and B. Robbins (eds.), *Cosmopolitics: Thinking and Feeling Beyond the Nation* (Minneapolis, MN: University of Minnesota Press 1998) pp. 216–233.

8. J. Sidaway, 'On the Nature of the Beast: Re-Charting Political Geographies of the European Union', *Geografiska Annaler B*, 88 (2006) pp. 1–14.

9. Bigo and Tsoukala (note 2); D. Bigo, 'The Möbius Ribbon of Internal and External Security(ies)', in M. Albert, D. Jacobson, and Y. Lapid (eds.), *Identities, Borders, Orders: Re-Thinking International Relations Theory* (London and Minneapolis: University of Minnesota Press 2001) pp. 91–116; also, D. Bigo, R. Bocco, and J.-L. Piermay (eds.), *Frontieres, marquages et disputes. Cultures et conflits* (Paris: L'Harmattan 2009).

10. See the contributions in M. Geiger and A. Pecoud (eds.), *The Politics of International Migration Management* (Basingstoke: Palgrave Macmillan 2010); for a discussion of the IOM, see R. Andrijasevic and W. Walters, 'The International Organization for Migration and the International Government of Borders', *Environment and Planning D: Society and Space* 28/6 (2010) pp. 977–999.

11. See, among others, L. Bialasiewicz et alia, 'The New Political Geographies of the European 'Neighbourhood', *Political Geography* 28 (2009), pp. 79–89; C. Browning and G. Christou, 'The Constitutive Power of Outsiders: The European Neighbourhood Policy and the Eastern Dimension', *Political Geography* 29 (2010), pp. 109–118; C. Browning and P. Joenniemi, 'Geostrategies of the European Neighbourhood Policy', *European Journal of International Relations* 14(2008), pp. 519–552; V. Kostadinova, 'The Commission, ENP and Construction of Borders' *Geopolitics* 14(2009), pp. 235–255; J. Rupnik, *Les Banlieues de l'Europe: Les politiques de voisinage de l'Union europeene* (Paris: Presses de la Fondation Nationale des Sciences Politiques 2007).

12. See L. Bialasiewicz, 'The Uncertain State(s) of Europe', *European Urban and Regional Studies* 15 (2008) pp. 71–82.

13. See T. Diez, 'Constructing the Self and Changing Others: Reconsidering 'Normative Power Europe', *Millennium: Journal of International Studies* 33 (2005) pp. 613–636.

14. See the specifications in the document 'Guidelines for Integrated Border Management in the Western Balkans', available on the EULEX website at <http://www.eulex-kosovo.eu/training/police/PoliceTraining/BORDER_BOUNDARY/DOCUMENTS>, accessed 14 July 2010.

15. J. Zielonka, *Europe as Empire: The Nature of the Enlarged European Union* (Oxford: Oxford University Press 2007).

16. See, among others, S. Lavenex, 'EU External Governance in 'Wider Europe', *Journal of European Public Policy* 11 (2004) pp. 680–700; S. Lavenex, 'Shifting Up and Out: The Foreign Policy of European Immigration Control', *West European Politics* 29 (2006) pp. 329–350; A. Zolberg, 'The Archaeology of 'Remote Control', in A. Fahrmeir, O. Faron, and P. Weil (eds.), *Migration Control in the North Atlantic World. The Evolution of State Practices in Europe and the United States from the French Revolution to the Inter-War Period* (New York: Berghahn 2003).

17. For further discussion see the special section of this journal on issue 16 (2011), including H. van Houtum and F. Boedeltje, 'Questioning the EU's Neighbourhood Geo-Politics: Introduction to a Special Section', *Geopolitics* 16 (2011) pp. 121–129.

18. 'Climate Change and International Security', Paper from the High Representative and the European Commission to the European Council, 14 March 2008, S113/08.

19. E. Guild, 'What is a Neighbour? Examining the EU Neighbourhood Policy from the Perspective of the Movement of Persons', (June 2005) available at <http://www.libertysecurity.org/article270.html>, accessed 14 July 2010.

20. W. Walters, 'Imagined Migration World: The European Union's Anti-Illegal Immigration Discourse', in M. Geiger and A. Pecoud (eds.), *The Politics of International Migration Management* (Basingstoke: Palgrave Macmillan 2010) p. 75.

21. See full details and statistics available at <http://www.unitedagainstracism.org/>, accessed 14 July 2010.

22. Most recently, FRONTEX (in collaboration with Europol and the ICMPD) has been compiling an internet-based digital 'I-Map' that seeks to map migratory movements in the Mediterranean 'in real time'; see <http://www.icmpd.org/>.

23. N. De Genova, 'Migrant Illegality and Deportability in Everyday Life', *Annual Review of Anthropology* 31 (2002) pp. 419–447. On the North American context, see also G. Rosas, 'The Thickening Borderlands: Diffused Exceptionality and 'Immigrant' Social Struggles During the War on Terror', *Cultural Dynamics* 18 (2006) pp. 335–349.

24. <http://www.acpsec.org/en/conventions/cotonou/>, accessed 14 July 2010.

25. CONCORD Cotonou Working Group Briefing Paper, 'The Revision of the Cotonou Partnership Agreement (CPA)', 2010; available at <http://www.concordeurope.org/>, accessed 14 July 2010.

26. UK Home Office, *New Vision for Refugees* (London: UK Home Office 7 March 2003). Countless scholars have written about what the notion of 'protection in the region' entails, so I will not try to unpick this highly problematic notion here. For a geographical perspective, see J. Hyndman, 'Preventive, Palliative, or Punitive? Safe spaces in Bosnia-Herzegovina, Somalia, and Sri Lanka', *Journal of Refugee Studies*, 16 (2003) pp. 167–185; J. Hyndman, 'Conflict, Citizenship, and Human Security: Geographies of Protection', in D. Cohen and E. Gilbert (eds.), *War, Citizenship, Territory* (London: Routledge 2007) pp. 241–257; also J. Hyndman and A. Mountz, 'Refuge or Refusal: Geography of Exclusion', in D. Gregory and A. Pred (eds.), *Violent Geographies* (London: Routledge 2007) pp. 77–92; in critical legal studies, C. Dauvergne, *Humanitarianism, Identity and Nation: Migration Laws of Australia and Canada* (Vancouver: University of British Columbia Press 2005); for a multi-disciplinary perspective, the edited collection by N. De Genova and N. Peutz (eds.), *The Deportation Regime: Sovereignty, Space and the Freedom of Movement* (Durham, NC: Duke University Press 2010).

27. UK Home Office (note 26) p. 20. See also the discussion in G. Noll, 'Visions of the Exceptional: Legal and Theoretical Issues Raised by Transit Processing Centres and Protection Zones', *European Journal of Migration and Law* 5 (2003) pp. 303–341.

28. T. Gammeltoft-Hansen, *Access to Asylum: International Refugee Law and the Globalization of Migration Control* (Cambridge: Cambridge University Press 2011).

29. T. Gammeltoft-Hansen, 'Outsourcing Asylum and the Advent of Protection Lite', in L. Bialasiewicz (ed.), *Europe in the World: EU Geopolitics and the Making of European Space* (Aldershot: Ashgate 2011).

30. Both quotations come from the Amnesty International Report 'Libya of Tomorrow: What Hope for Human Rights?', available at <http://www.amnesty.org/>, accessed 14 July 2010. Similar comments can be found in T. de Zulueta, 'Gaddafi Strips Off Diplomatic Fig Leaf', *The Guardian*, 11 June 2009, available at <http://www.guardian.co.uk/commentisfree/2009/jun/11/gaddafi-libya-italy>, accessed 14 July 2010.

31. See the full description in N. Ronzitti, 'Il Trattato Italia-Libya di Amicizia, Parternariato e Cooperazione', Senato della Repubblica, XVI Legislatura, Study nr.108, Jan. 2009.

32. Cited in Amnesty International (note 30).

33. See the analysis in R. Andrijasevic, 'Deported: The Right to Asylum at EU's External Border of Italy and Libya', *International Migration* 48 (2009) pp. 148–174; R. Andrijasevic, 'From Exception to Excess: Detention and Deportations across the Mediterranean Space', in N. De Genova and N. Peutz, *The Deportation Regime: Sovereignty, Space and the Freedom of Movement (Durham, NC: Duke University Press 2010).*

34. Amnesty International (note 30).

35. For a description, see F. Gatti, *Bilal: Il mio viaggio da infiltrato del mercato dei nuovi schiavi* (Milano: Rizzoli 2007); and J. Brachet, *Migrations Transsahariennes: Vers un Desert Cosmopolite et Morcele (Niger)* (Bellecome-en-Bauges: Editions du Croquant 2009).

36. E. Rigo, *Europa di confine. Trasformazioni della cittadinanza nell'Unione allargata* (Roma: Meltemi 2007).

37. See also the documentation produced by the Global Detention Project, available at <http://www.globaldetentionproject.org/countries/africa/libya/introduction.html>.

38. Cited in Amnesty International (note 30).

39. Italian Ministry of the Interior Communication, May 2009.

40. European Committee for the Prevention of Torture and Inhuman or Degrading Treatment or Punishment, 'Report to the Italian Government on the visit to Italy, 27–31 July 2009', available at <http://www.cpt.coe.int/documents/ita/2010-inf-14-eng.htm>, accessed 14 July 2010.

41. Ibid.

42. For a general discussion, see E. Guild, 'Jurisprudence of the ECHR: Lessons for the EU Asylum Policy', in C. Dias Urbano de Sousa and P. de Bruycke (eds.), *The Emergence of a European Asylum Policy* (Brussels: Bruylant 2004).

43. See W. Walters 'Anti-Policy and Anti-Politics: Critical Reflections on Certain Schemes to Govern Bad Things', *European Journal of Cultural Studies* 11/3 (2008) pp. 267–288.

44. On 25 June, the UNHCR was allowed to resume operations in Libya, though restricted only to its current caseload. Libya's Foreign Ministry, giving the official reasons for the mission's closure, 'accused UNHCR staff of serious misconduct, including the taking of bribes and sexual favours in exchange for the granting of refugee status to immigrants' – allegations that, according to UNHCR spokesperson Adrian Edwards 'remain unsubstantiated'. Edwards told journalists in Geneva that 'talks on the agency's future

in the country will resume shortly and that the expulsion order has not yet been formally lifted' (UNHCR communication, 25 June 2010). The Libyan authorities also claimed that UNHCR failed to comply with the country's requirement that asylum seekers should not be given refugee status, saying that nearly 9,000 refugees were registered illegally by the agency. 'No person who exists in Libya should be given refugee status whatever the reasons behind his stay', the statement reads, claiming all the supposed 'refugees' were illegal 'economic migrants' (*Tripoli Post Online*, 25 June 2010).

    45. European Commission, 'Concept Note: Libya Country Strategy and National Indicative Programme 2011–2013', (June 2010) available at <http://ec.europa.eu/world/enp/mid_term_review/final_concept_note_libya_en.pdf>, accessed 14 July 2010.

    46. Finmeccanica Comunicato Stampa, 'SELEX Sistemi Integrati firma accordo da 300 milioni di euro con la Libia per la protezione e sicurezza dei confini', 7 Oct. 2009, available at <http://www.finmeccanica.com>, accessed 14 July 2010.

    47. When Belgian-made projectiles (calibre 7.62) were found on the runway of El Beida airport attacked by Gaddafi's forces, the Belgian authorities suggested that these had originally been 'destined for the convoys protecting humanitarian aid shipments to Darfur'. For all figures on arms sales, see C. Bonini, 'Missili ed elicotteri, cosi l'Italia ha armato le milizie del rais', *La Repubblica*, 27 Feb. 2011.

    48. Frontex, 'Frontex-Led EU Illegal Immigration Technical Assistance Mission to Libya', 28 May–5 June 2007, Report (emphasis added).

    49. Zielonka (note 15).

    50. Andrijasevic, 'From Exception to Excess' (note 33) p. 8.

    51. Andrijasevic suggests that such a policy is indeed counter-productive in halting 'illegal' migration, for even those who would otherwise seek asylum are forced to become 'illegal' migrants due to the effective impossibility in accessing the asylum procedures. Andrijasevic, 'Deported' (note 33) p. 159; for a discussion of the broader EU context, see Noll (note 27).

    52. Andrijasevic and Walters (note 10).

    53. See A. Levy, 'The EUBAM and the Remote Control Border: Managing Moldova', in L. Bialasiewicz (ed.), *Europe in the World: EU Geopolitics and the Making of European Space* (Aldershot: Ashgate 2011). This is a 'style' of governance already experimented in the Western Balkans as part of the EU's CARDS programme for Integrated Border Management, which included a series of national 'action plans', 'capacity-building measures' and the coordination and harmonisation of border control procedures and technology. As previously, see 'Guidelines' (note 14).

    54. N. Vaughan-Williams, 'The Generalised Biopolitical Border? Re-Conceptualising the Limits of Sovereign Power', *Review of International Studies* 35 (2009) pp. 729–749; N. Vaughan-Williams, 'The UK Border-Security Continuum: Virtual Biopolitics and the Simulation of the Sovereign Ban', *Environment and Planning D: Society and Space* 28/6 (2010) pp. 1071–1083.

    55. *El Pais,* 'La ignominia de los europeos', 23 Feb. 2011. For a longer comment, see L. Bialasiewicz, 'Borders, above all?' *Political Geography* 30/6 (2011) pp. 299–300.

    56. Ibid. See also *Le Monde*, 'La fortresse Europe face au drame libyen', 26 Feb. 2011; D. Perrin, 'L'aveuglement de l'Europe a été criminel', *Liberation*, 23 Feb. 2011.

    57. It had to be pointed out to Frattini (by, among others, his Belgian counterpart Steven Vanackere) that 'recognising the Libyan authorities' full sovereignty in this very moment amounted to legitimising the massacre of protesters as simply an internal political affair within which [the EU] could not interfere'. For all citations see A. Bonnani, 'L'ira della UE contro la Farnesina: Non puo difendere un dittatore', *La Repubblica*, 22 Feb. 2011.

    58. IOM Press Briefing, available at <http://www.tsr.ch/info/monde/2979344-l-immigration-massive-de-la-libye-semble-improbable.html>.

    59. As reported by the press release of ANAFE (Association nationale d'assistance aux frontières pour les étrangers), 'Libye: la France rapatrie ses ressortissants mais tente d'y refouler. un résident étranger', *Press release*, Feb. 25 2011.

    60. See <http://www.enpi-info.eu/mainmed.php?id=26082&id_type=1&lang_id=450>, accessed 3 Nov. 2011.

    61. For an overview of the EU-Tunisia Partnership Agreements see <http://enpi-info.eu/mainmed.php?id=26548&id_type=1&lang_id=469> accessed 3 Nov. 2011.

Mixed Legacies in Contested Borderlands: Skardu and the Kashmir Dispute

ANTIA MATO BOUZAS
Zentrum Moderner Orient, Berlin, Germany

The article explores the sense of belonging of people from Skardu, a border town located in the Gilgit-Baltistan region, a territory administered by Pakistan but which is disputed by India for its being part of the former Princely State of Jammu and Kashmir. Neither full Pakistani citizens, nor identifying themselves with Kashmiri nationalism, the people of Gilgit-Baltistan lack of a common sense of belonging. The uncertain future of the territorial entity contributes to this, despite transformations already at work there. By examining the social and material landscape of Skardu town, and therefore using a micro-level perspective, the article aims to address issues of identity and security connected with broader constructed narratives of intrastate or interstate conflict, such as the Kashmir dispute within the wider geopolitical imaginary of India–Pakistan rivalry.

INTRODUCTION

Border people in contested borderlands are often caught between rivalries among states and subject to exclusive territorial nation-building processes that disregard their generally heterogeneous (and therefore non-exclusively territorially articulated) sense of belonging and their mixed loyalties. In some cases, border communities develop a degree of agency capable of altering these general centric-state narratives, as Kashmiri nationalism has done in the India–Pakistan conflict; in other situations their margin to influence those hegemonic representations is very limited, as the case of the population in Gilgit-Baltistan (northeastern Pakistan) in the same dispute exemplifies. Bordering is about difference, about representing and making identity but this,[1] in conflictive contexts, is done through material practices in which local populations are regulated by extraordinary and restrictive security measures (regimes) that do not merely delimit their activity but actually place them under an exceptional form of political control.

Borders also function as sites for exchange and cooperation. These activities, that involve a potential for transformation at different levels[2] – economic, political, cultural but also local, regional, national – depend very much on the state's influence and control over its boundaries. Many boundaries in the world today are characterised by being permeable and porous and it is just the opposite that seems less common. Globalisation processes have also accentuated cross-border mobility to the point that some scholars have postulated that 'state borders are becoming increasingly obsolete'.[3] The idea that international boundaries are vanishing has been articulated in two main ways: on the one hand, one trend of research considers that state boundaries are becoming 'virtual lines' but nonetheless, other cultural, economic barriers are emerging and need specific attention[4]; on the other hand, neoliberal approaches, particularly in the economic field, maintain that the world is becoming 'borderless'.[5] However, both these interpretations contrast with constant phenomena in which issues of power, security and identity intermingle to erect or reinforce boundaries as barriers. For example, the so-called war on terror and the subsequent military interventions in some countries,[6] policies of deportation of 'illegal' migration, or even the recent state responses in the European Union to the economic crisis, among others, constantly remind us how deeply bounded and territorialised the world is.

In border conflicts of partitioned and postcolonial states, territory and state control are still a matter of crucial concern because they are usually attached to ongoing discourses of nation-building related to the formation of particular national identities and, in the process, recreating a certain image of the Other, the neighbour. The cases of India and Pakistan and their respective arguments on Kashmir based on claims of achieving a 'secular' and 'Muslim' state to articulate a national identity are exemplary in this regard.[7] As a result of the animosity between both countries, the border is still a place to claim a national allegiance based on separation and alienation from the neighbour, as it is manifest in the 'cartographic anxiety'[8] displayed by the Indian state but also applicable to Pakistan.

However, proposals of border transformation and the creation of 'soft borders' have also penetrated the political discourse in various conflicts, including Kashmir, with the creation of confidence-building initiatives intending to reduce or alleviate the source of hostility between the contending parties. This has sometimes implied reconsiderations of the state as the sole sovereign over a concrete territory[9] but has also put into question important issues on state's identity and culture. Protracted disputes such as Kashmir have been affected by these new considerations of 'making the boundary irrelevant', as the former Pakistani president Musharraf publicly expressed one year later after the initiation of the India–Pakistan dialogue process in 2004.

The eventual relaxation of tensions among states and the adoption of decisions related to transforming the hostility of the border landscape (through facilitating cross-border mobility initiatives) can alleviate the situation of some groups on the ground but will hardly affect the whole understanding of the conflict by local populations, at least on a short-term basis. Opening boundaries is one thing, but the dismantling of the ideological framework in which border people in conflict areas have lived with and have been socialised for decades is another one. The scholar Anssi Paasi, in his work on the Finish-Russian border, argues that, despite the disappearance of the traditional enmity with the end of the Cold War and the opening of the boundary, symbols and practises of historical hostility still are present.[10]

However, in the context of the Kashmir dispute, the traditional enmity remains very much unsettled and occupies a central part of the respective national building processes in India and Pakistan. The problem rests on the fact that the Line of Control (hereafter LoC) is still mainly considered as a ceasefire line and therefore still can be challenged. Besides, conflict in Indian Kashmir has been part of the everyday life for the last two decades and thus the opening of the line only addresses part of the humanitarian problem but not the political one. The self-positioning of different border groups along the LoC on the dispute depends very much on the prevailing conditions of uncertainty in regard to the future settlement as well as other variable regional considerations. Indeed, these regional considerations, characterised by complex interrelations of 'agency, social relations and power',[11] are crucial in people's perceptions of belonging and have to be considered as rather strategic.

The present article focuses on the Pakistani area of Gilgit-Baltistan, a territory formally attached to the Kashmir dispute, although the experience of conflict and perceptions emerging from local populations there seem to indicate otherwise. It argues that issues of culture and self-identification of border people in this area play an important role in understanding the dispute, but these are shaped by specific state practices of authority and control over time resulting in particular social orders in this borderland, distinct from those being formed in the mainland parts of the state. The existence of these social orders – marked by the proximity to a contested boundary of variable regional reach – question the liberal approaches adopted in the India–Pakistan dialogue process to deal with the Kashmir dispute. These approaches emphasise that trade and cooperation will gradually attenuate the sources of the conflict, as a sort of positive evolution 'from conflict to harmony',[12] as it has been experienced in some European borderlands. However, such evolution depends to a large extent on the willingness of the state actors and the agency of the borderlanders to transform these specific border orders.

The article is structured as follows. First, it discusses the implications of adopting a borderland perspective to address the Kashmir dispute by looking at the history and the heterogeneous experiences of people living in the territory, as well as their own understanding of the geopolitical space they inhabit. Then, it examines the question of the lack of constitutional definition of Gilgit-Baltistan as a specific form of bordering. Third, state strategies of inclusion and exclusion, and the local self-identifications in relation to the conflict are explored through the case of Skardu, a border town close to the LoC in the division of Baltistan.

UNDERSTANDING KASHMIR AS A BORDERLAND

The Kashmiri historian Chitralekha Zutshi argues that adopting a borderland's perspective to explore Kashmir history, apart from the potential of liberating the region from the imperatives of national borders that misread history, can also give a boost to the academic work on South Asian borderlands.[13] Zutshi is right in her assessment but adopting a borderland perspective, as understood in the present article, implies engaging with certain considerations of the political space, of inclusion and exclusion, and a historically variable expression of agent power.[14] In other words, it is precisely this lack of questioning on national borders, borderlands and processes of nation-building and territorialisation that remains at the core of the problem when examining the Kashmir conflict in its present form. In the sub-field of Kashmir studies the focus on social borders (the identity and the ethnic plurality of the region) has not been related, with some exceptions,[15] to the analyses of the state's strategies of territorialisation in the periphery.

Besides, most of the published material deals with the Indian part of Kashmir as compared with the areas of Azad Kashmir and Gilgit-Baltistan[16] and few works have been produced by Pakistani authors regarding these territories.[17] Accounts by Indian authors on developments in the Pakistani Kashmir tend to focus on legal–constitutional matters and the historic evolution of the territories, usually adhering uncritically to Indian government positions and displaying a traditional animosity when observing how Pakistan deals with Kashmiri affairs.[18] Part of the problem lies in the fact that it seems almost impossible for Indian scholars to conduct fieldwork on the Pakistani Kashmiri–related areas, but important difficulties apply also for foreigners trying to do research on both sides of the LoC. Kashmir still belongs to the military realm.

The territories that were part of the former Princely State of Jammu and Kashmir constitute a vast borderland inhabited by a multitude of peoples belonging to different cultural groups that coexist and interrelate in various and complex ways. Previous to Partition of the subcontinent, the region could be described as a sort of frontier instituted by the Treaty of Amritsar in 1846 that later was expanded by further conquest on the North and Northeast (notably Gilgit, Baltistan and Ladakh). Different territories were amalgamated around the political control of the Dogra maharaja in the Kashmir valley, a Hindu prince ruling over a Muslim majority population.

In 1947 the Partition of the subcontinent took place and the indecision of the maharaja to join India or Pakistan, followed by the dramatic unfolding of events, led to an internal revolt against the ruler and in the aftermath caused the intervention of the Indian and Pakistani armies. After the 1947–1948 Indo-Pakistan first war on Kashmir, the former Princely State split up and its territories became peripheral areas of two large postcolonial states. Further conflict erupted in 1965, 1971 and 1999 – apart from different crises – exacerbating the rivalry between the two countries. The interstate dimension of the dispute has been complicated by the development of a nationalist insurgent movement in the Indian Kashmir, centred in the homonymous valley, in the late 1980s.

The 1949 ceasefire line, later converted in the LoC, remains the main source of dissent, not only between India and Pakistan but also between the divided territories of the former Princely State. The LoC has acquired tangible and symbolic meanings related to experiences and discourses of Partition and the building of a national identity at the wider state level, connected with claims to a past identity, a Kashmiri one, still very much disputed. It remains the most visible form of division and confrontation, although the existence of other territorial and social borders within these territories complicates the understanding of the conflict.

To examine Kashmir from a borderland perspective implies not only analysing the impact of interstate warfare and the humanitarian dimension at the border as an edge of the state,[19] to some extent a common feature shared by most of the conflicts. It is necessary to enquire how and in which ways local populations have been kept on one side of the line or the other and their experiences of it. It is the bordering process that affects interaction and cooperation and/or conflict[20] and hence, it is the role of the state as a powerful agent of territorialisation under different forms of social control that has to be considered.

India opted during decades for an integration policy of the Kashmir-related territories it acquired in 1947 and later, after the insurgency erupted in the late 1990s, it controlled the region through militarisation, even though it preserved a form of democratic government most of the period. On its part, Pakistan decided to maintain its own Kashmiri-related areas as not proper parts of the state in order to keep a solution to the conflict open but it differentiated between Azad Jammu and Kashmir and Gilgit-Baltistan, the first with a nominal federal status and the second in a constitutional limbo. Indeed, the case of the Pakistani Kashmiri–related areas serves to expose the contradictions of the state and nation-building processes, as well as the understandings of the dispute by people from these territories.

CONSTITUTIONAL UNDEFINITION AS A MODE OF BORDERING IN GILGIT-BALTISTAN

At first glance, the history of the Gilgit-Baltistan area of Pakistan could resemble that of many remote regions whose populations have had limited interaction with the state (colonial and postcolonial), a sort of 'Zomia'.[21] The territory is sandwiched between India, China and Afghanistan. People living in this area, surrounded by seemingly never-ending high mountains, often have more in common with the communities on the other side of the international boundary than with people within the neighbouring valleys. Gilgit-Baltistan is administered and territorially controlled by Pakistan through an executive order approved by the federal government but its legal–political status remains undefined and attached to the Kashmir conflict.[22] As a result of this situation, people's socialisation in the state can apparently be seen as marginal and therefore they can be regarded as relatively outside of the state's purview, both in a positive and negative sense.

However, the military presence, which exercises power and authority in the area, shows otherwise. Indeed, Gilgit-Baltistan poses an interesting case of territorialisation and state-making done through security discourses that evidence the paradoxes of Pakistani nationalism.[23] The interaction with the external threat, India, shapes the 'internal' dimension or state-making process, but this happens without a clear sense of community definition. Put differently, it is the Other that matters rather than a definition of a shared or inclusive 'We'. The enmity with India is articulated by resorting to the 'Kashmir' issue as a security problem through a *speech act* articulated by the bureaucratic and military elites in which the survival and the definition of Pakistan are at stake.[24] It is the maintenance of this order and this status quo that creates insecurity and uncertainty in the people living in the borderland territories.

Current developments seem to move in the direction of a progressive integration of the region within the Pakistani state, in line with the rest of the country's four provinces, but still with remarkable differences.[25] One major challenge for the Pakistani state in integrating Gilgit-Baltistan comes from its internal diversity and its lack of a single dominant cultural group, contrary to what happens in the main provinces of the country. This territory is sparsely populated, with perhaps little more than 1.5 million inhabitants, according to an estimated projection from the 1998 census (at the time of research, there was information that the elaboration of a new census would start in the near future),[26] still predominantly rural but with increasing urbanisation. Besides, the geographical and climatologic barriers that characterise the Karakoram Range or make interaction among these communities quite limited as compared with the populations living in the provinces. Baltistan represents the more homogeneous division, but in the whole territory there are significant differences in sense of belonging and emotional and cultural affiliations.

Thus, the current politico-economic scenario in the region can be best described by the existence of changes on the surface – some of them induced by the central state, others by supra-regional and supranational forces – and also by uncertainty as to the future status of Gilgit-Baltistan. This uncertainty is not only due to the link with the Kashmir dispute and Pakistan's claim to it, but to the frequent instability within the Pakistani state – even though it has not directly affected Gilgit-Baltistan to date as compared with the other four provinces of the state and also Azad Jammu and Kashmir – and the role of Gilgit-Baltistan as being a territory of regional encounter.

Pakistan took over the region after Partition, but without considering the claims of local actors who had been loyal to the creation of Pakistani state,[27] perpetuating a sort of colonial government through the figure of the Political Agent, who was later replaced by a Resident Agent. The first attempt to introduce a regional administrative body came in 1972 when Z. A. Bhutto abolished the raja system, thus extricating power from the regional rulers, who until then had exercised certain legal and administrative duties, and reorganised the administration of the area into districts by creating the posts of Resident Commissioner and Deputy Commissioner. He also established an elected Northern Areas Council to function as a sort of regional body, but with limited capacities.[28] Later, in 1994, a new order, the Northern Areas Legal Framework Order, came into force, by which the Minister of Kashmir and Northern Areas (KANA) now exercised executive powers over the area.

During the presidency of Pervez Musharraf's military rule, new problems arose due to the increasing sectarian violence in the former North West Frontier Province (now renamed as Khyber Pakhtunkhwa), which also affected the area of Gilgit. An internal controversy about the use of new textbooks, whose content condemned some important figures in the Shia religious mindset, arose in 1999 in Gilgit, causing a new period of violence and protest.[29] The problem was partially solved in 2005 when the authorities gave the option of not using the controversial chapters until a revised edition was supplied, but such new books never materialised.

The new Pakistan People's Party (PPP)-led government announced on 9 September 2009 a reform package, the Gilgit-Baltistan Empowerment and Self-Governance Order, which included the name change of the former Northern Areas in favour of the more concrete Gilgit-Baltistan. The name change has somehow added a new element to the image of self-identification of this territory, but the undefined constitutional status of the region within the Pakistani state remains. The 2009 reform is concerned only with the guarantee of maintaining some sort of figurative political representation in the area (still closely controlled by Islamabad) and to dealing with matters of administration and development, rather than giving answers to people's citizenship rights demands.[30] The ruling has to be understood also as a move of the PPP-led government to conciliate the official Pakistani stand on Kashmir without denying rights to a territory in which the majority of the population may have pro-Pakistani sentiments (as compared with the ambivalence of the nationalist-separatist leanings of the Azad Kashmiris).

As a result of compromise, the 2009 reform for Gilgit-Baltistan is no more than a ruling approved by Pakistan's Federal Cabinet. Gilgit-Baltistan has no representative in the National Assembly because the people of the area cannot participate in state elections. It creates the new figure of the Governor (in line with the other provinces of Pakistan) with wider powers to supervise the decisions of the Assembly and establishes a Supreme Appellate Court. However, despite some minor improvements, the main debate on the political characteristics of Gilgit-Baltistan persists with important implications in terms of rights for the local population. For example, Article 9.2 of the 2009 Order, which deals with the freedom of association, refers to limits of association or political expression regarding activities detrimental to the 'ideology of Pakistan'. This vagueness about 'how the ideology of Pakistan has to be interpreted' has clear implications for imposing restrictions on autonomist movements, apart from other religious or cultural considerations.

The Gilgit-Baltistan Empowerment and Self-Empowerment Order introduced by the PPP has met with opposition and criticism, especially from the political leaders of Azad Jammu and Kashmir, on the grounds that the Order could hamper Pakistan's position on Kashmir.[31] Some people in Gilgit-Baltistan have also questioned the resolution, but on different grounds – for extending a status that makes locals vulnerable and passive spectators to important transformations that are already taking place. In Skardu, for example, when interviewing some relevant local personalities after the reform was passed, reactions were mixed and cautious.[32] People recognised that the Order brought certain improvements, but still they were not regarded as Pakistani citizens like the rest. In their answers, they showed an ambivalence that indicated the ruling did not fulfil their expectations. Nevertheless, when enquiring about why the AJK Assembly were concerned about the measure, they too stated that the situation of Gilgit-Baltistan was different and they were somehow tired of the Kashmiri leadership voicing something that was not their own business. Among the interviewees, there were PPP and Pakistan Muslim League-Quaid-e-Azam (PML–Q) sympathisers, as well some with more nationalist leanings (closer to the Balawaristan National Front). What emerged from these interactions, irrespective of their political leanings, was a distinct regional sense of shared belonging or self-identification. They were reacting to the dominant narrative of 'being part of the Kashmir dispute' but without directly pointing at the Pakistani state as the sole actor responsible for it. If they do not openly question the ambivalent attitude of Pakistan, they admit to feeling that the 'government is doing its best', that they have some advantages in the current context[33] (notably tax exemptions and subsidised prices for basic products such as rice, wheat and petrol, among others) or perhaps, what is most probably the case, they cannot openly express themselves on this point.

Hence, the ambiguous constitutional status of Gilgit-Baltistan may be interpreted in the first instance as a relative autonomy or freedom for the communities living in the area, marginally socialised with the idea of Pakistan. However, power relations evidence state continuous practices of bordering and 'reimagining' of its borders.[34] The changes are connected with possible future alignments, particular in relation to a solution of the Kashmir dispute and the preservation of the LoC as an international boundary. Within this context, border people adjust to the uncertain circumstances by searching for non-conflictive forms of self-identification.

THE CASE OF SKARDU WITHIN THE 'KASHMIR BOX'

As has been said, the uncertain territorial status of Gilgit-Baltistan within the Pakistani state has clear implications for citizenship and raises questions of self-identification for the people living in the area. In articulating their sense of belonging, the state remains a contradictory and distant figure because statehood in a modern sense (after Partition) has not been experienced much in everyday life. By contrast, what prevails is a historical experience of shared neighbourhood and proximity with the Ladakh area that the separateness created by the LoC has not completely removed so far.

In order to understand the ways in which Gilgit-Baltistan has remained within the 'Kashmir problem', and therefore as an issue of disputation between India and Pakistan, it seems pertinent to observe the social landscape of the border area and the mixed affinities of their inhabitants. The local perspective of a border town such as Skardu offers a good example of the complexity of the area's wider geopolitical landscape because, as Anssi Paasi points out: 'Local life in the border area is constituted by socio-spatial boundaries that are simultaneously both local and non-local and are to a greater or lesser degree social'.[35]

Skardu town is located in a valley relatively near the LoC but well outside the military restricted zone, surrounded by mountains 3,000–4,000 metres high. At first glance, it could hardly be described as a border town in a disputed area except for the two military cantonments that denote the overwhelming presence of the army. The town does not conform to the typical image of violence and lawlessness associated with most of the Pakistani border areas, since criminality there is almost zero.[36] The representation of the Pakistani administration in the region is through the figure

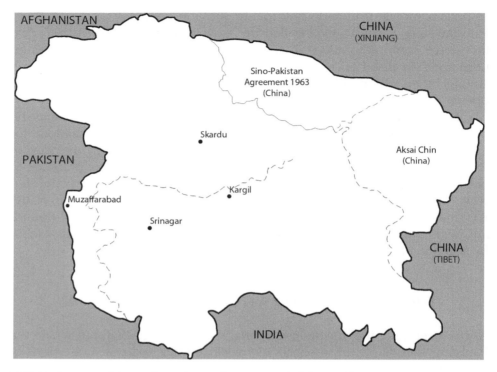

FIGURE 1 Map of the Kashmir disputed territories slightly modified by the author to show Skardu's location. Based on the map 'The Kashmir region' available at: http://www.lib.utexas.edu/maps/middle_east_and_asia/kashmir_region_2004.jpg

of the District Commissioner, who now resides at Gilgit and is assisted by a Deputy Commissioner and an Assistant Commissioner in Skardu. The Gilgit-Baltistan Legislative Assembly has its headquarters in Gilgit, and in November 2009 elected its first Chief Minister from Skardu, Mehdi Shah, a fact that was perceived locally as a sign of the increasing importance of Baltistan in regional affairs against a traditionally Gilgiti-dominated bureaucracy.

The population of the town, excluding the army, is mainly of Dard-Tibetan origin, who speak *Balti*, a dialect of Tibetan mostly employed in its spoken form. Nevertheless, Urdu is widely employed in the bazaar and in more formal contexts. With regard to the religious composition, most Skardu inhabitants belong to the Twelver Shia branch of Islam (around 70–80%) but there is a growing Nurbakhshi community as a result of a continuing labour migration from the eastern part of the region (Ghanche district).[37] Sunnis make up around 10% of the town's population. There are also some Shia Ismaili families from the Gilgit-Hunza area, most of whom are employed as skilled workers. To some extent, the Skardu human landscape offers a representative portrait of Baltistan as a whole, although perhaps the Skardu district is less homogeneous in terms of ethnicity (Tibetan), language (Balti) and religion, than the eastern part of Ghanche, where the Nurbakhshis dominate, along with Shias.

Language and ethnic and religious affinities are also shared with the other side of the LoC, especially in the Kargil area of Ladakh, on the Indian side. However, while the inhabitants of Kargil are seen by people from Skardu as part of their own cultural ethos, the broader region of Ladakh is perceived as more distant, mainly because of religious differences (given the predominance of Buddhism there) and cultural issues derived from these differences, such as the use of Tibetan script and vocabulary of Tibetan origin in the language as opposed to an 'Urdufied' or 'Persianed' Balti.[38] Acknowledgement of these differences is also reflected in the political dimension when views are expressed about 'the other side of the border' in relation to the disputed nature of the boundary. For instance, many in Skardu opine that Kargil people 'are like us'. Thus, the multicultural social landscape of the border area, part of an objective shared borderland,[39] shows the existence of other socio-spatial boundaries that are intertwined in various and complex ways. These do not necessarily coincide with general 'static' understandings of the conflict, in this case the reference to 'Kashmir', based on territorial, historic or identity aspects.

The Impact of the India–Pakistan Conflict at Local Level

Visible scars of conflictive and alienated border areas (gutted houses, soldiers deployed in the streets, propaganda, etc.) are not evident at first glance in Skardu town, but a closer look at the history of its inhabitants reveals definite episodes of confrontation between India and Pakistan and their impact on local populations near the LoC. For example, elderly people who moved in from neighbouring Ladakh in 1947 still live in town. Before Partition, they were mostly involved in trading activities. There is also a settled community of families in the southern part of the urban centre. These people, whom some locals refer as to 'refugees', moved from their villages in Chorbat La area in 1971, once the Indian forces took over that territory as a result of the third India–Pakistan war.[40] In addition, some families from the Siachen area moved to Skardu after conflict erupted there in the mid-1980s. More recently, two relatively new colonies were established in the outskirts of the town as a consequence of the 1999 Kargil conflict. The latter are made up of petty farmers who previously inhabited the areas located just off the LoC on the Pakistani side. Apart from these groups, some scattered families live in Skardu who are not necessarily from Baltistan but from adjacent areas such as Astore or Diamir. Some of them are headed by widows whose husbands used to work as porters for the army and who died as a result of crossfire episodes in the last three decades.[41]

Conflict-related migration in Skardu seems difficult to address and is sometimes minimised by social agents who argue that people tend to move to town from border sites because of the economic opportunities and the possibility of a better life, as a representative of a local NGO has suggested. Sometimes this can indeed be a motivation, but it is not always the case. During group interviews, women who had migrated from the border villages near Kargil (on the Pakistani side) as a result of the 1999 conflict, particularly stressed their preference for their former lifestyles, as opposed to the current lives they were leading in Skardu. While they recognised that their children had better educational facilities in town, their economic lives were substantially altered for the worse. As an example, the women pointed to the fact that now they were working as labourers for other families for paltry salaries whereas before, in their former villages, they had worked for themselves.

It is not clear whether inward migration from border sites is voluntary, encouraged or forced. This aspect was not openly explored during the fieldwork but there seem to be indications that situations vary according to army security and strategic needs. At times, the permanence of the local population on border sites can be encouraged for various reasons: for example, the army might persuade people in a sensitive territory to remain there as a proof of its control (however, these locals could be real hostages when fighting takes place); or the army might wish to use civilians as a source of labour. At other times, military needs may require seizure of land, participation in military campaigns and even fighting, all of which would encourage forced displacement.[42]

However, the government of Pakistan, or more specifically the army, has brought significant improvement to border villages and has an interest in keeping the population there. In group interviews conducted with people displaced from the border areas, especially those from the vicinity of Kargil, it became clear that the conflictive scenario in which they were living was the main reason for their decision to abandon their houses or livelihood and to move to Skardu. Intensive shelling, the need to spend periods in bunkers when fighting was going on, the problems of attending to and collecting crops and the Indians cutting off irrigation channels (during the Kargil conflict) were among the main reasons cited for taking the decision to move.[43]

The scars of interstate conflict significantly define the contours of the social landscape of border towns. They also provide useful information on how conflict is perceived by the population, in this case as a confrontation between the Indian and Pakistani armies, rather than as a 'Kashmir issue'. It certainly raises some questions about the perspective and the information that *borderlanders* have on the conflict for which they are not politically mobilised, but for which they suffer. In this sense, the border area seems to be a place where a regime of silence reigns, in which locals do not have any significant scope for action.

Social Control and Loyalties in Contested Borders

Border people along contested boundaries are dubious nationals; their loyalty to the state is under suspicion most of the time, even where locals take active part in national struggles, as the case of the Gilgit-Baltistan region shows. The conflictive environment worsens this condition because the crucial issues of belonging and self-identification have not been solved. The inhabitants of Skardu do not feel they are part of Kashmir but might reluctantly side with the imposed association with that dispute; they are kept within the Pakistani state but they do not enjoy full citizenship rights. In order to confront this situation of permanent uncertainty the unity of the community is preserved largely through religious forms of social control.

The significant military deployment and the heavy surveillance of the population impose a code of silence on many issues and especially on the manifestations of civilians' own worldviews. For example, it was not seen as controversial to enquire about people's opinions on Kashmir, when conducting interviews in Skardu, in trying to understand their views about the 'other side' of the LoC. Yet to ask about personal views of Pakistan's policy for the region and the fact that the Gilgit-Baltistan is not considered a proper part of the state was a sensitive issue. In this sense, the tight social control on the population poses some limitations to openly and freely addressing many problems, especially the state policies that affect them and, in particular, those related to the India–Pakistan dialogue process.

Contrary to what happens in the Kashmir valley and adjacent areas, the people of Baltistan and Ladakh seem to have no say in conversations between New Delhi and Islamabad and have limited agency to raise their own issues. They have been affected by the conflict but have never been involved in violent activities,[44] and have not even articulated political claims on the 'other side' of the line, as the Kashmiris of the valley have done. However, so far they have not benefitted from cross-border communication links. Strategic impediments have often been cited for this on both sides.

The army is present in Skardu and the border areas mostly to neutralise or to combat any external threat but also to closely monitor, through intelligence agencies, the local population's activities, as well as those of foreigners. In fact, beyond the idea that border areas constitute natural sites for spies and the spreading of rumours[45] the reality that seems to dominate on the ground, at least in this case, is that they are places where people do not enjoy the same political and legal rights as other citizens belonging to that state. In that sense, one may consider these places as exceptional territorial sites under specific border regimes.[46]

Although the long-term presence of the army acts as the primary instrument of social control inhibiting possible dissent, it has also a cooperative character that is sometimes seen as beneficial by the local population.

Indeed, the army represents a significant source of employment (as soldiers, assistants, tailors, etc.) and is a body that can defend the local population from possible threats from India. During interviews conducted in August–September 2009 and March 2010, most of the interlocutors underlined the existence of a relationship of 'mutual respect', but it is not clear whether this has something to do with the fact that a number of soldiers recruited are now locals. Some interviewees proudly reported that, during the Kargil mini-war, the local population was actively involved in organising food supplies for the troops, thus showing loyalty and support to the army, but they also remarked that there were local soldiers fighting in that conflict.[47] In any case, the relationship between civil and military forces remains complex and a discernible differentiation exists between the two sides.

In fact, against this security backdrop, it is the religious leadership of Skardu (and Baltistan by large) that is the one responsible for keeping the people together and thus defining the community. The clergy seems to play a moderating role between the military and the civil population,[48] but mediation is also articulated through the maintenance of rigid religious observance among the population, particularly participation in religious rituals (prayers, accepting legal opinions or fatwas, etc.), the preservation of gender segregation and limitation of women's role in public, among other things. Until now, this complex social order of civil-military relations has helped Skardu, and to a certain extent Baltistan, to escape the endemic problems of sectarian violence that affect the rest of Pakistan and, more concretely, the neighbouring area of Gilgit. Paradoxically, this seems to reinforce the sense of belonging to a community in which the contours of political identity appear highly debated or problematic, if not directly schizophrenic. In this sense, the proximity of the international boundary, where the boundary is located,[49] and its conflictive character can be seen as constitutive of specific socio-political orders.

A Society in Transformation

Despite the codes of silence that reign there, border towns are not merely static places located on the periphery of states but areas that cannot escape larger transformations happening at the state level or in the region. An overview of Skardu shows a society at an early stage of its socio-economic transformation from a traditional self-sustainable agrarian society to a more service-consumer oriented society. There is an increasing growth of population attracted by the possibility of finding jobs in the administration or public sector,[50] non-profit sector and also in tourism. As a result, economic activities such as construction for business purposes (mostly in the touristic sector) have become more noticeable. Communications have also improved significantly since 2007, when internet access and the use of mobile phones became operational. In addition, the widely visible presence of schools, mostly private, points to an important change for a region which had very low literacy rates just one decade ago.[51] The spread of education also brings implicit cultural changes, such as the diffusion of Urdu and English in the instruction and thus the perception of these two languages as being more 'refined' as compared with Balti and thus becoming the guarantors of socio-economic mobility.[52]

Skardu can be still regarded as a relatively isolated area, whose expectations for development (economic, political and cultural) are restricted by its condition of being a town near a disputed boundary. The communication infrastructure with the rest of Gilgit-Baltistan and Pakistan is poor, and this indirectly imposes restrictions on trade development as well as the possibility of establishing small industries due to high costs and distant markets. Only tourism has developed Skardu into a popular venue for foreign mountaineering, and this activity helps to employ local skilled workers and some educated youth as translators and guides as well as developing the wider tourist sector.

Attempts to end the relative isolation of this territory and to connect it with the wider Himalayan region seem to be under way. In 2009, Pakistani Prime Minister Y. Gilani announced the upgrading of Skardu airport to international level, allowing a flight connection with Katmandu,[53] with the aim of linking important sites of mountaineering tourism. Despite its clear economic aim, if the measure finally materialises it can also be seen as a first step to ending the imposed cutoff of Baltistan traditional ties with the Himalayan–Tibetan milieu.[54] The upgrading of the airport may also benefit some local entrepreneurs and indirectly help local inhabitants to develop a cultural affiliation, already at work and promoted by some local individual and groups,[55] with other Himalayan peoples as part of a shared sense of belonging to the Tibetan-Buddhist past.

Another issue concerns the improvement and development of certain major infrastructure projects such as the rebuilding by Chinese companies of the Skardu–Karakoram highway link, which is expected to start in the near future,[56] and the construction of major dams in the Gilgit-Baltistan region. Although these dams are not located in Baltistan, they might have implications for the mobility of the local workforce. In fact, plans for the Diamer-Basha dam remain highly controversial because of the potential effects on both the environmental and human landscape. This project has resulted in a displacement of population: some people from the affected areas have already moved to Baltistan. Also, the arrival of a workforce tens of thousands strong from other parts of Pakistan (probably Sunnis Muslims) may alter the fragile population balance in the area, especially if they settle there.[57]

The ongoing development and infrastructural activities taking place in the area suggest re-territorialisation processes in which old and new symbolic meanings are being developed to acquire tangible forms, thus reshaping the region's human and material landscape. Within these processes, Kashmir can represent only one reference among others (Xinjiang, Tibet, etc.). In short, the challenges faced by a border town such as Skardu, located in a disputed territory, are many. On the one hand, the conflictive character of the area imposes on the local population a strong imprint of silence, if not fear, to state agents' activities there, even when loyalty to the Pakistani state seems not to be in question. On the other, the changing scenario in a multitude of directions (changing the educational environment and its implications on culture, developmental activities and building of major infrastructure projects presented as politically unproblematic, movements of inward and outward migration) demands responses from the local population.

CONCLUSIONS

The examination of the social landscape of Skardu town, in relation to the legacies of the Kashmir dispute and the status of Gilgit-Baltistan and the Pakistani state, questions the commonly assumed macro-narratives associated with the dispute. The geopolitical imaginary of 'Kashmir' has led to a great sense of ambiguity for the local population living in the proximity of the LoC. It contradicts their own historic experiences during the colonial period and the subsequent Partition. Although past ties with that region are not denied, the whole dispute has been imposed on them from above, mainly from the Pakistani military-bureaucratic establishment, causing a great sense of frustration and uncertainty.

Being part of the Kashmir conundrum has implied for the inhabitants of the region the absence of a socialisation in the Pakistani state, since the latter does not consider them as full citizens, thus limiting their possibility of making claims based on political, legal and economic issues, among others. The control of the population by the state elites, mainly the military, has happened through the exercise of both despotic and paternalistic power. This power has been legitimated by security discourses articulated around the existence of an external threat, India and the Kashmir problem, and thus ignoring the lack of institutionalisation of the state for not integrating the region. The aim has been to conciliate the state claims on the whole of Kashmir while at the same time accommodating a local population which so far has not developed any autonomist leanings.

Yet, more than separation or differentiation from the other side, the proximity of the Line of Control has created a particular social order in the borderland marked by ambiguity and uncertainty. However, to counter this ambivalent situation, the existence of the provisional boundary has caused other group ties and cultural affinities to emerge at the local and regional level. These ties and affinities can be partially related to the process of bordering but also to a reaction to this context of uncertainty in which belonging and group affinities need to be assured. The case of Skardu as a border town in the Kashmir borderland highlights that issues of power, control and intervention by state institutions and other actors play an important role in shaping forms of self-identification of border people. This reality questions the predicament of the obsolescence of the state and its territorial markers.

Moreover, the significant infrastructural and development transformations taking place in Gilgit-Baltistan hint at territorialisation processes with the potential to impact the Kashmir borderland in various ways. The LoC remains an unsettled boundary but it divides peoples who, although they might have shared historical experiences, do not see themselves as part of a unique culture. Within this context, the possible opening of the LoC for mobility might be a referent for some groups, but not necessary for others whose intentions and expectations lie somewhere else.

ACKNOWLEDGEMENTS

I am grateful to comments posed by the anonymous reviewers of this article. This research has been supported by the German Federal Ministry of Education and Research (BMBF).

NOTES

1. See: Chris Brown, 'Borders and Identity in International Relations Political Theory', in Mathias Albert, David Jacobson, and Yosef Lapid (eds.), *Identities, Borders and Orders: Rethinking International Relations theory* (Minneapolis: University of Minnesota Press 2001); Corey Johnson, Reece Jones, Anssi Paasi, Louise Amoore, Alison Mountz, Mark Salter, and Chris Rumford, 'Interventions on 'Rethinking' the Border in Border Studies', *Political Geography* 30 (2011) p. 62.

2. Malcolm Anderson, *Frontiers: Territory and State Formation in the Modern World* (Cambridge: Polity Press 1996); Paul Nugent and A. I. Asiwaju (eds.), *African Boundaries: Barriers, Conduits and Opportunities* (London: Pinter 1996).

3. Thomas Wilson and Hastings Donnan, 'Nation, State and Identity at International Borders', in Thomas Wilson and Hasting Donnan (eds.), *Border Identities: Nation and State at International Frontiers* (Cambridge: Cambridge University Press 1998) p. 1; Arjun Appadurai, *Modernity at Large: Cultural Dimensions of Globalization* (Minneapolis and London: Minnesota University Press 1996) p. 19.

4. Vladimir Kolossov, 'Border Studies: Changing Perspectives and Theoretical Approaches', *Geopolitics* 10/4 (2005) p. 612.

5. Kenichi Ohmae, *The Borderless World: Power and Strategy in the Interlinked Economy* (New York: McKinsey 1999).

6. See for instance Stuart Elden, *Terror and Territory: The Spatial Extent of Sovereignty* (Minneapolis: University of Minnesota Press 2009).

7. Adrian M. Athique, 'A Line in the Sand: The India-Pakistan Border in the Films of J.P. Dutta', *South Asia: Journal of South Asian Studies* 31/3 (June 2010) pp. 473–477; Vali Nars, 'National Identities and the India-Pakistan Conflict', in T.V. Paul (ed.), *The India-Pakistan Conflict: An Enduring Rivalry* (Cambridge: Cambridge University Press 2005) pp. 178–201.

8. Shankaran Krishna, 'Cartographic Anxiety: Mapping the Political Body in India', *Alternatives* 19 (1994) pp. 507–521.

9. John Agnew, *Globalization & Sovereignty* (Plymouth: Rowman and Littlefield 2009).

10. Anssi Paasi, *Territories, Boundaries and Consciousness: The Changing Geographies of the Finnish-Russian Border* (Chichester: John Wiley & Sons) pp. 305–306.

11. Anssi Paasi, 'The Resurgence of the 'Region' and 'Regional Identity': Theoretical Perspectives and Empirical Observations on Regional Dynamics in Europe', in *Review of International Studies* 35 (2009) p. 133.

12. Julian V. Minghi, 'From Conflict to Harmony in Border Landscapes', in Dennis Rumley and Julian Minghi (eds.), *The Geography of Border Landscapes* (London: Routledge 1991) p. 18.

13. Chitralekha Zutshi, 'Rethinking Kashmir's History from a Borderlands Perspective', *History Compass* 8/7 (2010) p. 594.

14. Emmanuel Brunet-Jailly, *Borderlands: Comparing Border Security in North America and Europe* (Ottawa: University of Ottawa Press 2007) p. 4.

15. See the works of Ravina Aggarwal, *Beyond Lines of Control: Performance and Politics on the Disputed Borders of Ladakh, India* (Durham and London: Duke University Press 2004); Seema Kazi, *Between Democracy & Nation: Gender and Militarisation in Kashmir* (New Delhi: Women Unlimited 2009).

16. Leo Rose, 'The Politics of Azad Jammu and Kashmir', in Raju Thomas (ed.), *Perspectives on Kashmir: The Roots of Conflict in South Asia* (Boulder: Westview Press 1992); Cabeiri deBerg Robinson, 'Refugees, Political Subjectivity, and the Morality of Violence: From *hijarat* to *jihād* in Azad Kashmir (Ann Arbor: University of Michigan Press 2005); Martin Sökefeld, 'From Colonialism to Postcolonial Colonialism: Changing Modes of Domination in the Northern Areas of Pakistan', *Journal of Asian Studies* 64/4 (1995) pp. 939–973.

17. A notable exception is the columnist Ali Aziz Dad, who regularly publishes on issues of Gilgit-Baltistan in the Pakistani press.

18. An example can be: Debidatta Aurobinda Mahapatra, Seema Shekhawat, *Kashmir Across LOC* (New Delhi: Gyan Publishing House 2008).

19. Debidatta Aurobinda Mahapatra, 'Positioning the People in the Contested Borders of Kashmir', CIBR *Working Paper 21/2011*, Queen's University of Belfast, Centre for International Borders Research, available at <http://www.qub.ac.uk/research-centres/CentreforInternationalBordersResearch/Publications/WorkingPapers/CIBRWorkingPapers/Filetoupload,219140,en.pdf>, accessed 8 April 2011.

20. David Newman, 'The Resilience of Territorial Conflict in an Era of Globalization', in Miles Khaler and Barbara F. Walter (eds.), *Territoriality and Conflict in an Era of Globalization* (Cambridge: Cambridge University Press 2006) p. 101.

21. James C. Scott, *The Art of Not Being Governed: An Anarchist History of Upland Southeast Asia* (New Haven: Yale University Press 2009) pp. 14–19.

22. This is a rather controversial issue. While the Government of Pakistan officially maintains that the territory is disputed on the grounds it was part of the former Princely State of Jammu and Kashmir, on certain occasions it has been ambivalent and Islamabad's policy has been to progressively integrate the region into Pakistan, if with certain restrictions. The ambivalence rests on the assumption that only some parts of the now Gilgit–Baltistan would be disputed, while other areas could be considered as full Pakistan territory because at the time of Partition some former local elites agreed to the integration with Pakistan. For instance, the letter sent on 8 May 2007 by the Pakistani Ambassador to Baroness Nicholson on her report 'Kashmir: Present Situation and Future Prospects' notes that 'the whole of Northern Areas, which include Gilgit Agency and Baltistan Agency was not part of Jammu and Kashmir State in August 1947' and that the 'UNCIP resolutions are relative to the State of Jammu and Kashmir and do not, in any manner, apply to any part of the Northern Areas which were not included in the State of Jammu and Kashmir before 1947. From this perspective, integration of the Northern Areas with Pakistan is also not prohibited.' See also, European Parliament, P6_TA (2007)0214, European Parliament resolution of 24 May 2007 on 'Kashmir: Present Situation and Future Prospects' (2005/2242(INI)). Also, Aziz Ali Dad, 'The Case of Gilgit–Baltistan is Different', in *Kashmir Affairs*, available at <http://www.kashmiraffairs.org/aziz%20ali%20dad%20case%20of%20gilgit%20baltistan%20is%20different.html>, accessed 7 June 2010.

23. On state-making process as subjects see Agnew (note 9) pp. 106–107.

24. On this aspect, see Ole Wæver, 'Securitization and Desecuritization', in Ronnie Lipschutz (ed.), *On Security* (New York: Columbia University Press 1995) pp. 54–55.

25. Gilgit-Baltistan is the only Shi'a majority area and this might also be an obstacle for making it the fifth province in an increasing Sunni Pakistan. See Farzana Shaikh, *Making Sense of Pakistan* (London: Hurst and Co. 2009) p. 67; Vali Nars, *The Shia Revival: How Conflicts within Islam Will shape the Future* (London: Norton 2007) pp. 159–160.

26. Government of Pakistan, *1998 District Census Report of Gilgit* (Islamabad: Population Census Organization, Statistics Division 2000); Government of Pakistan, *1998 District Census Report of Baltistan* (Islamabad: Population Census Organization, Statistics Division 2001).

27. See Sökefeld (note 16) p. 959.

28. On the main political developments on Northern Areas since Partition: Hermann Kreutzmann, 'Kashmir and the Northern Areas of Pakistan: Boundary-Making Along Contested Frontiers', *Erdkunde* 62/3 (2008) pp. 209–212.

29. On this issue see Georg Stöber, 'Religious Identities Provoked: The Gilgit "Textbook Controversy" and its Conflictual Context', *Internationale Schulbuchforschung* 29 (2007) pp. 389–411.

30. Ali Aziz Dad, 'Discontents in Gilgit-Baltistan', *The Dawn*, 21 Jan. 2010, available at <http://www.dailytimes.com.pk/default.asp?page=2010%5C01%5C21%5Cstory_21-1-2010_pg3_3>, accessed 21 Jan. 2010.

31. Tariq Naqash (3 Sep. 2009) 'AJK Assembly Supports Gilgit-Baltistan Package', *Dawn*, available at <http://www.dawn.com/wps/wcm/connect/dawn-content-library/dawn/news/pakistan/09-ajk-assembly-supports-Gilgit-Baltistan -package--szh-13>, accessed 7 June 2010; Aziz Ali Dad (note 22).

32. These interviews were conducted in the first two weeks of September 2009, during fieldwork in the region.

33. During the government of Z. A. Bhutto, the area was declared as tax free and subsidies were introduced on some basic products for a period of thirty years that was later extended, and therefore, still in force.

34. Vali Nars, 'The Negotiable State: Borders and Power Struggles in Pakistan', in Brendan O'Leary, Ian S. Lustick, and Thomas Callaghy (eds.), *Right-Sizing the State: The Politics of Moving Borders* (Oxford: Scholarship Online 2003) p. 168.

35. Anssi Paasi, *Territories* (note 10) p. 214.

36. Interview with the District Attorney, Mr. Gulam Abbas Chopa, Skardu, 25 March 2010.

37. Nūrbakhshiyya can be considered as 'an offshoot of the Kubrawi Sufi order which functioned part of its existence as a distinct sect'. See 'Nūrbakhshiyya', H. Algar, *The Encyclopaedia of Islam*, online ed., Vol. 8 (Leiden: E.J. Brill 2004) p. 134a. On this community in Baltistan see Andreas Rieck, 'The Nurbakhshis of Baltistan: Crisis and Revival of a Five Centuries Old Community', *Die Welt des Islams* 35/2 (Nov. 1995) pp. 159–188.

38. See Hasnain Sengge Thsering, 'The Linguistic and Cultural Diversity of Kashmir: Baltistan's Tibetan Links', *South Asian Voice: Views from South Asia* (Sep. 2003), available at <http://india_resource.tripod.com/baltiyul.html>, accessed 24 June 2010. On this topic, different meetings were also held with Mr. Kazmi, Abbas and Mr. Yosuf Hussain Abadi, who kindly discussed with the author the sociolinguistic map of the area.

39. Victor Konrad, Heather N. Nicol, *Beyond Walls: Re-Inventing the Canada-United States Borderlands* (Aldershot UK: Ashgate 2008) p. 32.

40. Although the third major war between India and Pakistan erupted because of the crisis in East-Bengal (today Bangladesh), it was also fought along the cease-fire line in Kashmir. As a result, India gained some territories in the Ladakh–Baltistan eastern tract (Turtuk, Chulunka and Tyasik) that were never returned. This is a different situation from the position that developed in the Kashmir valley/AJK tract, where Bhutto and Gandhi agreed, during the negotiations at Simla, to go back to the positions of the 1949 ceasefire agreed line.

41. Interview held with a widow of a former porter who died in an episode of Indo-Pakistan confrontation, Skardu, 2 Sep. 2009.

42. Land grabbing by the army constitutes a source of concern that has been addressed in some interviews, even with people from the bureaucracy, but that cannot be openly questioned.

43. Group interviews conducted on 31 Aug. 2009, 1 Sep. 2009, and 3 Sep. 2009.

44. Mr. M spoke about events preceding the Kargil operation, events that were referred to by some other local interlocutors. His account reveals local disapproval of military-orchestrated activities along the border. He said that in the months before Kargil started, some 'outsiders' (it is not clear if they were Kashmiris) came to live in town, presumably for training. Some stayed in rented apartments, while others may have been in military areas (the narrator could not confirm this when asked about how many men came to Skardu). What happened was that some locals rented their apartments to them, but these men's behaviour was soon under question. They were 'noisy' and 'disrespectful' towards locals and they used to roam around in town with their jeeps at a great speed. Apparently, an incident happened between one of these men and a local old lady who had rented an apartment to them. It seems the man

threatened her when she asked him to leave the place. News of the incident spread quickly and the locals openly protested, requesting the army to make the 'outsiders' leave the place. Eventually, these supposed militants abandoned the town (interview, 26 March 2010).

45. For example, during my interviews I came across the importance of rumour in the perceptions of 'outsiders' and the wider world. I myself had to understand my position in this as an 'angrezi' which meant more than being identified as a 'foreigner'. A curious anecdote emerged when some locals tried to explain to me why they did not openly talk to 'outsiders'. In 2004 a rumour spread in town following the two visits of a high-ranking American official to the Deosai plains, an uninhabited plateau of 4,000 metres close to the Indian border and also not far from China. It was believed that the American military was about to occupy the Deosai to watch Chinese activities in the area.

46. Nick Vaughan-Williams, *Border Politics: The Limits of Sovereign Power* (Edinburgh: Edinburgh University Press 2009) p. 74.

47. They mainly referred to the Northern Light Infantry. The recruitment of locals in the army is also referred to in Stöber (note 29) p. 398.

48. Several interviewees have reported the role of mediator played by the religious leaders in moments of local unrest. For instance, during an episode of sectarian violence in Gilgit in 2005 that also spread to Skardu, certain local youths were imprisoned by the army. A section of the population grew angry and demonstrated in the streets to ask for the release of the boys. Apparently, the religious leaders interceded with the army and the problem was finally solved.

49. Henk Van Houtum, 'The Geopolitics of Borders and Boundaries', *Geopolitics* 10/4 (2005) p. 674.

50. The Pakistani administration is the main employer in the area. This seems to be a common feature of the entire disputed area between India and Pakistan.

51. According to 1998 Census, the literacy rate was 33.89% (Male 50.99%, Female 14.02%); Government of Pakistan, *Census Report of Baltistan* (note 26) pp. 29–31.

52. Sengge Thsering (note 38). Attitudes toward language were also explored in the interviews because language is a powerful instrument of power that can shape identity.

53. Taqi Akhunzada, 'Gilani Announces Uplift Projects for Gilgit–Baltistan', *The News*, 11 Nov. 2009, also, Government of Pakistan, Press Information Department, 'Wattoo for Expediting Development Projects in Gilgit–Baltistan', *Press Release* 215, 6 Feb. 2010, available at <http://www.pid.gov.pk/press16-02-2010.htm>, accessed 28 June 2010.

54. A similar policy seems to be taking place in the Gilgit region, after the demands of local trade associations to lift impediments and to facilitate trade with the neighbouring region of China. Northern Areas Chamber of Commerce & Industry, Gilgit (NACCI), 'Proposal for the Economic Development of the Northern Areas' (n.d.); Pakistan Peoples Party, 'The Last Hope of Gilgit-Baltistan'. Both documents were signed by Mr. Shehbaz Khan, advocate, former president of PPP in Gilgit and Chairman of the NACCI.

55. Ken Iain Macdonald, 'Memories of Tibet: Transnationalism, Transculturation, and the Production of Cultural Identity in Northern Pakistan', *India Review* 5/2 (April 2006) pp. 190–219.

56. At the time of research, the Chinese virtually stopped their reconstruction of the Karakoram highway because of security reasons, except for some areas in Gilgit. The enlargement of the Skardu–Gilgit road is expected to start once the highway work is completed. Interestingly, the Chinese government has also expressed its interest in linking Xinjiang and Gilgit by rail, a rather controversial project.

57. Interview with the spokesman of the Marafi Foundation, Skardu, 8 Sep. 2009. This NGO is active in providing vocational training to workers involved in these projects.

Towards a Multiperspectival Study of Borders

CHRIS RUMFORD

Department of Politics and International Relations, Royal Holloway,
University of London, UK

The paper develops a non-state centric approach to the study of borders, building upon Balibar's 'borders are everywhere' thesis. It offers a critique of the assumption of consensus (mutual recognition of borders) in border studies. It is argued that borders do not have to be visible to all in order to be effective. The case for a multiperspectival border studies is then outlined: borders cannot be properly understood from a single privileged vantage point and bordering processes can be interpreted differently from different perspectives. A key dimension of a multiperspectival approach to border studies is examined in detail: borderwork, societal bordering activity undertaken by citizens. This is explored at several UK sites in order to demonstrate the ways in which borders are not always the project of the state, that they can exist for some (but not all), and can link people to the world beyond the 'local' border.

INTRODUCTION

The 'Lines in the Sand?' agenda[1] has inspired the arguments for a multiperspectival study of borders outlined in this paper, which simultaneously advances the critical border studies agenda, and, at the same time, offers a critique of the 'Lines in the Sand?' project. As Parker and Vaughan-Williams note there is a real need to be critical of the time-honored idea that borders take the form of a line and that they are the property of the state (and located at its outer edges). This paper develops the 'Lines in the Sand?' agenda and notes that a particularly interesting thing about borders in the contemporary context is that they are often constructed in new ways, in a variety of locations, by diverse types of people. This means that looking afresh at some basic what, where and who questions is an important part of the Critical Border Studies agenda. Additionally, there is a case to be made for a broader Critical Border Studies agenda than exists at present. There is certainly every reason to phrase the study of borders in a more inclusive genuinely multi-disciplinary language. The 'Lines in the Sand?' document speaks to us in the language of political philosophy and this may restrict its audience in a way not intended by the authors. The present paper seeks to broaden the purview of Critical Border Studies by drawing upon a different range of disciplinary associations. It also aims to take seriously one of the stated aims of 'Lines in the Sand?': to understand the 'changing reality of borders'.[2] While 'Lines in the Sand?' does not have too much to say about how we might achieve this, this paper seeks to come to terms with the changing nature of borders, and in doing so attempts an alternative perspective on understanding borders.

Acknowledging the contribution of Balibar[3] to the field of enquiry by taking seriously the idea that 'borders are everywhere'[4] an essential component of the argument advanced here is that we should dispense with an exclusive nation-state frame when studying the border. The diffusion of borders traced by Balibar suggests not simply that 'national edges'[5] are spread more thinly across a territory, but that very different types of borders are also emerging. To investigate these 'different borders' we should endeavour to develop an approach which does not rely on the assumption that important borders are always state borders, representing divisions, and more importantly which does not reinforce the tendency to always 'see like a state' when viewing borders.[6] An approach which views the border as an instrument of exclusion constructed between two nation-states (a state centric view) has ready-made answers to questions such as 'What constitutes a border?', 'Where are borders to be found?', and 'Who is doing the bordering?' Rather, what is required, it is argued, is a multiperspectival border studies. Only then will we not be obliged to always 'see like a state' when viewing borders. In order to develop a multiperspectival border studies it is necessary to challenge some of the core assumptions associated with the study of borders, for example that (state) borders require mutual recognition (consensus) in order to exist and function, and that for a border to work properly it must be visible (to all).

Before critiquing the assumed consensus and visibility of borders it is necessary to elucidate the sort of research agenda promised by a multiperspectival border studies and the benefits that it will bring. It is also necessary to say something about the origins of this agenda and what has inspired it. I have already noted that the Critical Border Studies envisaged by the 'Lines in the Sand?' document has inspired this paper. In fact, the development of the multiperspectival borders thesis has been stimulated by an array of influences originating from several academic disciplines all of which have questioned why the study of borders is conducted in a certain way. The following can be singled out in a brief account. Newman and Paasi[7] have highlighted the connectivity of borders, thereby helping shift the discussion of borders away from an exclusive concern with division (a staple of state-centric border studies). More importantly perhaps in the present context they have recognised that locals do not necessarily see borders in the same way as governments.[8]. Sibley[9] understands borders as societal and notes that groups use borders symbolically to further their own ends (e.g., securing sociospatial/ethnic homogeneity). In parallel with Newman and Paasi's intervention, Balibar is the non-geographer who has done more than anyone to challenge geostrategic assumptions about the nature of borders. His agenda-setting work is reflected in the themes outlined by the 'Lines in the Sand?' authors. More recently, Ulrich Beck[10] has recast borders, rather provocatively, as 'mobile patterns that facilitate overlapping loyalties', probably the most fundamental re-imagining of the core function of borders yet encountered. A multiperspectival border studies is indebted to the innovative agendas proposed by these scholars and also aspires to emulate the boldness of their vision; the argument for doing border studies differently is still worth making.

This paper aims to demonstrate, through an exposition of a multiperspectival border studies, the case for studying borders differently. This involves generating a new set of questions about borders which do not presume that the borders in questions are necessarily seen as borders by all concerned, or in the same way. Newman and Paasi[11] include the following in their agenda for border studies: the need to acknowledge alternative boundary narratives from within different cultural traditions. It may be the case that alternative boundary narratives exist also *within* common cultural traditions. We do not have to step outside of our own culture in order to discover different accounts of borders. For example, one feature of the border studies literature in recent years has been the inclusion of 'auto-ethnographies' of borders.[12] Seeing the border from the perspective of Khosravi's 'illegal traveller' is an important dimension of a rounded border studies. But adding this perspective to a statist perspective and, say, a global or geopolitical perspective on borders, does not add up to a multiperspectival border studies. Framing borders as sites of 'cultural encounters'[13] is central to a multiperspectival border studies. This accords with Amin et al.'s[14] idea that territories should be seen as relational spaces in which 'all kinds of unlike things can knock up against each other in all kinds of ways'. Borders as sites of cultural encounter also makes it easier to study borders diffused throughout society and constructed/shifted by a whole range of actors. If the aim is to re-frame borders as cultural encounters rather than simply mechanisms of division then a key step is to undermine the underlying assumption of consensus – that borders have to be recognised as divisionary by all concerned – which does exist in border studies, and argued here to be the biggest factor inhibiting the development of a multiperspectival border studies.

THE PROBLEM OF CONSENSUS

The assumption of consensus is a key feature of the study of national (state) borders and is most evident for example when two countries deploy troops on both sides of a common border, or when the borders of a new nation-state gain international recognition (or are disputed), or when a conflict arises over territorial rights in a contested border region. Consensus is implicit when interested parties are all drawing the border in the same place on the same map of the world. Consensus is also evident when borders become accepted as 'world defining' borders; the 'Iron Curtain', the Mexico-US border ('tortilla curtain'), and the Israel-Palestine border are all widely thought to 'divide the world' in some sense. National borders, as with national sovereignty, rely upon the acknowledgement of others in order to become legitimate. Border disputes may occasion war but they also denote consensus: that it is a common border that is being disputed. On this line of thinking borders 'work' because more than one party recognises the existence, location and form of the border (even if that recognition takes the form of contestation). The logic of consensus is also reproduced in studies which emphasise bordering as a process rather than as 'lines in the sand'. Consider the following statement, which appears in a recent discussion of the changing nature of borders. 'Borders have become predominantly interpreted as the communication of practices, as stories narrated by some and contested by others'.[15] There is much to agree with in this formulation, which draws attention to the way in which borders can work to connect as well as divide.[16] The point to highlight in the context of understanding consensus is the way in which borders require mutual recognition, 'narrated by some and contested by others', and need to be recognised by all parties *as borders* in order to function. Consensus inheres in the recognition of the existence of the border, not agreement over its purpose and function.

During the Cold War everyone in Europe would have known, and agreed upon, where the borders of divided Europe were to be found, and which borders were the most important ones to the antagonistic blocs: the militarised lines dividing Germany and Cyprus, for example.[17] This consensus was not simply a product of the territorial fixity or physical presence of those borders or the political and military resources devoted to inscribing them upon the European landscape. The borders that divided Europe also divided the world; they marked the geopolitical division between East and West. There existed Cold War consensus on the global significance of borders, encapsulated in the following terms: 'While all borders are important, some borders are more important than others'.[18] For Balibar the fact that a border can have a significance that goes beyond its ability to mark territory in a particular location is termed 'overdetermination'.[19] For example, the border which separated West Germany from East Germany during the Cold

War was a national border and also a symbolic border between the Western world and the Eastern bloc whose representation took the form of an 'Iron Curtain'. The Iron Curtain both divided Europe, and, because this Cold War division was exported to other parts of the world, it was an overdetermined border, also working to signify a global division. Borders serve 'not only to separate particularities, but always also at the same time, in order to fulfill this "local" function, to "partition the world" to configure it. . . . Every map in this sense is always a world map, for it represents a "part of the world"'.[20] On this line of thinking, a national border is not always only a border between two states: local borders can also signify global divisions. In the contemporary context the legacy of such overdeterminations continue to be important. The 'Green Line' separating Northern Cyprus and the Republic of Cyprus has been reinforced by a new border between the EU and non-EU member states. The 'Green Line' now not only divides an island but demarcates EU from non-EU and as such represents a new kind of division.

The notion of overdetermination is proposed by Balibar as a way of explaining why some borders are deemed more important than others. It helps us understand why some borders have a symbolic significance which exceeds any local importance. According to Balibar the overdetermined border calls down civilisational differences and in that sense brings a 'world of difference' to bear on local demarcations.[21] But overdetermination is also a form of consensus-generation. A border that has a significance beyond the local requires a high degree of consensus as to its importance. However, this consensus is constructed at a remove from the actual border in question and is not related to any features of the border itself, except its ability to symbolise difference.

In the contemporary context far less consensus exists on what constitutes a border, where borders are to be found, or which borders are the most important. This is partly because we are no longer constrained to inhabit particular world views within which the symbolic meaning of borders are organised as 'givens'. It is also partly because important borders are no longer only nation-state borders. For example, the EU is active in establishing and shifting borders in Europe and indeed defining where Europe's border is located. The patrols carried out by Frontex, off the coast of Africa operationalise a border which is not mutually agreed by those on either side of it. The 'Frontex border' is a new sort of flexible border, deployed whenever and wherever it is needed and works to constitute the EU border as a world-defining frontier – the Great Wall of Europe, in Balibar's[22] formulation – projected some distance from the borders of EU member states. In the light of these developments, persisting with forms of border thinking which rely upon the idea that borders are easily identifiable, recognised by all parties, and that they are visible for all to see – and can be easily drawn on a map – will obscure key dimensions of bordering processes. It is for these reasons that an approach to borders and bordering which is sensitive to the multiplicity of borders that exist, their bespoke nature, and the range of actors who create them – a multiperspectival study of borders – holds much promise.

When we take seriously the idea that 'borders are everywhere' we must dispense with the assumption that consensus must exist. However, such assumptions have deep roots. Aristotle believed that there was an optimum size for a nation: its borders should be visible from a high point in the centre. This high point would be a city whose position would allow the whole territory to 'be taken in at a single view'[23] because 'in a country that can easily be surveyed it is easy to bring up assistance at any point'.[24] For Aristotle, the high point from which the territory can be 'taken in' or viewed is necessary for the security and military defence of the territory; 'a country which is easily seen can be easily protected'.[25] Military logic aside, Aristotle's 'high point' perspective on territorial rule has an enduring legacy: the idea that borders must be visible in order to function. van Schendel[26] holds that 'a border that is not visible to all has failed its purpose'. This paper questions the adequacy of understandings of borders which rely upon the assumption that borders must be visible in order to function.

It is certainly the case that the invisibility of (some) borders, including national state borders, is deemed desirable (by some). For example, in the last few years the UK government has invested heavily in e-borders, offshore borders, and juxtaposed borders,[27] developments designed to ensure that UK borders are 'open to business but closed to terrorists and traffickers'. The location of these borders remains invisible to many; not those attempting to cross them, for whom they are palpable, but certainly many living within these invisible borders. The maintenance of EU borders by Frontex, the EU borders agency, would be another good example (boat patrols in the Mediterranean and along the coast of West Africa), designed to contribute to a formidable physical barrier to those beyond the EU's border while not necessarily registering in the consciousness of, or impacting on, those living on the inside. Borders can be highly selective and work so as to render them invisible to the majority of the population, who do not recognise the border as a border, or for whom no such border is deemed to exist.

In order to study borders beyond assumptions of visibility and consensus it is argued that we must dispense with Aristotle's 'high point' from which everything, including borders, can be rendered visible and knowable. But this is easier said than done. The 'global frame' through which we must view borders now actually encourages 'high point' thinking as it is widely held that global space can be viewed in totality (one consequence of seeing the world as a single place). In other words, 'space is no longer that of a single country ... but that of the world as a whole'.[28] What we are witnessing, according to Elden, is a geographical extension of a pre-existing territorial calculus rather than a change in the way space is conceived. That this 'abstract space is now extended to the globe' means that the world 'can be divided, or ordered as whole'.[29] Another good example of a monoperspective on globality is the popularity of the idea of 'empire' associated with the work of Hardt and Negri[30] but also taken up recently in different ways by others, for example Zielonka[31] and Beck and Grande.[32] What these very different accounts of empire have in common is that they all posit the existence of a 'high point' from which perspective the novel spatiality of empire can be seen to have unity.[33] The idea of empire, while promising a novel understanding of space under conditions of globalisation, actually works to suggest that global spaces are integrated spaces given cohesion by the privileged vantage point from which the new imperial domain can be viewed.

RESOURCES FOR A MULTIPERSPECTIVAL BORDER STUDIES

The term multiperspectival requires some background and explanation. It has its origins in the idea that contemporary transformations cannot be properly understood from a single privileged vantage point and that events, processes, and actors can be interpreted differently from different perspectives.[34] In discussing the development of the modern state, Ruggie demonstrates that the Renaissance technique of developing a single perspective in art was quickly translated into state-craft, and territory became viewed from a single vantage point. In the world of nation-states, political space came to be defined as it appeared from a single fixed viewpoint (similar to Aristotle's 'high point'). On Ruggie's argument, the concept of sovereignty became 'the doctrinal counterpart of the application of single-point perspectival forms to the spatial organization of politics'.[35] In this way, Ruggie accounts for the development of the monoperspectival viewpoint associated with the politics of modernity, against which he offers us the European Union as possibly the 'first multiperspectival polity' to emerge since the advent of the modern era. 'Network Europe' has allowed for the creation of multiple perspectives as territorial nation-states now exist alongside non-territorial networks which do not necessarily fit together to form an integrated whole.[36] Ruggie's work opens up the possibility that different forms of linkages and flows can generate different perspectives on spatial integration/non-integration. Arjun Appadurai's multiperspectivalism, developed in his celebrated paper 'Disjuncture and difference in the global cultural economy',[37] is relevant in this context. He explores the ways in which the 'world in motion' associated with globalisation prevents cultural flows from crystallising into objective relations. For Appadurai 'scapes' (components of global cultural flows) do not look the same from every angle. 'They are deeply perspectival constructs, inflected very much by the historical, linguistic and political situatedness of different sorts of actors: nation-states, multinationals, diasporic communities, as well as sub-national grouping and movements (whether religious, political or economic), and even intimate face-to-face groups, such as villages, neighborhoods and families'.[38] In another context, Haraway reminds us that we should not romanticise or appropriate 'the vision of the less powerful while claiming to see from their position' in our attempts to 'see from the peripheries'.[39] The aim of a multiperspectival border studies is not to occupy the 'standpoint of the subjugated', which is but one perspective. Multiperspectivalism in this case is not synonymous with 'bottom up', although it may incorporate it. Moreover, the borders in question are by no means always at the periphery. A multiperspectival border studies is concerned with borders that are diffused throughout society as well as those at the edges.

Rajaram and Grundy-Warr[40] bring together the themes of multiperspectivalism, territory, and individual experience to bear on the study of borders in their edited collection *Borderscapes*. The idea of 'borderscapes' allows for the 'study of the border as mobile, perspectival, and relational',[41] thus pointing in the direction of a multiperspectival border studies. They hold that 'the border is a landscape of competing meanings'[42] thereby acknowledging the need to move 'beyond consensus'. They recognise the possibility that some borders may be invisible: 'Knowledge operates by making perceptible that which has reason to be seen . . . while making imperceptible that which has no reason to be seen'.[43] The role of borderwork – the ability of ordinary people to construct borders (see below) – is also alluded to with the acknowledgement that the state does not exhaust the meaning of the border. The work of Rajaram and Grundy-Warr has many affinities with the multiperspectival border studies advanced in this paper. However, they place continuing emphasis on the role of the state in processes of bordering. Borderwork stands at the centre of a multiperspectival border studies but Rajaram and Grudy-Warr, in contrast, gravitate more towards a study of national borders, and borderscapes are cast in relation to state borders. So for example while different interpretations of the border are possible it is the state border that is being contested rather than Balibar's diffused borders. Likewise, the border may be more complex than hitherto realised but the border in question is still a 'zone between states'.[44]

A multiperspectival border studies builds upon Balibar's innovations in studying borders, particularly the idea that borders exist at multiple sites within and between polities, that they mean different things to different people, and work differently on different groups. A multiperspectival border studies goes further though by drawing attention to the fact that some borders remain invisible, not usually to those on the outside but those living within, and that some borders exist for some people and not others. Rajaram and Grundy-Warr also make a significant contribution by acknowledging that borders can be viewed from a multiplicity of (sometimes contradictory) perspectives. These ideas are developed in this paper in an important new direction. Rather than 'seeing like a state' a multiperspectival border studies encourages us to 'see like a border,' or at least to encourage 'border seeing' as a counterpart to Mignolo's 'border thinking'.[45] This involves more than a recognition that it is possible to view a border from both sides, which simply reproduces the 'consensus' view of borders discussed above. Rather than 'looking both ways' across a border we need to aspire to look from the border and more importantly 'see like a border.' These ideas will be developed in the following section.

BORDERS BEYOND CONSENSUS

Wastl-Walter[46] writes that borders 'are manifested in diverse ways, and have various functions and roles. They can be material or non-material and may appear in the form of a barbed-wire fence, a brick wall, a door, a heavily armed border guard or as symbolic boundaries'. This is a bold attempt to represent the multiplicity of forms that borders can take, and she adds that 'while a brick wall may represent security for some, for others, it may be a symbol of suppression'. A multiperspectival border studies seeks to take these ideas further and incorporate yet further perspectives on, and understandings of, borders. There are several key components of a multiperspectival border studies, in addition to the idea that borders do not always need to be visible, or constituted through consensus. First, the potential of borders to connect as well as divide and constitute what Rovisco[47] terms 'sites of cultural encounter'. Second, the ability to 'see like a border'. Third, what I am calling borderwork, the ability of ordinary people to construct borders.

Borders as Cultural Encounters

The connective potential of borders has become a key theme in border studies in recent times, particularly in the context of borders working as both barriers and gateways, especially in cases where national borders are required to be both open for business and closed to terrorists and traffickers. It is in this context that we can understand Konrad and Nicol's idea of the Canada-US borderland, 'a zone of interaction where people on one side of the border share values, beliefs, feelings and expectations with people on the other side of the border'.[48] For Konrad and Nicol in the borderland the connectedness of the territory on either side of the border is emphasised: the borderland is a 'zone of interaction'.[49] However, the concept of the borderland is not the only way in which the networking potential of borders is emphasised.

The following example is illustrative. Border monuments and public art situated on or near borders are increasingly designed to celebrate cultural encounters and/or the ability of borders to connect as well as divide. Examples of such border monuments include the Schengen monument to a 'borderless Europe', the Dreilanderpunkt at Aachen, the Statue of Humanity on the Turkey/Armenia border, and the Star of Caledonia on the English/Scottish border. We can note the post-national nature of these monuments, contrasting this with earlier nationalistic attempts to monumentalise the border-as-division. Monuments have long been used by political elites to claim space and to mark the border as a division between proximate national realms.[50] Novel ways of monumentalising Europe's borders help generate multiple perspectives on borders. Monuments can 'communicate a range of values and meanings – meanings that vary based on the audience and the cultural and political context in which they are read'.[51] In other words, border monuments invite a multiperspectival study of borders and provide an important opportunity for studying the multiple interpretations of any border. A good example of the connectivity through the monumentalisation of the border is the 'Star of Caledonia' monument planned to be built on the Scottish/English border. In 2010 architect Cecil Balmond was announced by the Gretna Landmark Trust as the winner of a competition to design a public monument 'that celebrates and explores the border crossing [from England] into Scotland at Gretna'.[52] His winning design, 'The Star of Caledonia' will sit on the England-Scotland border on the A74 road at Gretna and will 'mark the point where the two nations meet'.[53] In the architect's own vision for the monument the theme of connectivity is very much to the fore. 'The Star of Caledonia is a welcome; its kinetic form and light paths a constant trace of Scotland's power of invention.'[54] It is 'designed to be welcoming to the people coming to Scotland.'[55] Its 'welcoming' function is only one dimension of its potential for connectivity: 'A border offers identity but one that is enriched by neighbours, so that it's not so much a line of separation as a local set of interconnected values.'[56] Reinforcing the theme of connectivity, the artist Andy Goldsworthy, commissioned by the Landmark Trust, is working on a complementary project, a walkway from Gretna to Canonbie, which will pass the monument and will incorporative a zig-zag design to show the knitting together of the two countries at the border.[57]

Seeing Like a Border

Although border scholars acknowledge that borders can be diffused throughout society there is still a tendency to look at borders from the perspective of the state, by considering for example the extent to which the development of borderlands is compatible with conventional notions of securitised borders. But what would happen if we were to adopt a different, non-state perspective? Rather than 'seeing like a state' what would it mean to 'see like a border'? 'Seeing like a border' shifts the emphasis in border studies in several important ways. First, as borders can be found 'wherever selective controls are to be found'[58] 'seeing like a border' does not equate to 'being on the outside and looking in' (or looking out from the watchtower to the wilderness beyond). In aspiring to 'see like a border' we must recognise the constitutive nature of borders in social and political life. Second, borders are not necessarily always working in the service of the state. When 'seeing like a state' one is committed to seeing borders as lines of securitised defence. Borders do not always conform to this model. In a desire to shore up what may be perceived as the ineffectual borders of the nation-state people may engage in 'local' bordering activity designed to enhance status or regulate mobility; gated communities, respect zones, 'resilient' communities of CCTV watching citizens. In such ways our anxieties and insecurities constrain us to 'see like a border.' Third, 'seeing like a border' does not necessarily mean identifying with the subaltern, the dispossessed, the downtrodden, the marginal. The border may be the project of those seeking to gain further advantage in society: entrepreneurs or affluent citizens, for example. Why remain passive in the face of other peoples' borders when you can obtain advantage by becoming a proactive borderer? If borders are networked throughout society and more and more people can participate in bordering activity, then the capacity to make or undo borders becomes a major source of political capital (see below). 'Seeing like a border' means taking into account perspectives from those at, on, or shaping the border, and this constituency is increasingly large and diverse.

Borderwork

It is possible to talk about the 'cosmopolitanization' of borders[59] wherein actors other than the state can be involved in bordering activity, the EU being one such actor. In addition, and more important in the context of this paper, ordinary people (citizens, non-citizens) are increasingly active in constructing, shifting, or even erasing borders. Citizens, entrepreneurs, and 'civil society' actors, amongst others, can engage in bordering, or what is here termed borderwork, the efforts of ordinary people leading to the construction, dismantling, or shifting of borders. The borders concerned are not necessarily those (at the edges) of the nation-state; they can be found at a range of sites throughout society: in towns and cities, in local neighbourhoods, in the countryside.[60] It should be noted that borderwork does not necessarily result in borders that enhance national security but it provides borderworkers with new political and/or economic opportunities: borders work to 'strengthen some people while disempowering others'.[61] The importance of borderwork is that it causes us to rethink the issue of who is responsible for making, dismantling and shifting borders, rather than rely upon the assumption that this is exclusively the business of the state. It also introduces us to a world of bordering which is not governed by consensus: there is no guarantee that the borders constructed by borderworkers will be recognised by everyone.

The role that ordinary people play in the construction of borders is under-represented in the border studies literature.[62] This statement requires further qualification. I am particularly concerned with the ways in which people construct, shift and dismantle physical borders. Constructing/dismantling borders rather than utilising existing borders: this is an important distinction. There have been many studies examining the ways in which people become involved in the business of the border or take advantage of the opportunities that borders offer: trafficking, smuggling, and other criminal activity[63] and tourism,[64] for example, but this literature confirms that the actors involved in border-crossing activity require the (state) border in order to function; they benefit from the border but do not seek to dismantle, shift, or construct it anew. Borderwork, as outlined here, centres on the ability of ordinary people to make borders, not the ability of people to opportunistically use borders to reinforce identity or seek material gain. There are many examples of the latter in the border studies literature: the work of Heymans, Herbet, Megoran, Nevins and Vila all demonstrate that people can utilise borders and/or draw upon borders in a particular way. There are other examples of this important work. Anzaldua[65] advances the idea that the borderlands-inhabiting, hybrid 'mestiza' subverts the border in order to resist the division of the mexicana community. Conversely, Wright's[66] 'maquiladora mestiza' experiences the border in a very different way, taking advantage of the border's ability to divide and fragment in order to increase social and economic standing: the border works to differentiate groups and individuals, and those in a position to take advantage of this can benefit at the expense of others. However, none of the authors mentioned above contribute exactly to our understanding of borderwork, as specified here.

Citizens increasingly make, shift and dismantle borders of all kinds, for example knocking down the Berlin Wall, building 'peace walls' in Northern Ireland,[67] and, in an example from an earlier period, constructing the Cutteslowe Walls to exclude the working classes from a middle-class housing development in Oxford in the 1930s.[68] In the contemporary context, Berwick-upon-Tweed is a prime borderworking site, but not because of the 'rebordering' which has occurred between England and Scotland in recent years, as a result of the devolved powers to the Scottish parliament and the recent attempts by some nationalist activists in the community to 'redraw' the Scottish border around Berwick. The nationalist dimension to the rebordering of Berwick is far less significant than the incredibly rich networking opportunities which borderwork generates. Berwick is a 'traditional' border which finds itself at the hub of a large amount of non-traditional borderwork activity. Constructing the border, not as a national divide between England and Scotland but as a gateway to the wider world is the thrust of local borderworking activity. Re-defining the border between England and Scotland would be an example of consensus bordering. Constructing the border as a staging post for global encounters is the product of a narrower, more exclusive, non-consensual form of borderwork. Examples of Berwick's embrace of international networks include membership of the 'slow cities' movement (Cittaslow), one of the first UK towns to gain this recognition.[69] Borderwork – the marking and re-marking of the border by ordinary people – lifts Berwick out of its local context and provides a link to the wider world.

A focus on borderwork, as one dimension of a multiperspectival border studies, shifts the debate on the contemporary nature of borders away from an association of borders and bordering with the state. It builds upon the insights that borders can be located 'away from the border' and dispersed throughout society and recognises that in many instances the construction of a border 'away from the border' may mean that borderwork is not necessarily working to enhance national security.[70] Borderwork alerts us to the wide variety of bordering activity that may exist, the diversity of interests at work in this bordering, and the varied spaces within which this activity occurs (and which can result from this activity). Borderwork is at the heart of the multiperspectival border studies approach: bordering processes which do not require consensus; borders which may be invisible to many, but extremely pertinent to a few; border as connective tissue – 'dividing what is similar, connecting what is different'[71]; and ordinary people (citizens) engaging in bordering activity.

CONCLUSION

A multiperspectival border studies is proposed as an alternative to the conventional focus on nation-state borders with its restricted monoperspective – or view from the 'brilliant space platforms of the powerful', in Haraway's[72] phrase – and its corollary, the assumption of consensus and visibility. The many shifts in border studies at work over the past decade or so have transformed the way we study borders, both in terms of shifting the focus away from the edges of a polity and also in the sense that border studies now has ambitions to greater interdisciplinary dialogue.[73] The argument here is that although these shifts are valuable, they are not by themselves sufficient. For example, the spatiality of borders which has been one key feature of the shifts has led to a heightened interest in the borderland as an object of study.[74] We can study the border as a region or zone which can extend far beyond the borderline (as with Konrad and Nicol's idea that Canada is a borderland stretching northward from the US-Canada border). But studying the borderland rather than the borderline does not necessarily challenge the need to 'see like a state' nor does it alter the perception that the borders of nation-states are the most important borders to study.

Importantly, a multiperspectival border studies places borders more centrally in relation to research on social and political transformations in the contemporary world and treats the border as an object of study in its own right rather than subsumed to national sovereignty or state security. The importance of borders seen in terms other than as a frontline of national defence has begun to emerge with the recent wave of interest in the airport, for example.[75] In this literature we can find the idea that the border can be studied outside of a narrow nation-state context; in the case of the airport the global connectivity of these 'non spaces'[76] is arguably of much greater importance. If a multiperspectival border studies is the ambition, freeing the border from an intrinsic relation to the nation-state is an important first step.

ACKNOWLEDGEMENTS

I am grateful for the comments of an anonymous referee on an earlier version of this paper.

NOTES

1. N. Parker, L. Bialasiewicz, S. Bulmer, B. Carver, R. Durie, J. Heathershaw, H. Van Houtum, et al., 'Lines in the Sand? Towards an Agenda for Critical Border Studies', *Geopolitics* 14/3 (2009) pp. 582–587.
2. Ibid., p. 583.
3. E. Balibar, *Politics and the Other Scene* (London: Verso 2002); E. Balibar, *We, the People of Europe? Reflections on Transnational Citizenship* (Princeton: Princeton University Press 2004); E. Balibar, 'Europe as Borderland', The Alexander von Humboldt Lecture in Human Geography, Institute for Human Geography, Universiteit Nijmegen, The Netherlands, 24 Nov. 2004, available at <www.ru.nl/socgeo/colloquium/Europe%20as%20Borderland.pdf>.
4. See A. Paasi, 'A Border Theory: An Unattainable Dream or a Realistic Aim for Border Scholars', in D. Wastl-Walter (ed.), *The Ashgate Research Companion to Border Studies* (Farnham: Ashgate Press 2011) pp. 22–23.
5. On the border as an 'edge concept' see V. Konrad and H. Nicol, *Beyond Walls: Re-Inventing the Canada-United States Borderlands* (Aldershot: Ashgate 2008) (especially ch. 2).
6. I. Abraham and W. van Schendel, 'Introduction: The Making of Illicitness', in W. van Schendel and I. Abraham (eds.), *Illicit Flows and Criminal Things: States, Borders, and the Other Side of Globalization* (Bloomington: Indiana University Press 2005) p. 6; J. Scott, *Seeing Like a State: How Certain Schemes to Improve the Human Condition Have Failed* (New Haven, CT: Yale University Press 1998).
7. D. Newman and A. Paasi, 'Fences and Neighbours in the Postmodern World: Boundary Narratives in Political Geography', *Progress in Human Geography* 22/2 (1998) pp. 186–207.
8. Ibid., p. 195.
9. D. Sibley, *Geographies of Exclusion* (London: Routledge 1995).
10. U. Beck, *What is Globalization?* (Cambridge: Polity Press 2000) pp. 51–52.
11. Newman and Paasi (note 7) p. 200.
12. Paasi (note 4) p. 16. Good examples include S. Khosravi, *Illegal Traveller: An Auto-Ethnography of Borders*, (Houndmills: Palgrave 2010); and G. Kapllani, *A Short Border Handbook* (London: Portobello Books 2009).
13. M. Rovisco, 'Reframing Europe and the Global: Conceptualizing the Border in Cultural Encounters', *Environment and Planning D: Society and Space* 28/6 (2010) pp. 1015–1030.
14. A. Amin, D. Massey, and N. Thrift, *Decentering the National: A Radical Approach to Regional Equality* (London: Catalyst 2003) p. 6.

15. N. DelSordi and D. Jacobson, 'Borders', in J. A. Scholte and R. Robertson (eds.), *Encyclopedia of Globalization Volume 1 A–E* (London: Routledge 2007) p. 100.

16. G. Simmel, 'The Bridge and the Door', *Theory, Culture and Society* 11/1 (1994) pp. 5–10.

17. This paper addresses contemporary Europe first and foremost and does not suggest that multiperspectivalism is equally grounded in all cultures, all places, all times.

18. E. Zureik and M. Salter, 'Global Surveillance and Policing: Borders, Security, Identity – Introduction', in E. Zureik and M. Salter (eds.), *Global Surveillance and Policing: Borders, Security, Identity* (Cullompton: Willan Publishing 2005) p. 1.

19. Balibar, *Politics and the Other Scene* (note 3).

20. Balibar, *We, the people of Europe?* (note 3) pp. 220–221.

21. E. Balibar, 'The Borders of Europe', in P. Cheah and B. Robbins (eds.), *Cosmopolitics: Thinking and Feeling beyond the Nation* (Minneapolis: Minnesota University Press 1998) p. 222.

22. E. Balibar, 'Strangers as Enemies: Further Reflections on the Aporias of Transnational Citizenship', *Globalization Working Papers* 06/4, Institute on Globalization and the Human Condition, McMaster University, Canada (2006), available at <http://globalization.mcmaster.ca/wps/balibar.pdf>.

23. Aristotle, *The Politics* (Cambridge: Cambridge University Press 1996) p. 164.

24. Aristotle, *The Politics* (London: Penguin 1992) p. 406.

25. Aristotle (note 23) p. 164.

26. W. van Schendel, 'How Borderlands, Illicit Flows, and Territorial States Interlock', in W. van Schendel and I. Abraham (eds.), *Illicit Flows and Criminal Things: States, Borders, and the Other Side of Globalization* (Bloomington: Indiana University Press 2005) p. 41.

27. Cabinet Office, 'Security in a Global Hub: Establishing the UK's New Border Arrangements', 2007, available at <www.cabinetoffice.gov.uk/media/cabinetoffice/corp/assets/publications/reports/border_review.pdf>; Home Office, 'Securing the UK Border: Our Vision and Strategy for the Future', 2007, available at <http://www.homeoffice.gov.uk/documents/securing-the-border>; Home Office, 'A Strong New Force at the Border', 2008, available at <www.ukba.homeoffice.gov.uk/sitecontent/documents/managingourborders/astrongnewforceattheborder/strongnewforce.pdf>.

28. S. Elden, 'Missing the Point: Globalization, Deterritorialization and the Space of the World', *Transactions of the Institute of British Geographers* 30/1 (2005) pp. 8–19.

29. Ibid.

30. M. Hardt and A. Negri, *Empire* (Cambridge, MA: Harvard University Press 2000).

31. J. Zielonka, *Europe as Empire: The Nature of the Enlarged European Union* (Oxford: Oxford University Press 2007).

32. U. Beck and E. Grande, *Cosmopolitan Europe* (Cambridge: Polity Press 2007).

33. C. Rumford, *Cosmopolitan Spaces: Europe, Globalization, Theory* (London: Routledge 2008).

34. D. Haraway, 'Situated Knowledges: The Science Question in Feminism and the Privilege of Partial Perspective', in D. Haraway, *Simians, Cyborgs, and Women: The Reinvention of Nature* (London: Free Association Books 1991).

35. J. G. Ruggie, 'Territoriality and Beyond: Problematizing Modernity in International Relations', *International Organization* 47/1 (1993) p. 159.

36. Ibid., p. 172.

37. A. Appadurai, 'Disjuncture and Difference in the Global Cultural Economy', in M. Featherstone (ed.), *Global Culture: Nationalism, Globalization and Modernity* (London: Sage 1990).

38. Ibid., p. 296.

39. Haraway (note 34) p. 191.

40. P. K. Rajaram and C. Grundy-Warr, 'Introduction', in P. K. Rajaram and C. Grundy-Warr (eds.), *Borderscapes: Hidden Geography and Politics at Territory's Edge* (Minneapolis: Minnesota University Press 2007).

41. Ibid., p. x.

42. Ibid., p. xv.

43. Ibid.

44. Ibid., p. x.

45. W. D. Mignolo, 'The Many Faces of Cosmo-Polis: Border Thinking and Critical Cosmopolitanism', *Public Culture* 12/3 (2000) pp. 721–748.

46. D. Wastl-Walter, 'Introduction', in D. Wastl-Walter (ed.), *The Ashgate Research Companion to Border Studies* (Farnham: Ashgate 2011) p. 2.

47. Rovisco (note 13).

48. Konrad and Nicol (note 5) p. 32.
49. Ibid.
50. N. Johnson, 'Cast in Stone: Monuments, Geography, and Nationalism', *Environment and Planning D: Society and Space* 13/1 (1995) pp. 51–65.
51. S. Mains, 'Monumentally Caribbean: Borders, Bodies, and Redemptive City Spaces', *Small Axe* 8/2 (2004) p. 182.
52. Official website blurb: <http://www.gretnalandmark.com/>.
53. M. McLaughlin, 'Is it a Star? Is it a Thistle? No, it's Scotland's New Welcome Sign', *The Scotsman*, 5 July 2011, available at <http://www.scotsman.com/news/Is-it-a-star-Is.6795931.jp>.
54. 'Urban Realm', 5 July 2011, available at <www.urbanrealm.com/news/2996/_%E2%80%98Star_of_Caledonia%E2%80%99_to_adorn_border_with_England.html>.
55. Balmond quoted on *BBC News*, 5 July 2011.
56. Balmond, quoted in 'Selection Finalists Announced for Iconic Scottish Landmark', 15 Dec. 2010; *Dumfries and Galloway Arts Press Release*, available at <http://www.gretnalandmark.com/uploads/downloads/PRSelectionLandmark.pdf>.
57. S. Liptrott, 'Star of Caledonia to Shine as Scotland's World Icon at Gretna', *Dumfries and Galloway Standard*, 6 July 2011, available at <http://www.dgstandard.co.uk/dumfries-news/local-news-dumfries/local-news-dumfriesshire/2011/07/06/star-of-caledonia-to-shine-as-scotland-s-world-icon-at-gretna-51311-28998268/>.
58. Balibar, *Politics and the Other Scene* (note 3), pp. 84–85)
59. C. Rumford, 'Does Europe Have Cosmopolitan Borders?', *Globalizations* 4/3 (2007) pp. 327–339.
60. L. Amoore, S. Marmura, and M. Salter, 'Editorial: Smart Borders and Mobilities: Spaces, Zones, Enclosures', *Surveillance & Society* 5/2 (2008) pp. 96–101; Multiplicity, 'Borders: The Other Side of Globalisation', in S. McQuire and N. Papastergiadis (eds.), *Empires, Ruins + Networks: The Transcultural Agenda in Art* (London: Rivers Oram Press 2005).
61. Van Schendel, 'How Borderlands' (note 26) p. 57.
62. C. Rumford, 'Introduction: Citizens and Borderwork in Europe', *Space and Polity* 12/1 (2008b) pp. 1–12.
63. Abraham and van Schendel (note 6); M. Naim, *Illicit: How Smugglers, Traffickers and Copycats are Hijacking the Global Economy* (London: Heinemann 2006).
64. H. Donnan and T. Wilson, *Borders: Frontiers and Identity, Nation and State* (Oxford: Berg 1999).
65. G. Anzaldua, *Borderlands/La Frontera: The New Mestiza*, 3rd ed. (San Francisco: Aunt Lute Books 2007).
66. M. Wright, 'Maquiladora Mestizas and a Feminist Border Politics: Revisiting Anzaldua', in U. Narayan and S. Harding (eds.), *Decentering the Centre: Philosophy for a Multicultural, Postcolonial, and Feminist World* (Bloomington: Indiana University Press 2000).
67. T. Diez and K. Hayward, 'Reconfiguring Spaces of Conflict: Northern Ireland and the Impact of European Integration', *Space and Polity* 12/1 (2008) pp. 1–12.
68. P. Collinson, *The Cutteslowe Walls: A Study On Social Class* (London: Faber and Faber 1963).
69. Ludlow in Shropshire was the first town in the UK to be admitted to Cittaslow (2003), Alysham in Norfolk was the second and Diss, also in Norfolk, was the third. Mold became the first Cittaslow in Wales (2006), and Perth the first in Scotland in 2007.
70. In extreme cases borderwork may take the form of vigilantism: see A. Sen and D. Pratten, 'Global Vigilantes: Perspectives on Justice and Violence', in A. Sen and D. Pratten (eds.), *Global Vigilantes* (London: Hurst and Co. 2008). In some instances, for example the 'Minutemen' patrols along the US/Mexico border, vigilantism is a form of borderwork which claims to *enhance* national security.
71. Van Schendel, 'How Borderlands' (note 26) p. 44; Simmel (note 16) p. 1.
72. Haraway (note 34) pp. 190–191.
73. D. Newman, 'Borders and Bordering: Interdisciplinary Dialogue', *European Journal of Social Theory* 9/2 (2006) pp. 171–186.
74. W. van Schendel, *The Bengal Borderland: Beyond State and Nation in South Asia* (London: Anthem Press 2004); Konrad and Nicol (note 5).
75. T. Cresswell, *On the Move: Mobility in the Modern Western World* (London: Routledge 2006); G. Fuller and R. Ross, *Aviopolis: A Book About Airports* (London: Black Dog Publishing 2005); M. Salter (ed.), *Politics at the Airport* (Minneapolis, MN: Minnesota University Press 2008).
76. M. Auge, *Non-Places: Introduction to an Anthropology of Supermodernity* (London: Verso 1995).

Index

Note:
Page numbers in **bold** type refer to figures
Page numbers followed by 'n' refer to notes

actorness 53
Adler-Nissen, R. 65; and Parker, N. 2–3, 4, 6, 47–70
Afghanistan 146
African, Caribbean and Pacific (ACP) countries 122–3
Agamben, G. 5, 8, 15–20, 24, 25, 34, 43
aid: EU 120–1
airports 4, 13, 155, 174; preclearance areas 10, 14
Alaska 93
America: discovery 36
Americanisation 58
Amin, A.: *et al* 163
amity lines 37
Amnesty International (AI) 128, 129
Amritsar Treaty (1846) 145
Andrijasevic, R. 134
Antarctic Treaty System 96–7
anti-illegal immigration policy (EU) 121
Anzaldua, G. 172
apartments 80, 87
Appadurai, A. 10, 167
Arctic 6, 92–116; Canadian 96; climate change 93, 95; Council 97; five states 97; geopolitics 94–8; ice cap 93, 95; international law 109, 111; maritime jurisdiction **106**; oil 95, 96; petroleum 95; Russian 96; sovereignty 93; Treaty suggestion 96–7
Arctic Ocean 97, **104**, 107, 110
Arendt, H. 17, 24
Aristotle 17, 18, 19, 20, 166, 167
armed forces 56
army presence 153–4
art: border 169–70
Ashton, C. 135
Asia 144
assimilation 23
asylum 123, 125, 128, 130; false claims 10; policy 132; processing 125–6, 129; seekers 128, 132
Atland, K. 96
authority 11, 13, 36
auto-ethnographies 163

Bachelard, G. 79
Badiou, A. 13
Balibar, E. 11, 161, 162, 163, 164, 165, 170
Balkans 119
Balmond, C. 170
ban 15, 16, 19, 20
barbarism 62
bare life (*zoe*) 17, 19
Barents Sea 93, 110
Bauman, Z. 62
Beck, U. 163; and Grande, E. 167
Belarus 121
Berlin Wall 172
Berwick-upon-Tweed 172–3
Bhutto, Z.A. 147
bi-lateral agreements 126–7, 129, 132, 134, 136, 137
Bialasiewicz, L. 4, 5, 6–7, 117–40
Bigo, D. 11, 118
biometric technologies 4
biopolitics 17–18, 54
Bird, K.J.: *et al* 95
border-making 8, 101
border-sustaining 51
bordering practices 3, 4, 13, 30, 31, 40–1, 42, 100; ethical implications 117–18; EU 118–19; political implications 117–18; state 47–70; theory 49–54; and violence 4–5, 7
borderlanders 152
borderlands 73, 173; contested 141–60; South Asia 144; zones of interaction 169
borderlines 11–12, 72, 73
borders 4, 11, 20–2; changing nature 31, 38, 40, 42, 162, 164; concept 3, 5–6, 31; definition 49–50; functions 51–4; inscription 54–60, 65, 67; reconstituting 50; role 20
borderscapes 73, 76–8, 88, 168
borderwork 3, 22, 161, 168, 171–3; EU 117–40
Bosnia 120
boundaries 21, 48, 67, 102–3, 142; definition 49–50; functions 51–4; narratives 163; natural features 105; sea 103; socio-spatial 151; spatial conditions 98–101

177

INDEX

boundary-making: cartopolitical view 94
Bouzas, A.M. 4, 5, 7, 141–60
Bowie, D. 82, 89
Brazil 102
British Academy 1
British Empire 109–10
Brown, W. 11–12, 42
Bubbles (Blasen) (Sloterdijk) 75
buffer zones 118

camps 15, 19; refugee 13
Canada 93, 95, 96, 108; -US borderland 169
Canadian Arctic 96
capital: social 9
cartography 92, 93, 101, 107, 108, 109, 111, 112
cartopolitics 92, 93–4, 100–3, 107, 112, 113n
Cavalletti, A. 38–9
cavity walls 82, 88
chain deportation 131
China 146
citizens: EU 58
citizenship 14, 16, 17, 23–4, 25, 149; rights 15–16, 153
Cittaslow ('slow cities' movement) 173, 176n
civil society 34
civil wars 37
civilisation 62
clergy 154
climate change 95, 120; Arctic 93, 95
co-operation 143, 145
coercive force 56, 61; legitimised 57
Cold War 7, 94, 96, 98, 143, 164, 165
collective identity 53
collectivities 52–3
Commission on the Limits of the Continental Shelf (CLCS) 105, 107, 109
communication technology 73
community 13; political 32, 33, 41
CONCORD 124, 125
conflict: interstate 152; -related migration 152
connectivity 163
consensus 164–7, 169, 173; bordering 172; borders beyond 169–73
Constitutional Courts: Czech Republic 64; Germany 70n
construction 172
container-box model 2
contested borderlands 141–60
contested borders 153–4, 164
Continental Shelf 103, 104, 108; Commissions (CLCS) 105, 107, 109; Convention (1958) 105; and law 92
control 63, 119, 120, 134, 137; social 153–4; state 142
Convention of the Continental Shelf (1958) 105

Convention on the Law of the Sea (UNCLOS) 92, 94, 95, 97–8, 103–5, 107, 109–10
Convention on the Status of Refugees (1951) 17, 128
Conventions of the Law of the Sea (1958) 98
cosmopolitanisation 171
Cotonou Agreement (2000) 123, 124, 125
Council of Europe: Committee for Prevention of Torture 130–1
courts 64; Constitutional 64, 70n
crime: organised 132
critical border studies (CBS) 1–2, 3, 10, 25; agenda 1, 5, 162; cartopolitical turn 6; multipersectival view 7
Croatia 120
cross-border dwelling 71, 86
cross-border regions 12
crossing: border 15, 23
cultural difference 99
cultural encounters: borders as 5, 163, 169–70
cultural flows 167
cultural policy: Europe 58
cultural proximities 58
cultural traditions 163
culture 143
Curzon, Lord (of Kedelston) 110
Cutteslowe Walls 172
Cyprus 164; Green Line 165
Czech Republic 66; Constitutional Court 64

Danish-German border 103
debordering 8, 10, 11–12, 51, 74, 83; USA 118
Debrix, F. 10, 13
decentring borders 2
decisions 53
decolonisation 16
Deleuze, G.: and Guattari, F. 74, 83
DelSordi, N.: and Jacobson, D. 164
demarcation 105
democracy 25; constitutional 53
democratisation 120
Denmark 93, 108
Derrida, J. 54
detention centres: Libya 128, 129, 132
Deutsch, K. 51
Diener, A.C.: and Hagen, J. 11
difference 141; cultural 99
disaggregation 11, 48, 59–60, 66, 67
disjuncture 10
dismantling borders 172
disputes 164; territorial 120
diversification: state 47–8
DNA 63
dream houses 81, **81**, 82
Dutch migrants 5, 72–3, 77, 78, 80–2; escapism 84–5; German borderlands 76, 88
Dutch-German border 4, 79–91

INDEX

dwelling 6, 74, 78–9, 83; as bubble and foam 85–7; cross-border 71, 72, 86; nomad (of becoming) 82–5; poetics 79
dwelling places 72, 74, 76, 78, 79; cross-border 72; multiple borders 71; transborder 88

e-borders 166
economic crisis 142
economic integration 69n
economic migrants 128, 132
economic relations 55
economy: global 37; world 39
education: higher 59
El País 135, 136
Elden, S. 93, 99, 100, 166–7
Empires 167; British 109–10; by Example 120, 134; Portugal 102; Spain 102
England 172
Eritrea 127, 129
estate agents 81, 82
ethics 13
EULEX 120
EURO-crisis 78
Europe 164; cultural policy 58; integration 64, 65–6, 67; President 78; renaissance 100; spatial order 37
European Charter for Regional or Minority Languages (ECRML) 58
European Commission (EC) 133
European Convention on Human Rights (ECHR) 128, 131
European Council 78
European Court of Human Rights (ECtHR) 131, 137
European Court of Justice (ECJ) 66
European Immigration Liaison Officers (ILOs) 123, 125
European Neighbourhood Policy (2003) 120, 121
European Union (EU) 12, 22, 56, 63, 72, 77–8, 111, 165, 167, 171; aid 120–1; anti-illegal immigration policy 121; Border Assistance Mission (EUBAM) 135; bordering practices 118–19; borderwork 4, 6–7, 117–40; citizens 58; cultural policy 58; economic crisis 142; geopolitical identity 118; law 70n; member states 65; norms 129–35; treaties 66
exclusion 12, 14, 18, 23, 24, 99, 144, 162
Exclusive Economic Zone (EEZ) 103–4
exclusiveness 11
exile 15, 16, 17
export tolls 55–6
extension 97

feudalism 62
film theory 13
fingerprint detection 41, 63
Finland-Russia border 143

fishing zones 104
flows: cultural 167
fluctuation 73
Foams (Schäume) (Sloterdijk) 75, 83
Foucault, M. 17, 56, 83
France 50
Frattini, F. 129, 136
FRONTEX 119, 119, 122, 126, 129; border 165, 166; Technical Assistance Mission to Libya (2007) 134
frontiers 23
functionalism 51

Gaddafi, M. 126, 136, 137
Galli, C. 5, 8, 9, 22–4, 25, 34, 42
Gammeltoft-Hansen, T. 125
Gauthier, D. 78–9
generalised biopolitical border 19, 54
Geneva Refugee Convention (1951) 17, 128
geography 109–10; social construction 107
geometrico-political borders 23
geopolitical identity: EU 118
Geopolitics 1
geopolitics 10, 13, 14, 93, 99, 107, 121; Arctic 94–8
Gerhardt, H.: *et al* 93
German borderlands: Dutch migrants 76, 88
German-Danish border 103
German-Dutch border 4, 79–91
Germany 50, 125, 164–5; Constitutional Court 70n
Giddens, A. 84
Gielis, R.: and van Houtum, H. 2, 3, 4, 6, 71–91
Gilgit-Baltistan (Pakistan) 141, 143, 144, 145, 153, 155, 156; constitutional status 146–9; Empowerment and Self-Governance Order (2009) 147–8; Legislative Assembly 150; population 146; sectarian violence 147
global economy 37
global order 43
global warming 6
globalisation 13, 21–4, 42, 47, 60, 73, 98, 142, 167
globe 36, 100
Globes (Globen) (Sloterdijk) 75
Goldsworthy, A. 170
governance 120, 121; at a distance 126
government 61
Grande, E.: and Beck, U. 167
Greece: Ancient 16
Greenland 108
Grundy-Warr, C.: and Rajaram, P.K. 168
Guantanamo Bay 13, 19
Guattari, F.: and Deleuze, G. 74, 83

Hagen, J.: and Diener, A.C. 11
Hans Island 93

INDEX

Haraway, D. 168, 173
Hardt, M.: and Negri, A. 167
Harper, S. 96
Harrison, P. 83
Heidegger, M. 74, 76, 78, 79, 83, 84, 86
higher education (HE) 59
Hitler, A. 39
homeland: nomadic 74
homo sacer 16, 17
houses 79, 80, 83, 84, 86–9; dream 81, **81**, 82; floating 84; national embeddedness 82; as vehicles 84
Houtum, H. van: and Gielis, R. 2, 3, 4, 6, 71–91
Howell, D.L. 62
human rights 24, 128, 131
human trafficking 63, 122, 132

identity 13, 65, 99, 141, 142; cards 4; collective 53; geopolitical 118; regional 22
illegal traveller 163
Ilulissat Declaration (2008) 97, 98, 109, 110, 111
imaginaries: border 2–5
immigration: illegal 10; policy 122
import tolls 55–6
in-betweenness 73
inclusion 12, 14–15, 17–18, 23–4, 99, 144
inclusiveness 11
India 5, 142–3, 145–6, 149, 151, 154, 156; -Pakistan rivalry 141, *see also* Kashmir
infrastructure projects 155–6, 157
institutions: and society 33
integration 60; economic 69n; Europe 64, 65–6, 67; theory 48
intelligence gathering 119
inter caetera divinae (1494) 37, 102
International Centre for Migration Policy Development (ICMPD) 119
international law: Arctic 109, 111
International Organisation for Migration (IOM) 119, 137
international relations 20, 31, 41; theory 64, 98
international spaces 93
internet 84
interpellation 10, 13, 15
interstate conflict 152
Inuit Circumpolar Council (ICC) 111
invisibility 166, 168
iris scanning 41
Iron Curtain 164, 165
Israel: Jerusalem 50
Israel-Palestine border 164
Italy 126, 127, 132, 133; Coast Guard 131; *Consiglio Italiano per i Rifugiati* 132; *Guardia di Finanza* 130, 131; International Centre for Migration Policy Development 132; Libyan migrants 136; military equipment sales 133; Navy 130, 131; push-back policy 127–8, 129–30, 131

Jacobson, D.: and DelSordi, N. 164
Japan 62
Jerusalem 50
Jong, E. 72
juridical-political order 37
jurisdiction: extraterritorial 131; marine 95, **106**
jurisdictional framework 57
jus publicum Europaeum 30, 31, 32, 34, 35, 36–7, 39, 40
juxtaposed borders 166

Kaika, M. 79
Kashmir 4, 7, 141–60, **150**; as borderland 144–6; Line of Control 143–5, 149, 151, 153, 156, 157
Khosravi, S. 163
Klaus, V. 66
Kolossov, V. 48
Konrad, V.: and Nicol, H. 169
Kosovo 120
Kranenburg 5, 76, 80, 81, 82, 85, **86**
Kratochwil, F. 51

La Russa, I. 136
labour: forces (cheap) 65; migration 150
Laidi, Z. 118
language rights 57–8
Latour, B. 6, 92, 93, 99, 100, 101, 108
law: and Continental Shelf 92; Convention of Law of the Sea (UNCLOS 1958) 92, 94, 95, 97–8, 103–5, 107, 109–10; EU 70n; international 16; maritime 108
League of Nations 17, 37–8
Levy, A. 135
Libya 7, 117, 126–40; Association agreement 133; asylum seekers 128, 132; civil war 133, 137; detention centres 128, 129, 132; economic migrants 128, 132; International Organisation for Peace, Care and Relief 132; irregular migrants 129; mass expulsions 128–9; migrants 136–7; Misratah Detention Centre 128; refugees 126, 128, 132; sovereignty 136
Libyan Revolution (2011) 126, 133, 135–7
Lines in the Sand 6, 10, 31, 33, 35, 48, 161, 162; Agenda 94, 112; metaphor 2–3, 41, 43, 44n, 98; research agenda 30
lingua franca 57
linguistic commonalities 57
Lisbon Treaty (2007) 65, 66
local knowledge 58–9
Lomé Convention (1975) 122
LOMROG I expedition (2007) 108
LOMROG II expedition (2009) 108

INDEX

McLaughlin, M. 170
Mains, S. 170
management 121, 135
Mann, M. 47
Marginson, S. 59
marine territory: expansion 98
maritime boundaries 103, 111, 112
maritime frontiers: deaths 122
maritime jurisdiction 95; Arctic 106
maritime law 108
maritime space 103–9
Maroni, R. 127
Mauritania 122
Mediterranean 117–40; migratory flows 122, **123**, 124
metacommunity 16–17, 18, 19, 20
Mexico-US border 164
Mignolo, W.D. 169
migrants 136–7; borderscape 77; economic 128, 132; irregular 129; Libyan 136, *see also* Dutch migrants
migration 123, 124; conflict-related 152; control 129, 134; Dutch 72–3; illegal 119, 127, 142; International Centre for Policy Development (ICMPD) 119; irregular 132; labour 150; management 119, 125, 135; re-admission 122, 123, 124–5; re-patriation 122, 123, 125, 137; short-distance 71, 88
migratory border movements 53
migratory flows: Libya 127; Mediterranean 122, 123, 124
MIGREUROP network 118
military: equipment sales 133; interventions 142
Minca, C.: and Vaughan-Williams, N. 4, 5–6, 30–46
mobility 41; controls 3; cross-border 142, 143; regulation 171; students 59
modern states 22, 32, 33–4, 38, 60, 167
modernity 12, 18; myth 59
Moldova 121, 135
Monroe Doctrine 39
Montenegro 119–20
monuments 169–70
Moreira, J.M.D. 58
Morin, M-E. 79
Morocco 122
multi-dimensionality 42
multi-perspectival study 161–76
multiple borders 12; dwelling places 71
multiplying borders 22
Musharrat, P. 147

narratives: boundaries 163
nation-building 142, 144
nation-states 4, 11, 34, 42, 77, 162, 171, 173; container-box model 2
national borders 164, 165

national constitutions 66
national insurance numbers 4
National Socialism 31
nationalism 51, 146
nations 33; security 51
Nature Geoscience 107
Nazism 38
Negri, A.: and Hardt, M. 167
neo-functionalism 51
nests: nomadic 86
Netherlands: Dutch-German border 4, 79–91, *see also* Dutch migrants
Network Europe 167
networked borders 12
New World 37
Newman, D. 11; and Paasi, A. 163
Nicol, H.: and Konrad, V. 169
Nietzsche, F. 83
nomad subjectivities 23, 24, 25
nomadic dwellings: of becoming 82–5
nomadic homeland 74
nomadic nests 86
nomadic places 86
nomadism 76
nomos 30, 31–2, 35–8, 39, 40; global 40–2; virtualised 41
non-aggregation 63
non-refoulement 128, 131
normality 34
norms: EU 129–35
Northern Areas Legal Framework Order 147
Northern Ireland: peace walls 172
Norway 93, 94–5, 107–8, 110
Nuuk Declaration (2011) 97
al-Obeidi, A.A. 126

off-shore borders 166
off-shoring 4, 6–7, 41, 117, 122, 134; asylum processing 125–6; migration management 125
oil 95, 96
order: and space (political) 30
ordering: and bordering 32–5
Organisation for Economic Co-operation and Development (OECD) 59
out-sourcing 4, 6–7, 117, 134; asylum processing 125–6, 129
overdetermination 164, 165

Paasi, A. 143, 149; and Newman, D. 163
Pakistan 5, 142–9, 151, 155, 156; ideology 148; -India rivalry 141; nationalism 146, *see also* Gilgit-Baltistan; Skardu
Pakistan Muslim League-Quaid-e-Azam (PML-Q) 148
Pakistan People's Party (PPP) 147, 148
Palestine-Israel border 164
Paris Peace Conferences (1918–1919) 37

INDEX

Parker, N.: and Adler-Nissen, R. 2–3, 4, 6, 47–70; *et al* 162; and Vaughan-Williams, N. 1–7, 10, 98
Partition 145, 147, 149, 151, 156
partition del mar Océano (1494) 37
passports 16–17, 24
patrols 63, 122
pax Britannica 40
peace 19, 23, 39
peace walls: Northern Ireland 172
people: free movement 65
performativity 8, 10, 12, 35, 43
petroleum 95
PISA tests 53, 59
places: nomadic 86
poetics: dwelling 79
police authorities: cross border co-operation 63
polis 18
political borders 11, 73
political community 32, 33, 41
political geography 31
political life (*bios*) 17–18, 19
political order: and space 30
political space 22–4, 99, 167
political territories: Medieval Europe 101
political theory 20, 21
politics 18–19, 20, 25; border 3
pooled sovereignty 64
population: concept 38–9; demarcation 61; Skardu (Pakistan) 150–1
ports 4
Portugal: Empire 102
postcolonial states 142
Powell, R.C. 92
power 35; blocs 40; sovereign 34
pre-frontier zones 4
Privileged Partnership agreements 137
psychoanalysis 12, 13
Pyrenees 105

Rajaram, P.K.: and Grundy-Warr, C. 168
rebordering 8, 10, 172
Redmond, R. 127–8
refugees 15, 17, 24, 151; adjudication process 24; camps 13; Geneva Refugee Convention (1951) 17, 128; Libya 126, 128, 132; status 14; UN High Commissioner (UNHCR) 127, 129, 131, 132
regionalisation 64
repression 48
Respublica Christiana 36
rights: citizenship 15–16, 153; human 24, 128, 131; language 57–8; sovereign 92, 103, 105
Rigo, E. 128
risk analyses 119
Rokkan, S. 52
Rovisco, M. 163, 169

Ruggie, J.G. 167
Rumford, C. 3, 5, 7, 22, 118, 161
Russia 93, 95, 108, 110; *Arktika* expedition (2007) 96; -Finland border 143
Russian Arctic 96

Salter, M.B. 2, 3, 4, 5, 8–29; and Zureik, E. 164
Sassen, S. 11, 12
Saunders, P. 80
Schendel, W. van 166, 171
Schengen: agreement (1985) 63, 65; border-free zone (1995) 56
Schmitt, C. 5, 6, 15, 22, 23, 30–46
Scotland 172
Scott, J.C. 7
Scottish Geographical Society 110
sea: boundaries 103; Convention of Law of the Sea (UNCLOS) 92, 94–5, 97–8, 103–5, 107, 109–10; patrols 127; territorial 103
sectarian violence 147, 154
secularisation 33
securitisation 7, 117, 120, 135
security 41, 141, 142, 173; deficit 63; nations 51; threats 10
security zone: US 39
segregation 23
self-identification 143, 147, 148, 149, 153, 157
self-sufficiency 18
Senegal 122
Serbia 120
Shaw, M.N. 107
Sibley, D. 163
Sidaway, J. 118
Skardu (Pakistan) 141, 144, 148, 149–57, **150**; airport 155; army presence 153–4; clergy 154; conflict-related migration 152; development 155–6, 157; infrastructure projects 155–6, 157; population 150–1; sectarian violence 154; transformation 154–6
slow cities movement (Cittaslow) 173, 176n
Sloterdijk, P. 6, 72, 74–7, 79, 80, 82–9, 118
smart borders 118
smuggling 55, 63, 132
social borders 144
social capital 9
social control 153–4
society: and institutions 33
Society and Space 76
socio-spatial boundaries 151
soft borders 142
Solana, J. 120
Somalia 127, 129
South Asia: borderlands 144
sovereign power 34
sovereign rights 92, 103, 105
sovereign spaces 93

182

INDEX

sovereignty 20, 21, 32, 36, 56, 61, 100, 111, 167; Arctic 93; games 6, 47, 48, 63–6, 67; Libya 136; pooled 64; practices 25; territorial 14, 62, *see also* state sovereignty
space 6, 92, 93, 98, 99, 100, 109, 166; and borders 92; global 100; international 93; land 111; maritime 103–9; measurement 100; networks 100; political 22–4, 99, 167; and political order 30; sea 111; sovereign 93
Spain: Empire 102
Sparke, M. 10
spatial order 39
spatiality 173
Sphären (Sloterdijk) 72, 74, 75, 83, 88, 89
Stanley, H.M. 92, 109–10
Star of Caledonia 170
state 33, 34, 54–5, 61, 80; bordering practices 47–70; borderline 11; borders 48, 77, 142, 162; control 142; diversification 47–8; extraterritorial jurisdiction 131; modern 22, 32, 33–4, 38, 60, 167; postcolonial 142; secularised 34, *see also* nation-states
state sovereignty 8, 9, 13–14, 21, 31, 37, 54, 57, 93, 101; borders 9, 60–6; disaggregated planes 61–3
state-building: Western 62
state-making 119–20, 126, 146
statehood 149
statelessness 17
status: economy 59; refugees 14
Steinberg, P. 103
Strandsbjerg, J. 6, 92–116
students: mobility 59
superpowers 40
surveillance 63
suture 8, 9, 10, 12–14, 15, 19, 21, 23, 25
Sweden 125

tax havens 68n
technology 42, 48, 84; biometric 4; communication 73; transportation 73
telecommunications 84
territorial disputes 120
territorial sovereignty 14, 62
territorialisation 144, 145, 146
territory 21, 33, 36, 56, 98, 100, 142, 163; protection 57
terrorism 132; war on 19, 22, 24, 40, 42, 43, 142
thinking: border 169
Third Reich 35
Thompson, G.F. 49, 52
Thrift, N. 99
tolls: export 55–6; import 55–6
topography 55
Tordesillas Treaty (1494) 102, 105
torture 57, 130–1
trade 143; international 56

traditions: cultural 163
trafficking: human 63, 122, 132
transborder dwelling places 88
transit zones 15
translatio imperii 118
transportation: technology 73
transworld 76
traveller: illegal 163
Treaty of Friendship, Partnership and Co-operation (2008) 127, 133
Tunisia 122, 136

Ukraine 121, 135
undecidability 6
UNITED 122
United Kingdom (UK): EU citizens 65; Home Office 125
United Nations Convention on Law of the Sea (UNCLOS) 92, 94, 95, 97, 98, 103–5, 107, 109, 110
United Nations High Commissioner for Refugees (UNHCR) 127, 129, 131, 132
United Nations (UN) 16, 17
United States of America (USA) 93, 136; -Canada border 173; debordering 118; -Mexico border 164; security zone 39
unity 33
universalism 37
university rankings 59

Valli, L. 39
Vaughan-Williams, N. 12, 19, 54, 135; and Minca, C. 4, 5–6, 30–46; and Parker, N. 1–7, 10, 98
vehicle registration databases 63
vigilantism 176n
violence 9, 34, 48, 57; and bordering practices 4–5, 7; sectarian 147, 154
virtual neighbourhoods 84, 85
visibility 166, 173

Walker, R.B.J. 5, 8, 9–10, 12, 20–3, 42, 48, 64
walling practices 32
Walters, W. 121
war 18, 19, 22, 23, 25; civil 37
Wastl-Walter, D. 169
Western state-building 62
Westphalian order 47
Williams, J. 10–11
world economy 39
world order 38, 41
World Trade Organisation (WTO) 56
Wright, M. 172

x-ray machines 41

Zielonka, J. 120, 134, 167

INDEX

Žižek, S. 13, 14
zones: border 5, 12; of interaction 169; of movement 55; pre-frontier 4; security (US) 39; transit 15
Zureik, E.: and Salter, M. 164
Zutshi, C. 144